KW-391-016

STATE CONTROL

Criminal Justice Politics in Canada

edited by
R. S. Ratner
and
John L. McMullan

WITHDRAWN
FROM
UNIVERSITY OF PLYMOUTH
LIBRARY

UNIVERSITY OF BRITISH COLUMBIA PRESS
Vancouver 1987

State Control: Criminal Justice Politics in Canada
© University of British Columbia Press, 1987
All rights reserved

Canadian Cataloguing in Publication Data

Main entry under title:
State control

Includes bibliographical references.
ISBN: 0-7748-0275-8

1. Criminal justice, Administration of - Canada. 2. Justice and politics - Canada.
I. Ratner, Robert, 1938-   II. McMullan, John L., 1948-
HV9960.C3S83 1987   364'.971   C87-091348-4

International Standard Book Number 0-7748-0275-8

Printed in Canada

PLYMOUTH POLYTECHNIC
LIBRARY

Acc
No   218203-4

Class
No   364.971 STA

            0774802758

70 0218203 4

TELEPEN

STATE CONTROL: CRIMINAL JUSTICE POLITICS IN CANADA

dedicated to the memory of
Geraldine McMullan
and
Joseph Ratner

Contents

CONCLUSION

Contributors

BRIAN E. BURTCH	Assistant Professor, School of Criminology, Simon Fraser University
ELIZABETH COMACK	Assistant Professor, Department of Sociology, University of Winnipeg
RICHARD V. ERICSON	Professor, Department of Sociology and Centre of Criminology, University of Toronto
EZZAT A. FATTAH	Professor, School of Criminology, Simon Fraser University
ROBERT G. GAUCHER	Assistant Professor, Department of Criminology, University of Ottawa
MICHAEL MANDEL	Professor, Osgoode Hall Law School, York University
ROSS HASTINGS	Associate Professor, Department of Sociology, University of Ottawa
MAEVE W. MCMAHON	Ph.D. Candidate, Department of Sociology, University of Toronto
JOHN L. MCMULLAN	Associate Professor, Department of Sociology, St. Mary's University and Dalhousie University
R. S. RATNER	Associate Professor, Department of Anthropology and Sociology, University of British Columbia
RONALD P. SAUNDERS	Associate Professor, Department of Law, Carleton University
IAN TAYLOR	Professor, Department of Sociology and Anthropology, Carleton University

Preface

The reasons for this volume of essays are fourfold. First, the plethora of theories about crime and social control have thrown correctionalist policy into disarray. While this has inculcated a healthy scepticism towards the ascendancy of any particular theory or "remedial" approach, it has also underscored the need to identify a perspective offering theoretical cogency and practical relevance. Second, the current and much-deserved emphasis on the state as both analytic category and crucial locus of relations between politics, culture, and economy has begun to pave the way for inquiry into the nature of state control in contemporary capitalist society, despite the longstanding acknowledgment of state monopoly over legal violence. Third, the revival of Marxist theory in western scholarship calls for the evaluation and further development of previous seminal work showing how it is germane to a theory of the modern state. And fourth, the leading contributions of contemporary European state theorists must be assessed for their relevance to a theory of the Canadian State, expecially in conjunction with the specific problems of social control.

Accordingly, we have adopted a conflict perspective as the conceptual fulcrum for generating new lines of inquiry leading to a theory of social control in the Canadian State. Groups in conflict are presumed to construct political strategies which reflect their specific interests. The state, too, is a creature of particular interests. The exercise of these interests is revealed through the manner in which the state performs its three cardinal functions: capital accumulation, legitimation, and coercion. In this text, we are mainly concerned with displaying the connections between the latter two, although we recognize the concrete inseparability of all three. Our particular focus on the state coercive apparatus is justified, we believe, by the increased capacity of modern states to dominate areas of civil society hitherto outside the compass of state control. State interventions can of course be beneficial and enhance public welfare, but they may also represent the victory of narrower private interests which come disguised in the form of the common weal. The meaning of "state control," therefore, is inherently ambiguous and can be clarified only by analysis of the competing interests in the arena of "criminal justice politics"—hence the title of this book.

Our intention is to promote a reconceptualization of the study of crime and social control within the emerging theoretical paradigm of the sociology of the state and of the Canadian State in particular. Until recently, criminological inquiry has been conducted outside such a framework, yielding theoretically dubious and ahistorical accounts, which fail either to organize and reconcile the findings of discrete studies or to link them to important new developments in theorizing about the state. This has produced a void in the criminological literature which this text is designed in part to fill. In doing this, we start out with a topical focus on the problem of criminal justice reform in Canada, pointing to some of the integral ties between reform movements and state control. This is followed by theoretical and empirical analyses of the "relative autonomy thesis" as it applies to the Canadian criminal justice system, and then by an historical and theoretical reconceptualization of the Canadian State, focusing again on problems of social control.

Our hope is that this text will usher in a more sophisticated and culturally grounded Canadian criminology, aware of its history and ideological directions and thus more capable of promoting social justice in Canadian society. The interdisciplinary nature of the text, as well as the professional backgrounds of the contributors—academics with distinctly theoretical orientations and legal experts directly familiar with criminal justice issues—should make the volume attractive to students and scholars engaged in advanced study and research in the fields of criminology, sociology, law, political science, and Canadian Studies.

We wish to thank our contributors for their patience during the preparation of these complex materials. We also thank the editors of UBC Press for seeing our manuscript through to publication. The exercise of doing so provided us with an object lesson in the dialectical journey from the theoretical to the concrete.

R. S. Ratner and John L. McMullan
1987

INTRODUCTION

Rethinking the Sociology of Crime and Justice

R. S. RATNER

THE PRESENT IMPASSE

Interest in the regulation of conduct has always been an absorbing one, traceable back to antiquity. Any design for collective living requires the establishment of social norms or rules governing behaviour, and this in turn necessitates the imposition of sanctions or penalties for any violation of these norms. In the history of criminological thought, we encounter a wide range of theories about deviance and crime which advance and recede in prominence, nearly all showing still active descendants. One effect of the successive waves of academic popularity experienced by competing theories of social control is the erosion of public faith in the validity of any and all "scientific" claims of their proponents. Since the late 1960's, the dominant theoretical hegemony of liberalism has been in decline, leaving an unsettled ideological terrain in which explanations of deviance vie for supremacy and enjoin contradictory measures of crime control. The resurgence of interest in Marxist theory has yet to provide an agreed-upon direction out of this theoretical impasse, especially in view of the longstanding reluctance of mainstream western intellectuals to regard Marxism as within the limits of valid inquiry. (Gurney, 1981). Furthermore, the "problem of crime" has been accentuated by the apparent demise of liberalism in correctional policy (Ericson, 1977). Accelerating crime rates and increasing costs of crime control have inspired a "get tough" mentality amongst legislators and erstwhile reformers. "Law and order" policies are now very much in vogue and resonate with public insistences on increased protection from "street crime." But these mounting demands involve costly remedies, and they do not address the root causes of criminality. Sorely absent is a conception of social control that goes beyond the immediate response to social infractions, one capable of accounting for the wider origins of and reactions to deviant behaviour (Taylor, Walton, and Young, 1973). It is the argument of this book that such an approach is urgently required, and it must be developed in conjunction with a theory of the state, given the centrality of the state in post-industrial society. Unfortunately, this emphasis has been badly neglected in the era of liberal criminology which dominated much of the theoretical thinking until now. But the grounds for constructing a sociology of the state framework arise out of the very failures of previous "correctionalist" orientations which lacked the theoretical scope to isolate the actual sources of "crime."

CHANGING PARADIGMS IN CRIMINOLOGY

Criminology has evolved from changing perspectives that represent crucial turning points in the understanding of crime and justice, perspectives which are associated historically with three major ideological camps: conservative, liberal, and radical criminology.

For conservative criminologists, the validity of the "social contract" is unquestioned. Individuals, not the existing social order, are the subjects of scrutiny and reproach. This image of deviance has two different forms, one in the Classical School of Criminal Law, and the other in Positivist Criminology.

The Classical School began, somewhat ironically, as a "liberal" reform, since it came as a reaction to the capricious and often barbarous manner in which justice was administered in Europe prior to the embodiment of Enlightment doctrine. Classical reformers such as Cesare Beccaria in Italy and Jeremy Bentham in England sought to introduce a precise classification of offences and corresponding penalties that would rationalize and remove the arbitrariness of judicial action. Such reforms were based on the assumption that man "contracts" intellectually with his fellows and thus has the power to choose right from wrong (Beccaria, 1764, 1963). The task of lawmakers and penologists was to contrive a magnitude of punishment that would counterbalance the pleasure derived from illegal behaviour, in the expectation that rational man would usually choose to obey the law. While such reforms marked the beginning of a naturalistic approach to human behaviour (in contrast to the demonological beliefs of the Middle Ages) and helped to usher in an era of mitigation with respect to criminal justice, the "rule of paper" also produced stiff formalism and legalistic thinking.

Moreover, the avoidance of issues such as criminal motivation and the social circumstances surrounding the offence falsely isolated the criminal from social problems. Beccaria, for example, presumed the justice of the social contract and defended equality, but did not attack the omnipresent inequality in property and rank. Moreover, if it could be shown that there was no *a priori* consensus on the morality and permanence of the existing distribution of property, then the criminal act could be seen as authentically inspired and rational. But the basic assumptions of the Classical School precluded this insight.

Despite this uncertain foundation, the major outlines of current Anglo-Saxon criminal law are consistent with classical arguments. But persistent deviation by some individuals in the face of mounting sanctions led scholars to question whether the will was truly free. The growing popularity of the biological sciences and the ascendancy of scientific method triggered a search for causal factors operating within individuals but outside their conscious control. Accordingly, the last quarter of the nineteenth century gave witness to a second major development in criminological thought, one in which interest shifted from the offence and its punishment to the offender and his treatment. Although this positivist quest for the explanation of crime mainly attested to the excessive zeal of its advocates—from the early bio-anthropological "discoveries" of Lombroso (1876) to the current psychobiological theories of criminal aggression (Eysenck, 1970)—emphasis on the peculiarities of the offender did stimulate a new approach to penology. The aim was not merely to punish wrong-doing, as in the classical era, but to consider the nature and circumstances of the offender and devise measures to obviate the likelihood of further unacceptable behaviour, in order to ensure the future "protection of society." These measures could range from reform or cure to incapacitation or even elimination. In focusing on the violations of criminal law, rather than on the legal system itself, the criminal question was depoliticized. The doctrine of free will was flatly rejected, but the neglect of sociocultural factors in the work of biological and psychological positivists again isolated the criminal from social context and led to an excessive correctional emphasis. In seeking the truth about crime in the behaviour of the offender rather than in the criminal law itself, criminology became almost exclusively concerned with the tendentious question of why certain individuals became criminals and what kinds of penal institutions might reform them. Although the futility of the approach was evident in subsequent failures to reduce recidivism, proponents of the perspective resisted change.

While European studies into the causes of crime were biologically oriented, by the turn of this century interest in the United States centered on the sociological or psychiatric points of view. American social scientists eschewed the biological notions introduced by Lombroso, preferring to stress the theme of conflict or disorganization, either cultural or emotional. Psychiatrists focused on the "rejected personality," while the sociologists addressed problems of the "socially maladjusted individual" dramified by the New World immigrants searching for cultural stability in a changing urban milieu. This more distinct sociological orientation represented a third turning point in criminological theory and research. A strong correctional emphasis was maintained, but the social order was now implicated in criminality to some extent through the concepts of ecological plague areas (Shaw and McKay, 1942), anomic breakdown of social order (Merton, 1938), differential association (Sutherland, 1924), and deviancy amplification via societal reaction (Becker, 1963).

In all of these approaches, structural pressures toward norm-violation were conceded, but social mobility and cultural assimilation were still viewed as attainable, bolstered by measures such as decriminalization and guaranteed opportunity. Therefore, an amalgam of piecemeal social and legal reforms were undertaken in the context of the unchallenged institutional framework of a society in which crime was seen as more or less "normal," an inevitable by-product of social diversity. Thus while the primacy of individualism was no longer underscored (as in conservative criminology), state definitions of crime were rarely questioned, and continued attention to individual offenders served to deflect criticism of social structure. Despite cynicism about outcomes, reformism through the extension of welfare state capitalism was the chosen vehicle for rehabilitating offenders and ameliorating social problems.

The major shortcoming in all of the above variants of liberal criminology was the reluctance to extend notions of causality into a fully social analysis of deviance involving a radical critique of power and inequality. None of these liberal theories could substantiate a pluralistic conception of social control against the class-dominated practices of the capitalist state. Even the societal reaction (or "labelling") approach lacked a concrete analysis of the indispensable relationship between class power and state enforcement (Manders, 1975). Growing recognition of this inadequacy led to another major change in perspective, introducing the "conflict" approach to criminological theory (Vold, 1958; Turk, 1969). The liberal tendency to refer abstractly to the interests of society was rejected by a new school of thinkers who focused on particular and conflicting interests *within* society and who acknowledged the role of value choices, political strategies, and the exercise of power in the control of deviant behaviour and the shaping of criminal justice. Criminologists could no longer limit their concerns to examining criminals and crime, to formal aspects of criminal law, or to insular and partial analyses of social disorganization. Rather, they had to consider the total political process, if only to demonstrate the applicability of their work to those who administered the system. This entailed a thorough debunking of "social adjustment" strategies and corresponding modes of rehabilitation. Individual deficits were now traced to structural inequalities which spawned the behaviours that contravened legal statutes. Consequently, the theoretical emphasis shifted to the interplay of political economy and law as they influenced both the creation of the behavioural category of crime and the application of criminal labels and sanctions. Consensus (or "pluralist") theoreticians tended to conceive of law as legitimate authority, of conflict as unnecessary struggle, and of the state as a neutral mediator. However, conflict (or "coercion") theorists now perceived law as the exercise of official power, conflict as ubiquitous struggle, and social order as the dynamic equilibrium resulting from a balance of power (Turk, 1976). These observations of conflict theorists foreshadowed a criminology which focused on the relation of justice and the wider political economy, an emphasis articulated in the "new criminology" (Taylor, Walton, and Young, 1973, 1975) and further developed in Marxist criminology, with its more explicit materialist analysis of crime (Greenberg, 1980).

In sum, radical criminologists, unlike their conservative or liberal counterparts, adopt a more macrosociological approach to criminality. They reject state definitions of crime and view the reduction of crime as possible only through a more equitable distribution of wealth and power. Crime is not seen as normal or necessary to social order, but its abolition requires a dramatic change in present economic and political arrangements. Both deviance and conformity are seen as problematic, and it is argued that criminological inquiry should focus on the agents of social control, on the processes by which laws come to be formulated and enforced, and on the larger political and economic crimes of the elites or ruling classes of bourgeois democracies, rather than on the relatively trivial personal and property crimes of lower class deviants. Conservative and liberal criminologists are viewed as blocking social change and preventing the wider realization of social justice, since they divert political opposition and help to implement repressive government policies. The proper role of the criminologist is to seek a comprehensive understanding of the larger political economy in order to promote a revolutionary transformation of society, one that would eliminate the structural causes of deprivation, greed, and misery.

Of course, we must be cautious about the chronology of this account. The various intellectual themes in criminology intersect at so many points throughout its development and have such active descendants that use of any straight-line evolutionary model in cataloguing its history inevitably distorts. This poses the question of whether the different frames of reference are simply incommensurable (Kuhn, 1970), or whether some notion of progress in criminological theory may be sustained, providing methodological grounds for the assessment of theoretical adequacy (Lakatos, 1970), even allowing us to judge whether perspectivial changes in criminology represent "progressive problemshifts" (Downes, 1978). This problem of specifying relevant epistemological criteria is obviously crucial to an evaluation of the current interest in the Marxist paradigm.

END OF ETIOLOGY

Recent advances in radical criminology have been blunted to some extent by the repressive impact of economic crisis on crime control. The economic stagnation of the 1970's meant declining surplus revenues, which, in turn, meant fewer social programmes for the rehabilitation of offenders. Rehabilitation seemed pointless anyway, since a faltering economy could not absorb those who might have reformed. With Keynesian policies apparently bankrupt, domestic austerity policies were introduced, along with ideologically congruent strategies of crime control. The significance of ordinary street crimes was exaggerated, fostering "moral panics" that served to legitimate more coercive forms of class rule (Hall et al., 198). This led to a rejection of the "rehabilitative ideal" that had dominated correctionalism in the 1950's and 1960's, on the dubious claim that "nothing works" (Martinson, 1974). This change ignited a fundamentalist revival in criminal justice predicated on the assumption that "wicked people exist" (Wilson, 1975). A justice model of sentencing and corrections, with appeal to liberals and conservatives, was devised to replace the ideologically obsolete rehabilitative model (Fogel, 1979). This new model revitalized the ideas of rationalism and utilitarianism associated with the classical school of criminology of the late eighteenth century. It defended the utility of deterrence and incapacitation, advocated a general hardening of penalties, stressed individual responsibility, and shifted concern from the plight of incarcerated offenders to the rights of victims (van den Haag, 1975). Approving liberals believed that the justice model would eliminate the discretionary excesses of sentencing and parole; conservatives envisioned harsher sentences and swift retaliation by the state against those whose acquiescence under the yoke of increased austerity was more uncertain.

This advocacy of punitive control was rationalized by academic criminologists as a result of the alleged failure of the "root causes" approach. Since competing theories of crime causation did not point to any singularly relevant interpretation, and since government was not inclined to rectify the structural conditions generating crime, the neo-classical theorists abandoned the search for etiology and narrowed inquiry to "practical" concerns and "feasible" solutions which would control, if not eradicate, social disorder. In the context of fiscal austerity, policy reforms expanded the formal networks of crime control without a commensurate expansion of public payrolls. Under the ideology of deinstitutionalization, this resulted in the privatization and profitization of social control (Spitzer and Scull, 1977).

Of course, the morally correct flavour of the "just deserts" model exhibits much less probity when applied to actual class-divided and distributively unjust societies. But the essence of the neo-classical school lies in its criminological apology for the status quo. As a neo-conservative offensive against the welfare state, it is unsurprising that the debate over punishment has been cast in terms of its necessity and utility, rather than in terms of its contribution to social justice.

The present conjuncture is one in which the resurgent interest in crime and punishment lacks critical understanding. Neo-classical criminology rejects any consideration of alternatives to the existing conventional order. The rehabilitative ideal has been denigrated and prematurely discarded (Cullen and Gilbert, 1982), paving the way for a move to the right in crime control (Fattah, 1978). But this movement is not only a response to economic recession. As Hall observes:

> It also has its roots in the much augmented power and presence of the State. . . . Its counterpart, at the popular level, is what can only be defined as a blind spasm of control: the feeling that the *only* remedy for a society which is declared to be "ungovernable" is the imposition of order through a disciplinary use of the Law by the State. (1980, p.3)

So the construction of the new "law and order" consensus owes much to the existence and machinations of the state, a curiously underinvestigated topic in the annals of criminological research.

STATE AND SOCIAL CONTROL

Liberal-pluralist ideologues have paid little attention to the role of the state because pluralism itself has served as a mystifying apologia for the concentration of massive political power in the capitalist class. Analysis of the concrete workings of the capitalist state would have exposed its inherent bias, undermining claims of political neutrality (Mankoff, 1970). But the task of dissecting pluralist theory and thereby delegitimizing the capitalist state became less mutinous with the growing centralization of administrative power and a corresponding decline in public participation. In academic circles, the debunking analyses of Miliband (1969) and Domhoff (1967) stimulated wide interest in the explanatory importance of the state. No longer were states regarded as mere arenas of decision-making in which individual choices aggregated into collective interests and action; they were now visualized as potent and autonomous organizational actors able to formulate and pursue goals not always harmonious with the demands of specific interest groups (de Jasey, 1985). Indeed, it is now obvious that states are inextricably involved in the economic political and cultural development of all contemporary nations, so that social scientists can no longer avoid considering the state's role (Skocpol, 1982).

Although neither pluralist analyses nor the orthodox Marxian tradition offered any explicit theory of the role of the state in the function of law and social control in capitalist society, important questions revolved around the integral ties between class, state, and social control (Giddens, 1982). In the legal field, sociological jurisprudence gave way to a reconceptualization of the law-state relation grounded in a political economy approach. Under bourgeois legal ideology, the law is treated in a relatively unproblematic manner—citizens are expected to obey the law on the assumption that the legal system and the state are neutral institutions seeking to advance the common good of society by rational and efficient means. This implies, however, an uncritical acceptance of the legal system and of the political economy upon which that system rests. Consequently, the sociology of law has developed into an important subfield of legal studies, one which aims to understand the relationship between law and other social and economic factors. The early phases of the sociological movement in law were concerned mainly with questions of legal effectiveness, but later developments, influenced by neo-Marxist scholars, have elaborated the theoretical foundations of jurisprudential systems (Hunt, 1978). Much of this recent work examines the extent to which the content of legislation is shaped by the demands of dominant socioeconomic groups. Approaches range from those that grant the legal order unqualified autonomy from society, to those that deny the legal order any autonomy from the influence of exogenous factors. Systematic exploration of the linkages also involved analysis of the form as well as the content of law, particularly in those studies which parallel the commodity-exchange and legal forms under capitalism in order to expose the class basis of bourgeois law (Balbus, 1977; Fine, 1979; Pashukanis, 1980). The overarching question of whether law is a product of consensus, struggle, or coercion in turn relates to the question of whether the law can contribute to radical social transformation (Sumner, 1979; Beirne and Quinney, 1982). Is law synonomous with control, such that liberal rights only weaken oppositional solidarity and mystify the process of lawmaking? Or is the retention of bourgeois rights an important step in effecting legal and social change? These pivotal questions underscore the crisis in legal ideas and ideologies since the mid-1970's, a crisis which has left the sociology of law oscillating between the mainstream empiricism of the "legal realists" of the 1950's and 1960's and the "left idealism" characterizing much of the neo-Marxist scholarship of the past decade (Sugarman, 1983). Although the integration of legal theory and empirical research has not yet been achieved, it does appear that this next phase will involve the continuing revival of a critical neo-Marxist perspective, one that stresses the sociology of law and the state as a new framework for examining social control, crime and penal policy, and ideological views of crime and community.

As a separate and well-defined field of inquiry, the sociology of the state is only just beginning to flourish. But enough has already been written to suggest that it will provide the theoretical scaffolding for a reformulation of the sociology of crime and justice. The already impressive contributions of European state theorists have offered convincing analytic challenge to the bourgeois description of power in society as diffuse and fragmented and to the idealized view of the criminal justice system as operating with popular consent. Within the parameters of dialectical materialism, four major neo-Marxist interpretations of the capitalist state have been distinguished: instrumentalist (Miliband, 1969, 1970); structuralist (Poulantzas, 1969, 1978); class-conflict (Gramsci, 1971); and capital-logic (Holloway and Picciotto, 1978). Cutting across these theoretical variants are the vital, systemic processes of accumulation, legitimation, and coercion (O'Connor, 1973); the ordered state interventions of the ideological and coercive apparatus (Althusser, 1971); and the longterm trajectories of normal (liberal) or exceptional (authoritarian statist) democracies (Hall et al., 1978). Needless to say, the task of identifying the relevant substantive and methodological criteria for evaluating (and possibly integrating) the major state theories is monumental (Jessop, 1982).

Theorization along lines within a sociology of the state framework has been given impetus within Canada by an indigenous political economy tradition which converges to some extent with Marxist perspectives (Clement and Drache, 1978). Some of this work purposefully sets out to develop a theoretical problematic relevant to the Canadian State (Panitch, 1977; Chorney and Hansen, 1980; Stevenson, 1983), one sensitive to the distinctive features of a resource-based dependent economy, weak legitimation function, and evident use of coercion. Indeed, if this new intellectual movement is to bear fruit, then it must establish a research agenda suited to the particulars of Canadian society.

Regrettably, the converging interest in state theory, new criminology, and Canadian political economy has not yet significantly transformed the status quo crime-prevention ideology which defines the criminology field in Canada today (Ratner, 1984). Liberal and conservative criminologists are institutionally entrenched and in command of most of the research disbursements. It seems doubtful that they will offer challenge to the legal establishment that sustains their professional existence, partly because this would be incongruent with their own value-preferences and partly because their own reformist arguments for the gradual democratization of legal norms within the existing polity are not completely worn out. On the other hand, radical criminologists, though operating almost exclusively from a precarious, institutionally dispersed university base, are unlikely to abandon their goal of structural rather than transient reformist changes. For them, criminology cannot be insulated from sociology in general and from social theory itself. At the same time, there is a growing insistence that the study of crime and social control be tied more directly to the Canadian context (Gaucher, 1983). This poses questions of whether European-derived, neo-Marxist theories of the state are germane to Canada. Relevant applications are likely, since the state is pivotal in both contemporary European theories and the metropole-hinterland political economy studies of class formation in Canada. Until recently, however, there has been almost no concerted application of a political economy model to problems of social control in this country (Snider and West, 1980).

This state of affairs is now changing, however. Schematic formulations and new theories have been offered for undertaking analyses of social control phenomena in Canada based on neo-Marxist theories and on examination of the history of Canadian criminology in ideological context (Ratner and McMullan, 1982, 1984). A detailed analysis of the relationship between bourgeois state hegemony and crime control in Canada has been published (Taylor, 1983), and new texts containing both theoretical critiques and empirical research in the "critical criminology" genre have appeared (Fleming, 1985; MacLean, 1986; Brickey and Comack, 1986; Boyd, 1986). Although it many never achieve respectability with officialdom, radical criminology in Canada is no longer relegated to a subsidiary awareness. It has been the subject of occasional diatribes and some instructive critiques, but its intellectual foundations are incontrovertible. The current task is to enhance its credibility through conceptual development, empirical illustration, and historical specificity: in sum, to clarify the linkages between state and social control in Canada. That is the purpose of this book.

Following this introductory article, which has described the current theoretical impasse in Canadian criminology and posed the newly conceived problematic, the contributions to the volume are divided into three major sections.

The first section analyzes the dominant motifs of social control operative in the Canadian criminal justice system. Ericson's essay examines the reality of criminal justice reform in the Canadian State. After outlining the liberal-pluralist conception of the state and the reform process it entails, Ericson develops an instrumentalist conception of the state and argues that it provides the most insightful framework for understanding the contemporary reform process. This instrumentalist view, in turn, provides the framework for the following chapter by McMahon and Ericson, which reveals the intrinsic flaws in a specific effort at reforming the police in a Canadian city. Throughout both chapters, criminal justice reform is seen as a central component of the state's control efforts. Reform groups are shown to be deeply involved with state control authorities in maintaining the dominant order. The rhetoric of reform on the part of both the reform groups and the authorities who assert that "something is being done" merely reinforces the dominant order.

Fattah's critique of this position raises important questions about the meaning of reform and its relationship to ideology. Defending reformist efforts, Fattah seeks to counter the pessimism inherent in Ericson's instrumentalist view. Reforms that perpetuate authoritarian social control may be the result of "unanticipated negative consequences" rather than intentional strategies; some unintended effects do lead to positive consequences. Furthermore, the compromises involved in the give-and-take of reform are often not as important to participants as obtaining concrete goals, so concessions need not be equated with co-optation, and change should not be regarded as impossible. Of course, "practical considerations" are themselves indicative of ideological bias, a point Fattah ignores or overlooks within his own perspective.

The second section of the text moves beyond both the fatalistic implications of instrumentalism and the disingenuous liberal defence of reform. Ratner, McMullan, and Burtch explore the meaning of the "relative autonomy of the state" thesis by examining the internal arrangements of the state specific to criminal justice in Canada. Different levels of state autonomy are identified, which connect the operations of the justice sector to class practices and show how the relative autonomy thesis can clarify the complex and often contradictory processes operating toward and away from state autonomy in the criminal justice system. Hastings and Saunders examine the relative autonomy thesis in conjunction with the work of the Law Reform Commission of Canada (LRCC) and its contribution to the current initiative of the federal government to revise the Canadian Criminal Code. They argue that the LRCC has experienced an erosion of autonomy over time, resulting in a more limited vision of reform than was implied in its original mandate. In his chapter, Mandel interprets this as supporting his skepticism about the relative autonomy thesis, which he rejects in favour of an augmented instrumentalist approach.

The three chapters in the final section of the text relocate the parameters of inquiry through an historical and theoretical reconceptualization of the Canadian State primarily in terms of the capital-labour relation and its effects on social control. Gaucher's article contends that an understanding of Canadian political and economic development has been distorted by an over-reliance on theoretical constructs derived from consideration of European societies. He argues that the early and sparing development of state-based disciplinary institutions in central Canada supports his characterization of Canada as a "quintessentially bourgeois nation-state," one which had relatively few difficulties in moulding a compliant capitalist labour force. Taylor accepts this reading of the relatively uncontradictory bourgeois character of the Canadian social formation, treating it as more compatible with Habermas's "legitimation-crisis" theory than with Gramsci's writing on ideological hegemony, since the latter implied the existence of a political culture more like those of class-divided European societies than of the liberal quietest ideology pervasive in Canada.

In her critique of Gaucher's and Taylor's interpretation, Comack disputes the thesis that Canada may be understood as a throughly bourgeois social formation. She identifies numerous instances of regional class conflict and working-class consciousness in Canadian labour history, which suggest that consensus ideology is neither continuous nor uniform and is certainly not unproblematic. Consequently, she is more optimistic than either Gaucher or Taylor about the possibilities of a liberative "counter-hegemony" developing out of the class-based nature of the crisis in Canada. The creation of this counter-hegemony would necessarily include new ways of understanding and responding to crime.

The text ends with McMullan's epilogue, which critically surveys the various contributions and outlines some new directions for a sociology of the state and social control. In providing suggestions for an alternative criminal justice politics, McMullan seeks to counter the pessimistic outlook of some of the authors with a "left realist" agenda that embraces the rule of law as a human good and which can help to protect the vulnerable and establish social justice. Ultimately, this is what our enterprise, and this book, must be about.

REFERENCES

Althusser, Louis. 1971. "Ideology and Ideological State Apparatuses." In *Lenin and Philosophy and Other Essays*. London: New Left Books.

Balbus, Isaac D. 1977. "Commodity Form and Legal Form: An Essay on the 'Relative Autonomy' of the Law." *Law and Society Review* 2: 571-88.

Beccaria, Cesare. 1963. *On Crime and Punishments* (1764). Translated by Henry Paolucci. Indianapolis: Bobbs-Merrill.

Becker, Howard. 1963. *Outsiders: Studies in the Sociology of Deviance*. New York: Free Press.

Beirne, Piers, and Richard Quinney, eds. 1982. *Marxism and Law*. New York: John Wiley and Sons.

Boyd, Neil, ed. 1986. *The Social Dimensions of Law*. Scarborough, Ontario: Prentice-Hall.

Brickey, Stephen and Elizabeth Comack, eds. 1986. *The Social Basis for Law in Canada: Critical Readings in the Sociology of Law*. Toronto: Garamond Press.

Chorney, Harold and Phillip Hansen. 1980. "The Falling Rate of Legitimation: The Problem of the Contemporary Capitalist State in Canada." *Studies in Political Economy*, no. 4: 65-98.

Clement, Wallace, and Daniel Dracher. 1978. *A Practical Guide to Canadian Political Economy*. Toronto: James Lorimer.

Cullen, Francis T., and Karen E. Gilbert. 1982. *Reaffirming Rehabiliation*. Cincinnati, Ohio: Anderson Publishing.

de Jasay, Anthony. 1985. *The State*. London: Basil Blackwell.

Domhoff, G. William. 1967. *Who Rules America?* Englewood-Cliffs, New Jersey: Prentice-Hall.

Downes, David. 1978. "Promise and Performance in British Criminology." *British Journal of Sociology* 29, no. 4: 482-505.

Ericson, Richard. 1977. "From Social Theory to Penal Practice: The Liberal Demise of Criminological Causes." *Canadian Journal of Criminology* 19: 170-91.

Eysenck, Hans. 1970. *Crime and Personality*. London: Paladin.

Fattah, Ezzat A. 1978. "Moving to the Right: A Return to Punishment?" *Crime and/et Justice* 6, no. 2: 79-91.

Fine, Bob, et al., eds. 1979. *Capitalism and the Rule of Law*. London: Hutchinson.

Fleming, Thomas, ed. 1985. *The New Criminologies in Canada: State, Crime, and Control*. Toronto: Oxford University Press.

Fogel, David, ed. 1981. *"We are the Living Proof": The Justice Model for Corrections*. 2d ed. Cincinnati, Ohio: Anderson Publishing Co.

Gaucher, Robert. 1983. "On the Need for Specificity in Marxist Criminology: An Illustration." *Canadian Criminology Forum* 6 (Fall): 35-47.

Giddens, Anthony. 1982. "The State: Class Conflict and Political Order." In *A Contemporary Critique of Historical Materialism*. California: University of California Press.

Gramsci, Antonio. 1971. *Selections from the Prison Notebooks*. London: Lawrence and Wishart.

Greenberg, David, ed. 1980. *Crime and Capitalism.* Palo Alto, California: Mayfield Publishing Co.

Gurney, Patrick J. 1981. "Historical Origins of Ideological Denial: The Case of Marx in American Sociology." *The American Sociologist* 16 (August): 196-201.

Hall, Stuart. 1980. *Drifting into a Law and Order Society.* London: The Cobden Trust.

_____., et al. 1978. *Policing the Crisis: Mugging, the State, and Law and Order.* London: MacMillan.

Holloway, John, and Sol Picciotto, eds. 1978. *State and Capital: A German Debate.* London: Edward Arnold.

Hunt, Alan. 1978. *The Sociological Movement in Law.* New York: Academic Press.

Jessop, Bob. 1982. *The Capitalist State.* Oxford: Martin Robertson.

Kuhn, Thomas. 1970. *The Structure of Scientific Revolutions.* 2d ed. Chicago: University of Chicago Press.

Lakatos, Imre. 1970. "Falsification and the Methodology of Scientific Research Programmes." In Imre Lakatos and Alan Musgrave, eds. *Criticism and the Growth of Knowledge.* London: Cambridge University Press, pp. 91-196.

Lombroso, Cesare. 1876. *Criminal Man.* Milan: Hoepli, 5th ed., Turin: Bocca.

MacLean, Brian, ed. 1986. *The Political Economy of Crime: Readings for a Critical Criminology.* Scarborough, Ontario: Prentice-Hall.

Manders, Dean. 1975. "Labelling Theory and Social Reality: A Marxist Critique." *The Insurgent Sociologist* 6, no. 1: 53-66.

Mankoff, Milton. 1970. "Power in Advanced Capitalist Society: A Review Essay on Recent Elitist and Marxist Criticism of Pluralist Theory." *Social Problems* 17: 418-30.

Martinson, Robert. 1974. "What Works?: Questions and Answers about Prison Reform." *Public Interest* (Spring): 22-54.

Merton, Robert K. 1938. "Social Structure and Anomie." *American Sociological Review* 3: 672-82.

Miliband, Ralph. 1969. *The State in Capitalist Society.* London: Weidenfeld and Nicolson.

_____. 1970. "The Capitalist State: Reply to Nicos Poulantzas." *New Left Review* 59: 53-64.

O'Connor, James. 1973. *Fiscal Crisis of the State.* New York: St. Martin's.

Panitch, Leo, ed. 1977. *The Canadian State: Political Economy and Political Power.* Toronto: University of Toronto Press.

Pashukanis, E. B. 1980. "General Theory of Law and Marxism." In Piers Beirne and Robert Sharlet, eds. *Pashukanis: Selected Writings on Marxism and Law*, pp. 37-131.

Poulantzas, Nicos. 1969. "The Problem of the Capitalist State." *New Left Review* 58: 67-78.

_____. 1978. *State, Power, Socialism.* London: New Left Books.

Ratner, R. S. 1984. "Inside the Liberal Boot: The Criminological Enterprise in Canada." *Studies in Political Economy,* no. 13: 145-64.

_____., and John L. McMullan. 1982. "Radical versus Technocratic Analyses in the Study of Crime: Critique of *Criminal Justice in Canada.*" *Canadian Journal of Criminology* 24, no. 4: 483-94.

————. 1984. "Ideological Foundations of Criminology in Canada: A Framework for Analysis." Paper presented at the 1984 annual meetings of the Canadian Sociology and Anthropology Association, Montreal, Canada.

Shaw, Clifford, and Henry McKay. 1942. *Juvenile Delinquency and Urban Areas*. Chicago: University of Chicago Press.

Skocpol, Theda. 1982. "Bringing the State Back In." *Social Science Research Council* 36, nos. 1 & 2: 1-8.

Snider, Laureen, and W. G. West. 1980. "A Critical Perspective on Law in the Canadian State: Delinquency and Corporate Crime." In R. J. Ossenberg, ed., *Canadian Society: Power and Conflict*. Toronto: University of Toronto Press.

Spitzer, Steven, and Andrew T. Scull. 1977. "Privatization and Capitalist Development: The Case of the Private Police." *Social Problems* 25, no. 1: 18-29.

Stevenson, Paul. 1983. "The State in English Canada: The Political Economy of Production and Reproduction." *Socialist Studies: A Canadian Annual, 1983*: 88-128.

Sugarman, David, ed. 1983. *Legality, Ideology, and the State*. New York: Academic Press.

Sumner, Colin. 1979. *Reading Ideologies: An Investigation into the Marxist Theory of Ideology and Law*. New York: Academic Press.

Sutherland, Edwin H. 1924. *Criminology*. Philadelphia: Lippincott.

Taylor, Ian. 1983. *Crime, Capitalism, and Community*. Toronto: Butterworths.

Taylor, Ian, et al. 1973. *The New Criminology*. London: Routledge and Kegan Paul.

————. 1975. *Critical Criminology*. London: Routledge and Kegan Paul.

Turk, Austin. 1969. *Criminality and the Legal Order*. Chicago: Rand McNally.

————. 1976. "Law, Conflict, and Order: From Theorizing toward Theories." *Canadian Review of Sociology and Anthropology* 133, no. 3: 282-94.

van den Haag, Ernest. 1975. *Punishing Criminals: Concerning a Very Old and Painful Question*. New York: Basic Books.

Vold, George B. 1958. *Theoretical Criminology*. New York: Oxford University.

Wilson, James Q. 1975. *Thinking About Crime*. New York: Random House.

PART ONE:

Criminal Justice Reform

2

The State and Criminal Justice Reform

RICHARD V. ERICSON

LIBERAL PLURALISM AND THE REFORM PROCESS

Pluralist (such as Dahl, 1963) and managerialist (such as Weber, 1917; Veblen, 1921) views provide the basis for conventional approaches to criminal justice reform. The state is "above" civil society, neutral and independent of partisan or class interests, as it regulates and mediates the interests of various social groups. This regulation and mediation is undertaken by professional managerial experts, who have in recent decades expanded in numbers and authority as *the* administrators of the rational-legal society. These administrators employ the discourse of the conventional reform trinity—cost, effectiveness, and humaneness—in their constant efforts to refine the state on behalf of the "public interest." The administrators "run" the political system, judging their degree of neutrality and legitimacy by the level of passive acquiescence among citizens. The majority of citizens participate politically only through the electoral process, which tends to reinforce their sense of the neutrality of it all.

In these models, reform means improving something by changing imperfections, faults, errors, abuse, or malpractice. It entails "forming again" in a manner that is different from before and somehow better. It is intimately linked with the idea of progress, in that successive reforms are part of a perpetual quest for a more efficient and humane system. In the criminal justice sphere, efficiency refers to the ability of a particular reform to prevent crime by deterrence and to be relatively cost-effective; humaneness refers to the reform's conformity with the moral sensibilities of its time. The common view is that we have progressed since the eighteenth century through stages of increasing efficiency and enlightenment: from the "bloody code" of capital punishment, for example, through the penitentiary, or the "museum of order," as the ideal form of control, to the proliferation of penal options in the twentieth century, the most recent examples of which are community programmes (such as community policing and community corrections) and increased legalism.

Within a state which professes to operate within pluralist and managerialist conceptions it should come as no surprise that criminal justice reform is at the forefront of state efforts and that the primary impetus to reform comes from state agents, the essence of whose job it is to be reformers. Reform is not outside the state's control apparatus but is integral to it, part of its very programme. The traditional private agencies of reform, if they continue to exist at all, do so by contracting with government to undertake control services. Especially in the corrections sphere, the contemporary move to the private sector is more the "publicization" of the private agencies than the privatization of justice.

Since the emergence of the managed liberal state, there has been an enormous expansion in legislation, law enforcement agents and agencies, programmes, and various types of expertise involved with criminal justice. Furthermore, crime control has been used by reformers to justify a variety of health, education, and welfare measures, so that it is not easy to separate crime control from other aspects of governmental social control.

Within the pluralist and managerial model, the state has responded to a variety of occupational interest groups, all of whom vie for a slice of the crime control pie by arguing that they can do the job more efficiently and humanely. As each new reform is proposed, it is seen as an improvement, and its predecessor is cast in a negative light. Among professionals there is a continued sense of progressive enlightenment. However, built into this is also constant talk about failure, because without the display of failure one cannot have the continual process of reform and sense of progress. Thus, a dominant sense is created that "nothing works," that reform is always in need of reform, that we have not progressed, that we need to make more changes.

Within this context of institutionalized failure, the liberal pluralist response is a professional one, even if it is contradictory. This is exemplified in correctional reform at the federal level over the past decade (see Ericson and Baranek, 1984). In response to disorder in penitentiaries and high levels of recidivism among ex-inmates, every possible professional solution has been advocated or implemented: increased surveillance (Ouimet, 1969, regarding mandatory supervision), psychiatric treatment (Advisory Board of Psychiatric Consultants, 1973); three-quarter way houses and one-quarter way houses along with half-way houses (Law Reform Commission, 1975a; Outerbridge, 1973); alteration of the sentencing structure toward lower maximums and more determinate sentencing (Law Reform Commission, 1974, 1975b); bringing of the rule of law to corrections (MacGuigan 1977); professionalization of guards (ibid.); reorganization of management (ibid.); and education (*Let's Talk,* 1981). Many of these proposals involve fundamental contradictions in terms of models of man (such as the Advisory Board of Psychiatric Consultants' deterministic, individual pathology versus the Law Reform Commission's and MacGuigan's free will, individual responsibility). It is not surprising that they also result in conflicts and contradictions in practice.

What we have progressed to, using the effectiveness-cost-humaneness discourse of liberal pluralism and its professional solution, is not peace of mind and a feeling of security, but incessant demands for more of the same, a belief that more will work where less has not. Thus the heated debates among reformers kindle the expansion of the crime industry (as one would expect, since they are an integral component of that industry).

What we have progressed to is a state that is still viewed as inefficient. We have continuing high rates of crime and recidivism, along with a public perception that the situation is even more serious than the official record suggests (Doob and Roberts, 1982). Reforms proposed in the name of alternatives to formal and more coercive sanctions have frequently proven to be "add ons" which intensify the numbers under control and the severity of sanction (Hylton, 1981; Chan and Ericson, 1981). In Ontario, this has been the case with victim-offender restitution programmes (Dittenhoffer and Ericson, 1983) and most recently with community service orders, which are the current favourite among judges, who appear to be using them to put some "bite" into probation orders rather than as an alternative to incarceration. In Ontario between 1975 and 1980 there was a threefold increase in probation orders in proportion to the population, and in 1981 a 50 per cent increase in community service orders as part of probation orders. All of this is likely to result in intensified surveillance over those under community sentence, thereby increasing the chances that more will be prosecuted for breaches and moved into prison.

We have progressed to a state with an increasing number of options which entail an increasing degree of discretion for the professionals who administer them (Rothman, 1980). This discretion is based on both the actual number of options and the increased range of justifications which go along with these options. In allowing for multiple causes, both scientifically and in terms of professional interests, liberal pluralism also allows for multiple control techniques and attendant rhetorics of justification. Multidisciplinary criminology provides for multidisciplinary techniques.

We have also progressed to a bifurcation of the correctional system, posing a fundamental contradiction for liberals (see Matthews, 1979). At the same time that there has been a liberal "hands off" push toward decarceration and diversion, toward using the least severe option, there has arisen in relation to the penitentiary an increased sense that it contains the uncontainable, the dangerous. This has resulted in a "hands on" push within prisons—prisons within prisons, including protective custody, psychiatric units, special handling units, administrative dissociation, and punitive dissociation, as well as arguments for administrative devices to keep the "dangerous" there (such as via "gating") even when previous administrative practice and the law suggest otherwise. So the carceral continuum stretches very deeply inside the prison and very widely into the outside community, according to an administrative model of who is more or less dangerous, more or less free. Even if the pluralist state could manage a truly uniform, determinate sentencing structure (which appears doubtful from the American experience [Alschuler, 1978; Brewer et al., 1981]), it would still fail to alter the fact that between two persons treated equally at the point of sentence, one could end up in "the hole" at a maximum security penitentiary while the other could live where the action is in a downtown, minimum security, community corrections centre.

We have also arrived at a state where the moral sensibility that informs humaneness considerations is increasingly defined by law. If everyone can be treated equally under the law (bracketing out structured inequality in society and in the law itself), then the state can congratulate itself for being a reasonable regulator and mediator. Arguments for making sentences more "fixed" exemplify this view of humaneness. Of course, this is not a new sensibility if we consider distant history, but it is substantially different from the sensibility of less than one hundred years ago. For example, Charlton Lewis, in an address on "The Indeterminate Sentence" to the U.S. National Prison Association in 1900, stated [fixed sentences] . . . the method of apportioning penalties according to degrees of guilt . . . is as completely discredited and as incapable a part in any reasoned system of social organization, as is the practice of astrology or . . . witchcraft. . . . [The] time will come when the moral mutilations of fixed terms of imprisonment will seem as barbarous and antiquated as the ear-lopping, nose-slitting and hand amputations of a century ago" (cited in Rothman, 1980, pp. 59-60). Presently, the public culture (Gusfield, 1981) is swelling with humane reform debate related to the law, no doubt given an impetus in Canada by the passing in April 1982 of the supreme legal document, the Constitution, and its *Canadian Charter of Rights and Freedoms*. Pushing for human rights within legal discourse is seen as the latest progression of the maturing state, the way forward for a more humane criminal justice system (Ericson, 1985).

We have progressed to a state wherein the management of pluralism is expensive indeed, with a burgeoning government deficit and the government services side of the gross national product approaching 50 per cent. Among the various governmental functions which have expanded recently, crime control has stood at the forefront; between 1961 and 1975 the rate of increase in crime control employment was twice that of the federal sector as a whole. In the same period the proportion of police personnel in relation to the population grew over 50 per cent, with a nineteenfold increase in expenditure. The prison system now looks after an equal number of staff and inmates. This can be compared to California, a state of relatively equal population and standard of living to Canada, where there is a 1:3 staff-inmate ratio (Chan and Ericson, 1981).

This is the pluralist and managerialist state of contemporary criminal justice reform, of changing imperfections, faults, errors, abuse, and malpractice in the name of progressing toward a more efficient and humane system. But what other changes are happening? This question, and the series of questions which flow from it, can be addressed from an instrumentalist viewpoint.

INSTRUMENTALISM AND THE REFORM PROCESS

An instrumentalist model of the state, whether based on non-Marxist elite theories (see Mills, 1956; Porter, 1965; Clement, 1975) or materialist conceptions (see Miliband, 1969, 1977), looks at ways in which the state serves as an instrument of elites to achieve domination over the lower orders. "The intervention of the state is always and necessarily partisan: as a class state, it always intervenes for the purpose of maintaining the existing system of domination" (Miliband, 1977, p. 91). Elections are part of "democratic make-believe" because voters are manipulated to believe that they are participating in the construction of democratic order when in fact they have minimal political purchase (see Bay, 1981).

In the main, those who employ the instrumentalist view separate out intentions and effects and concentrate mainly on effects, thereby avoiding a conspiratorial view. That is, state operatives are seen to have the effect of acting on behalf of the elites, but not necessarily at the direction of the elites. Institutions, such as the law and attendant criminal justice apparatus, are aids to domination, but there is no direct link between the elites and the institutions. Furthermore, there is a connection between state institutions and those which are part of civil society (such as schools or the media). The focus is upon the ways in which institutions intersect to reproduce social, political, economic, and cultural consensus, ensuring that "right" thinking and acting people support the prevailing order of things, the existing hierarchy, the status quo.

Of course, in any particular instance, state agents may take actions against the interests of an elite member or a larger segment of the elite. However, what counts in the long run is the legitimization of the state agents, agencies, and rules in contributing to the stability of the status quo. Furthermore, it might be argued that the member's position has improved socially, politically, materially, and culturally. For example, prisoners are no longer whipped or put in a ball and chain; they have increased communication outside the prison with visits, letters and temporary absence; and they can seek legal representation in some circumstances. All of these changes may be seen as improvements in the prisoner's lot over time, but they can also be seen as instruments of control in sustaining the prisoner's relative position in the social hierarchy. In other words, reforms that are concessions to improve the lot of those at the lower end of society's scheme of things are also instruments for reforming or reordering the structure of domination (Ericson and Baranek, 1982).

Within an instrumentalist view, reform is simply the favourite programme of a particular interest group at a particular time. Since, as stated earlier, the bulk of present-day reformers are agents of government, reforms are the latest adjustments to serve state interests on behalf of the status quo. The idea of progress is largely a vehicle for making people think that reforms are in the "public interest," that is, that they are improvements. Progress may be seen not in terms of progressing to something better for most people, but rather progressing toward a goal that may serve only narrow interests and have unintended or negative ramifications. In this respect, there are links to other thinkers on the idea of progress, people whose work is beyond the "instrumentalist" position. For example, George Steiner (1983) argues that the working hypothesis for discovering the current state should be "the fall of man." Northrop Frye (1967) observes that "some of the most horrible notions that have ever entered the human mind have been 'progressive' notions: massacring farmers to get a more efficient agricultural system, exterminating Jews to achieve a "solution" to the "Jewish question," letting a calculated number of people starve to regulate food prices. . . . Hence for most thoughtful people progress has lost most of its original sense and has become simply progression toward a goal more likely to be a disaster than an improvement."

The instrumentalist view places emphasis on ideology, core beliefs, and legitimizing state actions. Liberal pluralism is seen as an ideology of vested interests, the opposite of the freedom it professes. As Bay (1981, p. 16) expresses it, liberalism is "the ideology of special pleading for priorities of liberty of special concern to already privileged social classes." The state is involved in "engineering consent" (Miliband, 1977) through both coercive and ideological work (Althusser, 1971).

Even state agents who have a more explicit coercive function, such as the military or police, are used as educators in the public culture. This has been evidenced in Britain where the Conservative government managed to whip up enormous popular support first via the war in the Falkland Islands and then in their use of police in the year-long miners' strike. It seems that in Canada in recent years the law, police, and prisons—domestic "law and order"—has a much more dominant place than the military and international order as a vehicle for the reproduction of dominant ideology. As evidenced by the recent enormous expansion in the crime control industry, relative to other government sectors, the coercive arm of the Canadian state and that arm's educational function are mobilized around internal order much more than external threats. This seems to be one way in which Canadian culture is different from the American and British, where the international threat and military are much more dominant physically and culturally. In Canada, concern about the international threat is certainly there, especially in relation to the nuclear arms issue, but it tends to be played out culturally much more in relation to issues such as immigration rather than the military and threat of war.

In examining the state of criminal justice reform from an instrumentalist viewpoint, the focus for analysis is on the social, political, economic, and cultural dimensions of reform within the public culture. Specifically, reform debates and the process of implementation should be read as part of the separate reality of the state's legitimation work, crime and its control.

REFORM AS SOCIAL INSTRUMENT

Reform debates can be read as ideology which serve as an instrument of social control. This is evidenced by some of the major illusions which are part of public culture debates about crime control. Perhaps the master illusion is the belief that state authority is *only* a bridge to the control of private behaviour. The effect of this illusion is to make reformers, and other citizens, perceive perpetual inefficiency and inhumaneness in terms of the gap between ideals and reality. As Gusfield states:

the hiatus between the public and private sides of reality is interesting or shocking or provocative only as the observer expects or demands a closer fit, assumes that public authority is a means to a private end— control of the behavior of persons. Suppose that instead, or in addition, public acts—laws, legislation, official speeches, mass media descriptions, brochures and other mechanisms of public action—can be considered *sui generis,* as events in and of themselves without reference to possible functions as means to ends. (1981, pp. 20-21)

An illusion which has received considerable attention in criminology is that there is a fundamental dichotomy between rehabilitation and punishment of offenders. Sides have been taken and lines drawn: psychiatrists, social workers, and other specialists on the rehabilitation side opposed to those who embrace legalism and principles of just proportion on the other side. For a long time each side missed the point that rehabilitation is *for* punishment, or more broadly, *for* the efficient suppression of crime and criminality. This could have been gleaned from even a cursory examination of the rule system which enables administrative discretion within the Canadian penitentiary system. The *Penitentiary Act* and the hundreds of pages of directives and standing orders it enables are justified in the name of offender rehabilitation. Even the recent introduction of certain due process legal rights for inmates following upon the MacGuigan Report (1977) are justified in the written rules in the name of rehabilitation of the offender (Feltman, 1981). Debates about rehabilitation versus punishment simply miss the point that the bottom line is social control; they lead many to believe otherwise, thus relieving public conscience over what is convenient administrative practice for suppression, even repression, of troublesome people.

Another illusion in the same vein is the one of accused and offender rights protected by due process of law and procedure versus crime control through efficient and expeditious law enforcement procedures (the classic formulation is Packer, 1968). This debate has pitted civil libertarians on the due process side and law and order advocates on the crime control side. Both miss the point that there are many ways in which due process is *for* crime control in that the law as written, interpreted, and enforced legitimizes the efficient suppression of crime without much formality (Black, 1972; McBarnet, 1981; Ericson and Baranek, 1982).

For example, there is an illusion that plea bargaining is a widespread practice caused by heavy caseloads and is evil because it results in concessions or bargains to accused persons. There is much debate over the practice which ignores some fundamental structural features: the law itself is written to encourage guilty pleas, such as allowing a guilty plea to be a legitimate basis for mitigating a sentence; the rights that are available are frequently more costly to the offender to invoke than if he simply pleads guilty, so that the "process is the punishment" (Feeley, 1979); and, the guilty plea has been the norm for decades in spite of variations in caseload and number of judges available (ibid.; Heumann, 1978). For the vast majority of accused going through the provincial courts, where 90 per cent of criminal cases in Canada are heard, the "trial" takes place in a closed setting, in the absence of the accused: the police, crown attorney, and defence lawyer reach a guilty plea settlement that often also includes a sentence recommendation. These decisions are individualized regarding the accused, whose confession to the police and confirmation thereof in pleading guilty are not seen as a violation of a right against self-incrimination and a right to a trial; rather, they are rewarded as the first step toward rehabilitation. The informality of it all, out of the public eye, resembles the procedures in court for juveniles and certainly has less formality than many diversion projects ostensibly established to encourage a more informal resolution of disputes (Feeley, 1979; Ericson and Baranek, 1982).

In the public culture debates among due process civil libertarians and crime control law and order advocates, there is the related illusion that any legal change or particular reform will have a direct impact on the phenomenon or behaviour involved (McBarnet, 1982). This has characterized the debates over the effects of entrenching rights and freedoms in the Constitution (Ericson, 1985). There has been much rhetorical reference to high crime rates in the United States, as if the only or major cause is the entrenchment of rights in their constitution. There is also much rhetorical reference to individual, isolated cases in the United States where the accused apparently "got off" on a constitutional point.

There is little or no consideration of the fact that the law does not stand still but is constantly interpreted; many of the American decisions, most notably *Miranda,* are a central feature of American popular culture. However, the popular conception is of the law as it was passed almost two decades ago, not as it has been interpreted since (McBarnet, 1982a). There is little or no consideration of the post-*Miranda* studies, which show how the rules are incorporated into existing practice and do not impair police ability to secure confessions and other evidence (see Ayres, 1970; Medalie et al., 1968; Wald, 1967). There is little or no consideration of the fact that in Canada the vast majority of accused plead guilty without trial and therefore the police construction of the case is not even discussed in open court, let alone subject to challenge. There is little or no consideration of the fact that the *Canadian Charter of Rights and Freedoms* has escape clauses both for particular cases at the discretion of the court (Section 1) and for governments who want to opt out of particular sections from time to time (Section 33). Furthermore, in specific areas such as the admissability of illegally obtained evidence, the matter remains within the discretion of the judge. There is little or no consideration of the fact that only an incompetent police officer could fail to show the legality of a search given the array of enabling legislation and practice at his disposal (see, for example, Ericson, 1981). Indeed, practice in this area is apparently so lax that the Law Reform Commission (1983) found in a panel study of judges asked to examine warrants already processed, that over one-half of the warrants were "fatally defective" because they lacked signatures or adequate details on the grounds for the searches. It should also be noted that a few months after the passing of the *Canadian Charter of Rights and Freedoms* in April 1982, it was revealed that the solicitor general was actively considering a "dial-a-warrant" system whereby a police officer can carry blank, numbered warrants and obtain his authorization over the telephone rather than be required to appear in person to have the paper rubber-stamped. Perhaps this connotes that a touch of criminal control culture realism has percolated up to state hired reformers who operate in the public culture reality. However, this is rather difficult to connect with all the noise about the imagined cataclysmic effects of giving too many concessions to the citizenry in the *Canadian Charter of Rights and Freedoms.*

Of course, such inconsistencies are not peculiar to Canada. Many contemporary states use the formal declaration of human rights as ideological camouflage. It is instructive to consider what states have formally adopted the United Nations Charter of Human Rights and use it in the international forum when someone blows the whistle on their repressive practices. Formal adoption has typically occurred only among the most totalitarian states, such as Argentina and South Africa (who have taken it on word for word) (del Russo, 1978). These states can refer to their adoption of the United Nations standards to show that any inhumane practice is not in accordance with official policy, and they can thereby label it as an isolated aberration rather than as normalized repression.

The message is clear: as with the treatment-punishment debate, the "rights"/due process/crime control debate is more understandable in the context of the state's ideological work in the public culture concerning how it should proceed in relation to troublesome citizens than in terms of how it does proceed. It creates illusions, displacing reform talk away from social control and serving as an instrument of that control. (I am not suggesting that this is experienced as an illusion by everyone, for one of the great skills in the art of statesmanship is to realize that such illusions can also be constituted as realities in the public culture [Friedenberg, 1975; Gusfield, 1981].)

REFORM AS POLITICAL INSTRUMENT

This discussion of criminal justice reform as an instrument of social control indicates that there is also a political dimension. Criminal justice reform is a key arena for defining the nature and extent of state power over the citizenry and for legitimizing that power as authority. For citizens in civil society, it is a primary basis for assessing the role of the state as a moral agent.

A key aspect of this process is the definition of what constitutes a problem or issue and what might be appropriate techniques for dealing with it. Given the fact that many reformers are employed by the state, many problems or issues are raised by them. This allows them to set the agenda and define the reality of the problem and legitimate solutions. If issues are raised from outside their direct sphere of influence, they can nevertheless manage to keep them expressed as a series of single issues rather than as related phenomena requiring action on several fronts. Moreover, a given issue can cut across pressure group interests and class interests, allowing the demonstration of an essential consensus (for examples, see Schur, 1980; Taylor, 1981). At the same time, alliances are rarely multi-issue and longstanding, so that conflict among various interest groups can be used to disperse a sustained groundswell for more fundamental reform which might create major schisms within the state or within civil society.

Reformers of the state constantly define sources of potential harm to the "public interest." They construct definitions of who are the "dangerous" and work to stigmatize and exclude them, thereby ensuring that they remain politically powerless. This process has been well-documented within criminology in the case of dangerous individuals, showing how the state often drops its assumed standards of formal legal rationality in order to incapacitate dangerous people (see Price, 1970; Klein, 1976; Menzies et al., 1981). It has been less well-documented in the case of dangerous organizations, although criminologists abroad have given attention to it (see Wynn and Anderson, 1982; Erman and Lundman, 1982; Carson, 1982) as did the Canadian media in the Ontario apartment "flip" case involving Cadillac-Fairview Corporation and a number of trust companies.

On a broader level, and one intimately connected with reform as an economic and cultural instrument, criminal justice reform activity is a useful vehicle for political rationalization. Accepting the instrumentalist view that the state exists to rationalize on behalf of the status quo, the nature of criminal justice reform efforts in the Canadian state can be appreciated. To quote Wolin, "the legendary vices of bureaucracy—to be slow-moving, unimaginative, obsessed by routine and legal norms—are, in effect, the virtues needed if it is to perform the function of rationalizing and controlling economic life. To expect the opposite virtues is to confuse the public domain of rationalization with the private domain of innovation. In a political economy the state rationalizes, the economy modernizes" (1980). In this context, it should come as no surprise that reform of juvenile justice in the form of a new act of parliament took twenty years; that the Law

Reform Commission spent the first five years doing nothing but rationalization work without producing any legislation; that a federal bureaucracy, the Canadian Unity Information Office (that is, office of domestic propaganda) had a budget of over thirty million dollars to advertise the virtues of the supreme legal reform, the Constitution (Johnson, 1982). The various levels of government in Canada are by far the biggest source of advertising revenue for the media (Royal Commission on Newspapers, 1981) an aspect of complementarity between state and civil institutions that is predictable from an instrumentalist viewpoint.

REFORM AS ECONOMIC INSTRUMENT

In addition to a general rationalization on behalf of the economic sector, which includes ensuring structured legal inequality between upperworld and lowerworld economic crime in the law as written, interpreted, and enforced (Snider, 1977; Goff and Reasons, 1978), there are other economic dimensions to the state's involvement in criminal justice reform. Significant among these is the interests of state-employed or contracted workers who earn their living by administering the criminal justice apparatus. While from an instrumentalist viewpoint criminal justice reform may do nothing more than generally reform the existing order of things, it can alter which occupational groups obtain relatively more resources to ply their trade for crime control. In any reform, occupational interests are always at stake; as related earlier, within liberal pluralism there is a similar discourse from each occupational group concerning why their approach has the most appropriate blend of efficiency and humaneness and, therefore, why they should be paid to do the job. "Resource problems" allow crime control occupational groups to explain why they do not appear efficient or humane and why they need more resources. For example, the police use crime rates rhetorically to argue why they need more resources, ignoring the complicated nature and meaning of crime rates as an artifact of police organization (Ericson, 1981, 1982); the courts underscore caseload pressure and its presumed effects on such things as plea bargaining and the right to a trial within a reasonable length of time, ignoring the fact that the historical record suggests reduced caseloads have little bearing on the rate of guilty pleas, or the waiting time for, length of, or fairness of trials (Heumann, 1978; Feeley, 1979). Of course, to the extent that perpetual evidence of failure can be seen to justify more doses of the same, the system is at least successful in enhancing the interests of the middle-class persons who run it. Saying nothing works keeps a lot of people working in the control business (Chan and Ericson, 1981).

Criminal justice reform is also a means of sustaining the principle of less eligibility, thereby disciplining the working classes, in Foucault's (1977) sense of making them docile and useful. No matter what reform is introduced, criminals and other deviants must appear to be worse off than the rest of the population, even if the state must spend high sums for facilities and labour to ensure that this is the case. Consider that professors manage to live quite well, and even to support children and pay for a home (albeit mortgaged), on salaries no greater on average that the operating (let alone capital) cost of maintaining a federal penitentiary inmate. But we have earned our way and prisoners have not, and that is why it would be considered "undisciplined" thinking to even suggest that prisoners should be given the money to support their children and to buy a modest (mortgaged) home.

REFORM AS CULTURAL INSTRUMENT

As suggested, criminal justice reform debate in the public culture is a vehicle for communicating the core values of a moral education. In this respect it is similar to other cultural products: crime news, mystery novels and films, and police serials on television (see Hurd, 1979). In some spheres of operation, the state explicitly legislates its agencies and agents to undertake reproductive work on behalf of the status quo. For example, the *Broadcasting Act* directs broadcasters to "safeguard, enrich and strengthen the cultural, political, social and economic fabric of Canada." Similarly, the criminal law, its apparatus of criminal justice, and the reform component built into this apparatus, provide a reading of values which are instrumental in reproducing images of order (Ericson, 1985).

Reform measures which "sell" are likely to be those which affirm the core values to an equivalent or greater extent than those they replace. It is arguable that imprisonment became an ideal punishment to replace capital punishment and transportation to penal colonies at the time of the industrial revolution because it cohered with the attendant cultural shift toward the values of liberty and equality. Its punishments are measurable and can be meted out equally in doses of deprivation of liberty according to the social harm (including loss of liberty to the victim) caused by the crime (see Foucault, 1977). Imprisonment has remained a dominant punishment and this is likely to change only if there is a fundamental shift in cultural values attendant upon the move to a post-industrial communications-based society or if there is a substitute punishment which reflects the persistent cultural emphasis on liberty and equality. The recent expansion of community service orders, mentioned above, may relate to the fact that this punishment has features similar to imprisonment: a measurable number of hours of service, the discipline of time and place, and other visible restrictions on liberty.

It must be kept in mind that there are fictive aspects to criminal justice reform as a cultural vehicle for sustaining an orderly, morally directed society (see Gusfield, 1981). One way in which these aspects are revealed is in the key words of reform. For example, the word "justice" itself is no more than the representation of an ideal, which we are unlikely to ground empirically in actual instances of realization. As George Eliot contemplates in her novel *Romola,* "Who shall put his finger on the work of justice, and say, 'Is it there'? Justice is like the kingdom of God—it is not without us as a fact, it is within us as a great yearning" (1980, p. 639).

CONCLUSION

Each reform effort must be seen in terms which go beyond the immediate goal of correcting a particular problem in order to progress toward a more efficient tomorrow. Reforms must be scrutinized within an instrumentalist framework so that the cultural, technical, and scientific discourse used to sell them, and the efficiency and improvement they promise, are understood in terms of wider moral, political, and social ramifications and interests. Researchers must direct their questioning to the public culture of reform debate as a reality in itself. They must ask: where do reforms come from? How are they transmitted in governmental, scientific, and mass media? What is the nature of evidence used? What are the rhetorical and fictive features of the discourse? What are the social, political, economic, and cultural processes by which reforms are accepted or rejected? Whose interests are served? What are the wider implications for a morally directed, politically responsible, economically viable, and socially satisfying existence? Addressing these questions will allow at least some reasonable assessment of what *progression* has been made by embracing a particular reform or set of reforms, and whether this represents *progress* in the sense of making collective life better or if it simply reproduces the structure of inequality and the interests that structure serves.

REFERENCES

Advisory Board of Psychiatric Consultants. 1973. *Report to the Solicitor General of Canada.* Ottawa: Information Canada.

Alschuler, A. 1978. "Sentencing Reform and Prosecutorial Power: A Critique of Recent Proposals for 'Fixed' and 'Presumptive' Sentencing." *University of Pennsylvania Law Review* 126: 550-77.

Althusser, L. 1971. "Ideology and Ideological State Apparatuses." In L. Althusser, ed., *Lenin and Philosophy and Other Essays.* London: New Left Books.

Ayres, R. 1970. "Confessions and the Court." In A. Niederhoffer and A. Blumberg, eds., *The Ambivalent Force.* Waltham, Massachusetts: Ginn.

Bay, C. 1981. *Strategies of Political Emancipation.* Notre Dame, Indiana: University of Notre Dame Press.

Black, D. 1972. "The Boundaries of Legal Sociology." *Yale Law Journal* 81: 1086-1100.

Brewer, D., et al. 1981. "Determinate Sentencing in California: The First Year's Experience." *Journal of Research in Crime and Delinquency* 18: 200-31.

Carson, W. G. 1982. *The Other Price of Britain's Oil.* London: Heinemann.

Chan, J. and R. Ericson. 1981. *Decarceration and the Economy of Penal Reform.* Toronto: Centre of Criminology, University of Toronto.

Clement, W. 1975. *The Canadian Corporate Elite.* Toronto: McClelland and Stewart.

Dahl, R. 1963. *Modern Political Analysis.* Englewood Cliffs, New Jersey: Prentice-Hall.

del Russo, A. L. 1978. "Prisoners' Right of Access to the Courts: A Comparative Analysis of Human Rights Jurisprudence in Europe and the United States." *Journal of International Law and Economics* 13: 1.

Dittenhoffer, T., and R. Ericson. 1983. "The Victim/Offender Reconciliation Program: A Message to Correctional Reformers." *University of Toronto Law Journal* 33: 315-47.

Doob, A., and J. Roberts. 1982. *Crime: Some Attitudes of the Canadian Public.* Ottawa: Report to the Ministry of Justice.

Eliot, George. [1863.] 1980. *Romola.* Middlesex: Penguin.

Ericson, R. 1981. *Making Crime.* Toronto: Butterworths.

————.1982. *Reproducing Order.* Toronto: University of Toronto Press.

————. 1985. "Legal Inequality." In S. Spitzer and A. Scull, eds., *Research on Law, Deviance and Social Control.* Greenwich, Connecticut: JAI Press.

————. and P. Baranek. 1982. *The Ordering of Justice.* Toronto: University of Toronto Press.

————. 1984. "Criminal Law Reform and Two Realities of the Criminal Process." In T. Doob and E. Greenspan, eds., *Perspectives in Criminal Law: Essays in Honour of John L. J. Edwards.* Toronto: Canada Law Book Company, pp. 255-76.

Erman, M. D. and R. J. Lundman. 1982. *Corporate and Governmental Deviance.* New York: Oxford University Press.

Feeley, M. 1979. *The Process is the Punishment.* New York: Russel Sage Foundation.

Feltman, S. 1981. "The Common Law Breaks Out of Prison." *The Advocate* 16: 2-10.

Foucault, M. 1977. *Discipline and Punish: The Birth of the Prison.* New York: Pantheon.

Friedenberg, E. 1975. *The Disposal of Liberty and Other Industrial Wastes.* New York: Doubleday.

Frye, N. 1966. *The Modern Century.* Toronto: Oxford University Press.

Goff, C. and C. Reasons. 1978. *Corporate Crime in Canada.* Scarborough: Prentice-Hall.

Gusfield, J. 1981. *The Culture of Public Problems.* Chicago: University of Chicago Press.

Heumann, M. 1978. *Plea Bargaining: The Experience of Prosecutors, Judges and Defence Attorneys.* Chicago: University of Chicago Press.

Hurd, Jeffrey. 1979. "The Television Presentation of the Police." In Simon Holdaway, ed., *The British Police.* London: Edward Arnold, 118-34.

Hylton, J. 1981. "Community Corrections and Social Control: The Case of Saskatchewan, Canada." *Contemporary Crises* 5: 193-215.

Johnson, Bryan. 1982. "Self-Promotion Ottawa Style: Spend Money." *The Globe and Mail,* 8 May 1982, p. 10.

Klein, J. 1976. "The Dangerousness of Dangerous Offender Legislation: Forensic Folklore Revisited." *Canadian Journal of Criminology and Corrections* 18: 109-22.

Law Reform Commission of Canada. 1974. *Principles of Sentencing and Dispositions.* Ottawa: Information Canada.

_____. 1975a. *Diversion.* Ottawa: Information Canada.

_____. 1975b. *Imprisonment and Release.* Ottawa: Information Canada.

_____. 1983. *Police Powers: Search and Seizure in Criminal Law Enforcement.* Ottawa: Ministry of Supply and Services.

Let's Talk. 1981. Newspaper of the Correctional Service of Canada.

McBarnet, D. 1981. *Conviction: Law, the State and the Construction of Justice.* London: MacMillan.

_____. 1982. "Legal Form and Legal Mystification: An Analytical Postscript on the Scottish Criminal Justice Act, the Royal Commission on Criminal Procedure, and the Politics of Law and Order." *International Journal of the Sociology of Law* 10: 409-17.

_____. 1982a. Seminar, Centre of Criminology, University of Toronto.

MacGuigan, M. 1977. *Report to Parliament by the Sub-Committee on the Penitentiary System in Canada.* Ottawa: Ministry of Supply and Services.

Matthews, R. 1979. "'Decarceration' and the Fiscal Crisis." In B. Fine et al., eds., *Capitalism and the Rule of Law.* London: Hutchinson.

Medalie, R., et al. 1968. "Custodial Police Interrogation in our Nation's Capital: The Attempt to Implement Miranda." *Michigan Law Review* 66: 1347-422

Menzies, R., et al. 1981. "Legal and Medical Issues in Forensic Psychiatric Assessments." *Queen's Law Journal* 7: 2-40.

Miliband, R. 1969. *The State in Capitalist Society.* London: Weidenfeld and Nicholson.

———. 1977. *Marxism and Politics.* Oxford: Oxford University Press.

Mills, C. W. 1956. *The Power Elite.* New York: Oxford University Press.

Ouimet, R. 1969. *Toward Unity: Criminal Justice and Corrections.* Report of the Canadian Committee on Corrections. Ottawa: Queen's Printer.

Outerbridge, W. 1973. *Task Force on Community-Based Residential Centres.* Ottawa: Information Canada.

Packer, H. 1968. *The Limits of the Criminal Sanction.* Stanford, California: Stanford University Press.

Porter, J. 1965. *The Vertical Mosaic.* Toronto: University of Toronto Press.

Price, R. 1970. "Psychiatry, Criminal Law Reform and the 'Mythophilic' Impulse: On Canadian Proposals for the Control of the Dangerous Offender." *Ottawa Law Review* 4: 1-61.

Rothman, D. 1980. *Conscience and Convenience.* Boston: Little, Brown.

Royal Commission on Newspapers. 1981. *Final Report.* Ottawa: Ministry of Supply and Services.

Schur, E. 1980. *Politics and Deviance.* Englewood Cliffs, New Jersey: Prentice-Hall.

Snider, L. 1977. *Does the Legal System Reflect the Power Structure? A Test of Conflict Theory.* Ph.D. diss., Department of Sociology, University of Toronto.

Steiner, G. 1983. "The Roots of the Inhuman." Public Lecture. University of Toronto, 6 April 1983.

Taylor, I. 1981. *Law and Order: Arguments for Socialism.* London: Macmillan.

Veblen, T. 1921. *The Engineers and the Price System.* New York: Heubach.

Wald, M., et al. 1967. "Interrogations in New Haven: The Impact of Miranda." *Yale Law Journal* 76: 1521-648.

Weber, M. 1917. "Parliament and Government." In G. Roth and C. Wittich, eds., *Max Weber on Economy and Society.* Berkeley, California: University of California Press.

Wolin, Sheldon. 1980. "Regan Country." *New York Review of Books* 27 (18 Dec): 9-12.

Wynn, S. and N. Anderson. 1982. "The Useful Myth of Organized Crime." Paper presented to the American Society of Criminology, Toronto, 3-6 November 1982.

3

Reforming the Police and Policing Reform

MAEVE W. McMAHON and RICHARD V. ERICSON *

In the previous chapter it was argued that criminal justice reform is a key instrument through which social, political, economic, and cultural dominance is accomplished in the Canadian state. It was stressed that most efforts at reform now rest with state agents. Further, when signs appear that citizens might be organizing for reform, state agents move in to monitor developments, participate in events, and ultimately bring the reform effort within their sphere of influence. In the process they convert the property of the outside reform group into its instrumental value for the state.

This chapter traces the development of the Citizens' Independent Review of Police Activities (CIRPA), an organization established to reform the police in Toronto (for a more detailed analysis see McMahon and Ericson, 1984). The evolution of CIRPA demonstrates how reform efforts by groups outside the state apparatus can fail as a result of instrumentalist co-optation by state agents and agencies. Citizens' efforts at reforming the police are met with state agents' efforts at policing reform; the two become inseparable. Although limited by the fact that it is a case study, the story of CIRPA reveals some of the processes and mechanisms by which instrumentalist co-optation is achieved.

REFORM ISSUES AND THE FORMATION OF CIRPA

The police in Canada remain legitimacy incarnate, and it is only when there is a major problem that there is public questioning of the police. As has been the pattern with police reform in general (regarding Britain, see State Research Bulletin, 1981; Taylor, 1981; Brogden, 1982; regarding Canada, see McDonald Commission, 1981; Brodeur, 1983), there were serious and highly visible allegations of wrong-doing which served as the catalyst to reform efforts in Toronto. During the 1970's in Toronto and other parts of southern Ontario, there were serious and recurring allegations of police wrong-doing which led both citizen reform groups and official state reformers (see Maloney, 1975; Morand, 1976; Pitman, 1977) to seek an institutional reform that might process and resolve allegations against the police in a more just manner. The preferred mechanism was civilian review of police wrong-doing, in spite of cogent evidence that this had been unsuccessful in the United States (Goldstein, 1967; Skolnick, 1969; Chambliss and Seidman, 1971; Punch, 1983). Two highly publicized incidents provided the impetus for actual reform activity.

On 26 August 1979, Albert Johnson, a black immigrant from Jamaica, was shot by the police in his own home and died in hospital a few hours later. Johnson had had repeated encounters with the police and at one point had complained to the Ontario Human Rights Commission about police harassment and violence against his person. In subsequent inquiries, the police officers who shot Johnson said they were acting in self-defence after Johnson came at them with a lawn edger. Others gave competing versions, including Johnson's daughter, who said her father was told to kneel as he came down some stairs and then was shot while in a kneeling position

The Albert Johnson Committee Against Police Brutality was formed, supported by representatives of various minority and community groups. They engaged in street demonstrations and made submissions to the police commission and local politicians. They argued that Johnson was not an isolated case and drew links with Buddy Evans, another black who had been shot and killed by a police officer on 9 August 1978.

The authorities mobilized their response, initiating an investigation by the Ontario Provincial Police and appointing a cardinal of the Catholic church to mediate and report on police-minority relations. The cardinal reiterated calls for reform that had been made earlier, but there was no immediate or obvious impact. The Attorney-General promised legislation to give civilians a role in dealing with complaints against the police, but this legislation did not get past second reading. The police charged the two officers involved with manslaughter, but they were subsequently acquitted.

At the municipal level, a resolution was put to Toronto City Council saying the council had lost confidence in the Board of Commissioners of Police to be responsive to the community and initiate reforms; the council urged provincial government reform initiatives to change the structure of the board and undertake a judicial review of particular police policies and practices. More moderate voices argued that citizens were generally well-served by the police, although problems should not be ignored and modest reforms were in order. In extreme opposition, one alderman labelled police critics as radical, saying "a few are openly communist." He cited a report of the "Internal Security Subcommittee of the United States Senate" to support his suggestion that some critics may "have fallen into the trap set by the international communists" to discredit the police as a means of undermining state authority. He also argued that the low crime rate in Toronto was "due entirely" to the police commission. Overall, however, there was considerable support for police reform at city hall, as reflected in the passing of a vote of non-confidence in the commission and accompanying calls for reform.

On 5 February 1981, four gay bathhouses in Toronto were raided by over two hundred police officers (see Fleming, 1983). Over three hundred people were charged, including two hundred and eighty-nine as found-ins, twenty bawdy house keepers, twenty-two with drugs, four obstructing police, two for buggery, and one for assault on police.

The gay community and its supporters quickly organized public meetings and large-scale protest marches directed at the provincial legislature and at the 52 Division police station. Arguments were made that this raid was consistent with past police harassment of homosexuals, including criminal charges against a newspaper for homosexuals, previous bathhouse raids and bawdy house charges, police use of entrapment techniques, police informing school boards about gay employees, and the finding of anti-gay literature on the police station counter. Also cited was the fact that at one of the protest rallies following the bathhouse raids, "five of the people behind the front banner on that occasion turned out to be undercover cops, and other plainclothesmen were photographed carrying placards" (*Newsbreak*, Supplement to *The Body Politic*, July/August 1981).

Representatives of the gay community attended a police commission meeting on 12 February and were joined by other critics, including politicians, the Canadian Civil Liberties Association, the Working Group on Minority-Police Relations, and more supporters than the police commission would or could accommodate at their public meeting (Right to Privacy Committee, *Action!*, n.d.). They called for a public inquiry into the raids and raised again the question of democratic accountability and civilian review, saying the provincial government should reverse its trend of central control over municipal policing and establish a local citizen control and accountability system. The chairman of the police commission read from a prepared statement, saying that he and the Solicitor/Attorney-General agreed there was no need for a public inquiry and no basis to allegations of police harassment. Subsequently, city council voted for a public inquiry, but the metropolitan council voted against it, as it had following the Johnson incident. City council then commissioned a study of police-gay community relations (see Bruner, 1981).

The Right to Privacy Committee swelled from less than two hundred to over nine hundred members within two months following the raids. They promised co-operation "with other gay and non-gay organizations and individuals in activities designed to promote the best interests of the gay community and its members in relations with law enforcement and other regulatory agencies" (Right to Privacy Committee, *Action!*, n.d.). Several months later the police subsequently conducted more raids. They laid twenty-two more charges in connection with the February incident, charged another gay man with keeping a bawdy house in his own home, accused gay bars of liquor violations, and raided two more bathhouses.

Accounts from several sources indicate that all these incidents were a major catalyst to *Bill 68—An Act for Establishment and Conduct of a Project in the Municipality of Metropolitan Toronto to Improve Methods of Processing Complaints by Members of the Public Against Police Officers on the Metropolitan Toronto Police Force, 1981*. One political effect of the bill's introduction was to channel debate into the constitution of the legislation and citizen review mechanisms that were appropriate and away from the specifics of the incidents of harassment against particular minorities. The metropolitan chairman and the police chief were said to have "greeted the news jubilantly" (*Toronto Star*, 3 April 1981) regarding Bill 68; however, a coalition of approximately forty groups led by the Urban Alliance on Race Relations formed to lobby on the matter. The lobby focused on a provision which would allow the police to conduct initial investigations of a complaint, effectively giving them a thirty-day start over what the Public Complaints Commissioner might do by way of his own investigations. While a provision was available for the commissioner to intervene within thirty days, this was seen as being "so restricted as to be virtually useless" (Coalition leaflet, n.d.). The coalition called for a new bill that would enable investigation to be entirely in the hands of citizens and that would generally offer less protection to police officers than was available under Bill 68.

The coalition's criticisms were echoed by some opposition members in the legislature, but the majority Progressive Conservative government appeared satisfied that this was an instance of their "progressive" label. The Solicitor/Attorney-General commented that the legislation involved "a degree of accountability to the public that we have not seen in any other jurisdiction" (*Hansard*, 17 November 1981). He criticized the critics by asserting that "what they were really seeking to do through their amendments was to drive a significant wedge between the public and the police force that serves that public. They want to hamper in an unfortunate fashion the ability of police forces, not just to police themselves, but to resolve these issues directly with the citizens they serve" (ibid.).

Compared with American mechanisms for civilian review there were some progressive features. For example, in a review of seven civilian review boards in the United States, the Hartford Institute (1980) found only one that could "recommend specific disciplinary actions"; none of them could "implement specific disciplinary actions e.g. suspend or discipline officers." In contrast, Bill 68 empowered the Police Complaints Board to impose penalties, including dismissal from the force, on officers "found guilty." Furthermore, six of the seven boards examined by the Hartford Institute did not allow for public hearings, while the Toronto hearings could be public.

In the face of this impending legislation, a group of citizens decided to form an organization to press for further reform. Since The Working Group on Minority Police Relations had become dormant, and recommendations around Bill 68 had not been accepted by the Ontario government, a small group of municipal political figures decided to establish CIRPA. They were guided by an ex-alderman, who was supported by several politicians at city hall. In late May 1981, a draft proposal for "an independent citizens' review mechanism to deal with allegations of police misconduct" was sent to "interested parties" through the offices of two aldermen. Following discussion over several meetings, a revised proposal was drawn up. The purposes of CIRPA were:

1) To systematically obtain and review allegations of police misconduct in Metropolitan Toronto.
2) To assist complainants in pursuing their allegations through the most appropriate channels.
3) To publish periodically statistics on the number and nature of complaints and on their disposition and also on counter-charges laid by the police. These statistics should include divisions, names and numbers of police officers.
4) To press for reforms to ensure that both complainants and police officers receive fair and impartial treatment.
5) To conduct research into and to press for needed reforms in the organization and conduct of the Metropolitan Toronto Police Force.
6) To give information to other sympathetic groups and individuals (e.g. lawyers) approved by the board of directors.
7) To be concerned with public education.
8) To initiate legal and other actions which are consistent with the goals of the organization as well as intervening in and sponsoring litigation. (Revised proposal, 8 July 1981)

CIRPA stated that "a wide range of organizations must be involved in the structure. Minority communities, civil liberties groups, social service organizations, progressive legal bodies . . . all must be encompassed." However, as we document subsequently, CIRPA developed into a group of middle-class, liberal, professionals, especially lawyers; in terms of minority involvement, adult gay men were predominant.

INITIAL OPPOSITION TO POLICING AUTHORITIES

CIRPA set out to establish an unofficial, alternative citizen complaint mechanism. In the revised proposal, the impending Public Complaints Office was described as a "mock function" under "an ineffectual commissioner" and it was asserted that the Attorney-General, police commission, and metropolitan politicians seemed "not only unsympathetic, but downright hostile to the notion of a rational and fair set of checks and balances on police conduct." The same document also included an attack on the police complaints bureau, describing it as a "dangerous farce" and stating that complainants to that bureau are frequently "charged by the police with public mischief and malicious prosecution or sued by civil court."

CIRPA's oppositional stance was indicated further by its position regarding membership and attendance at meetings. While members called for more openness, democratic control, and accountability of police, their own territory was strictly policed. The original draft proposal permitted open membership to persons who "agree with the purposes of the organization subject to approval by the Board of Directors" and limited access by "members of the police department and their immediate families." Furthermore, at the discretion of the board of directors, any membership could be cancelled "at anytime without cause." At a 29 June meeting, two "professionals" (not police officers) attended a CIRPA meeting, and a debate ensued on whether they should be allowed to remain and what the attendance policy should be. The two were eventually invited to become members on condition that they agreed with the purposes of CIRPA and undertook not to report CIRPA affairs to their employers without approval from the steering committee. A subcommittee on attendance was struck and at an 8 July meeting a position on attendance limitations was adopted. This position was justified in terms of CIRPA's "obligation to protect complainants," especially minorities who face "often hostile police and government agencies . . . and often hostile people within those agencies," and with reference to "the unfortunate history of some elements in police and government agencies to interfere with legitimate community processes." Furthermore, until the official founding meeting, "only those invited to attend by the interim chairman will be entitled to attend . . . [and at] the direction of the meeting a chairperson might revoke an invitation previously extended." This was rather ironic for an organization which had occasion to criticize the accessibility of police commission meetings and which stressed "an obligation to develop strategies on behalf of the entire community which will result in opening locked doors, removing stubborn and wilfull obstructions and prevent the systematic use of recriminatory tactics against ordinary persons seeking justice."

At the outset, CIRPA used the tactic of bringing details of individual complaints, and sometimes the complainants themselves, directly to police commission meetings. It also planned to prepare comprehensive reports on complaint patterns, policing trends, and reform needs.

CIRPA also used the media. It issued a press release in connection with its inaugural meeting which described CIRPA as a "real alternative" to the proposed civilian review "farce" supported only by the police association and police commissioners. This drew a response from the police commission chairman, who accused CIRPA of "encouraging a system of espionage and sabotage on law enforcement officers who are sworn to uphold the law. What are these? Vigilante activities?" (*Globe and Mail*, 14 July 1981). He went on to belittle the CIRPA coalition of community groups, saying "they're always groups upon groups, and when you look into them you find they can hold their meetings in a telephone booth" (ibid.). Similar barbs from the police commission chairman and metro chairman punctured press accounts several months later as CIRPA made submissions to the provincial justice committee on Bill 68. The police commission chairman pointed out, "you don't see Kinsmen and the Rotary Club down here to protest" (*Globe and Mail*, 6 October 1981).

Part of CIRPA's preparation for its initial deputation to the police commission was a letter from a city alderman to the chairman dated 7 October 1981. In the letter CIRPA advised the chairman that it would attend the 22 October meeting of the commission to assist clients who wished to complain against the police and to present some lawyers' statements about "problems with one of the units in your department." It informed the commission that CIRPA clients had been advised not to use the police department complaints bureau or the new Public Complaints Commissioner's office but instead to bring complaints directly to the public police commission meeting. CIRPA also asserted, "your Commission has an obligation to hear complaints in public and to follow up on them" and advised that the meeting be held in a larger room than usual.

A week later, the chairman of the police commission replied, undercutting the alderman's requests. The chairman opened by saying he was replying to the letter in which "you purport to represent CIRPA" and continued by asserting that it was "totally impossible" for the police commission to schedule "your matter" for the 22 October meeting which is "now overloaded with items of importance." He concluded by stating, "the Commission will consider your request and you will be notified in due course as to its decision about the hearing of your deputation."

The alderman replied immediately, saying ample notice had been given for CIRPA's deputation and that, in anticipation of such a response from the police commission, copies of the 7 October letter had been sent to all members of the city council and to the provincial secretary of the justice committee. The chairman of the police commission was asked to specify the matters seen as "more pressing." He was then reminded that "justice delayed is justice denied" and told "we will be attending and asking to be heard. . . . We will see you on October 22, 1981." The chairman was also told that the police commission had an obligation to hear complaints from the public and warned that if it were planning to refuse, it would have to do so in public.

The chairman responded two days later, reiterating the commission's position and counteracting CIRPA's assertions. He said "the correspondence between us has already become public information and the reasons we are unable to hear you on that date are therefore a matter of public knowledge." He then argued that if there was any delay or denial of justice, it was at the hands of CIRPA for "refusal to avail yourselves of the well-established opportunity to utilize the facilities of our Citizens Complaint Bureau or the new procedures which are being put into place by Bill 68 of the Ontario Legislature." The chairman concluded by saying the board would consider CIRPA's request and would communicate further.

CIRPA responded immediately, again through an alderman's office, reiterating its main points and asserting that a deputation would attend the 22 October police commission meeting. This letter was especially confrontational, making personal comment about the chairman and warning the commission about private meetings: "we appreciate your well-known and strong personal feelings about not hearing complaints about your police officers, but we respectfully submit that you do not speak for the entire board and that the full board will have to deal with this matter in a public setting. We hope you won't resort to meeting ahead of time privately with no public notice and out of the public eye to make a board decision to refuse to hear us. You might note that the Kincardine Ontario Police Commission is being investigated for holding private meetings on public matters." There was no further reply from the police commission.

CIRPA members and lawyers arrived at the 22 October meeting equipped with a lengthy written submission, which included details about CIRPA;

comments about the police commission; documents relating to sixteen cases of alleged police abuse; correspondence from lawyers about abuse on the part of the Toronto police hold-up squad; correspondence from a ward community organization about local policing problems; and CIRPA recommendations for action regarding all these matters. The tenor of the contents was very confrontational. CIRPA was said to be "appalled" at comments made by commission members. In particular, reference was made to the "biased and hostile" attitude of the metropolitan chairman and the police commission chairman. It was asserted that if these officials could not act fairly and even-handedly to citizen groups they did not like, "then it is no wonder some of your officers believe that they can operate the same way on the street." CIRPA criticized the commission for discouraging complaints against the police by bringing lawsuits and reasons were enumerated as to why the commission should hear CIRPA's and other deputations.

The meeting opened with the chairman of the police commission presenting citations to citizens who had assisted police officers. When the CIRPA head announced he was going to deliver a detailed list of allegations of police brutality, a motion was passed that the commissioners would only meet CIRPA *in camera*. A lawyer argued "it was 'unprecedented' for the commission to insist on closed doors," to which the chairman of the police commission replied, "your appearance is unprecedented" (*Now*, 29 October 1981).

Against all of its previous arguments on the need for a public meeting, and against specific instructions from its complainants that their cases were to be presented in public before the board of police commissioners, CIRPA agreed to a private meeting with commission members. The commission subsequently announced that three senior police officers appointed by the police chief would "investigate accusations from lawyers that officers on the police department's hold-up squad use 'widespread torture'—including suffocation—to pry information out of prisoners" (*Toronto Star*, 23 October 1981). CIRPA had not only compromised on the matter of a public hearing but had also participated in the process leading to police officers conducting the investigation of the hold-up squad, after having explicitly stated in its submission that the investigation would have to be conducted by "some outside and impartial body." The authorities' framework for policing reform prevailed, and CIRPA's transition to eventual co-optation by the authorities was underway.

Having been party to these arrangements did not keep CIRPA from criticizing them. It wrote to the police commission five days after the meeting to restate its demand for a public inquiry, while conceding that the investigation by the three senior police officers might be useful "insofar as they recommended technical procedure and management changes." It also prepared a statement saying the investigation by the three officers, in keeping with all those conducted by the police force complaint bureau and Public Complaints Commissioner's office, "is essentially a private investigation," precisely the opposite of what CIRPA complainants wanted.

CIRPA continued to oppose the police commission and some of its members. At its inaugural meeting in February 1982, CIRPA members undertook to reform not only the police department but also the police commission itself, resolving "that CIRPA endorse the calls for the resignation of the current Commission and that the Province of Ontario be requested to restructure and expand it to make it more representative of the community, ensuring, as a minimum, representation of women, visible and other minorities."

CIRPA also initiated opposition to policing authorities on other fronts. It accelerated its formation in order to oppose and establish an alternative to the Public Complaints Commissioner's office, apparently seeing itself in a competitive race with that office. Ten days before the official announcement of an interim Public Complaints Commissioner's Office, CIRPA held a press conference attacking the "farce proposed by Queen's Park" and promoting CIRPA as the "real alternative review process."

From the outset CIRPA actively discouraged complainants from going through the Public Complaints Commissioner's office, although it agreed to assist complainants who became "enmeshed" in these procedures. In its own manual for helping complainants, CIRPA members were advised to take one of three options—no formal action, publicity, legal action—but no mention was made of the public complaints alternative. Furthermore, a CIRPA leaflet for complainants urged them to call CIRPA first and explicitly advised avoiding both official routes, stating:

> *Avoid the Police Complaint Bureau:* In our view, it is extremely dangerous to complain to the police complaint bureau. Too many people who have gone this route have later been charged or sued by the police and most others have been unhappy with the way their complaints have been handled. . . . *Avoid the Commissioner of Citizens Complaints:* This new operation is, in our view, simply a window-dressing exercise. Most complaints are still investigated by the police with the same potential problems as in the complaint bureau.

CIRPA repeated its opposition to the Public Complaints Office in varied contexts, including its submissions to the police commission, as documented earlier. The more detailed and legalistic arguments are apparent from an October 1981 submission by CIRPA to the police commission, calling for a public inquiry into allegations of wrong-doing. This document points out that Bill 68 does not prevent law suits and/or public mischief charges against complainants, a problem which is accentuated because under the Police Complaints Bureau system there was a "balance of probabilities" standard of proof, but under Bill 68 it is a "beyond reasonable doubt" standard. When combined with the fact that under Bill 68 a statement given by a police officer will no longer be used in court, "the effect is that it will be even more difficult for people to sustain complaints under the new system."

EVENTUAL CO-OPERATION WITH POLICING AUTHORITIES

By the summer of 1982, CIRPA had changed substantially in both its focus of concern and in its relations with policing authorities. It turned its attention from police abuse to police organization, administration, and policy issues; from controversial issues to those the police commission itself felt were in need of reform. In the process, CIRPA became a useful part of the state's reform efforts. As a police commission member remarked in an interview, "every organization needs not only a gadfly to keep them honest and to keep them thinking, but a horsefly, something that will come in and bite and hurt and draw some blood from time to time. I think it's very valuable, it's part of the system. . . . I'm glad they're there."

One indication of the transformation was CIRPA's approach to six major incidents which involved police control of large crowds and, in some cases, use of force, including billyclubs. On 7 July 1981, CIRPA wrote a letter to the police commission asking to appear at the 15 July commission meeting to consider the "most unsatisfactory trend" indicated by these incidents and how this might be remedied via review of police policies, guidelines, and training. The tenor of this letter was that of supplicant, in marked contrast to the letters of a few months earlier which had been insistent and oppositional. Moreover, events were tied to remedies, and the remedies took priority over specific allegations regarding, for example, the use of billyclubs. Indeed, this letter did not include the word "allege" or its derivatives, but rather "complaints" and "statements" by witnesses, one of whom "says" that some youths are "badly worked over by police."

The 15 July 1982 police commission meeting was the first to formally include CIRPA. Apparently the deferential language and tone of the letter had been enough to indicate that CIRPA would conform to the official framework. At the meeting, CIRPA focused on one of the six incidents outlined in the letter. This incident was referred to as the Scarborough party and involved approximately 50 police officers who had attempted to deal with an unruly house party of an estimated 300-500 people. An altercation ensued and some police officers indiscriminately beat youths with their billyclubs. Officers had taken off their identification badges, and a warrant was later executed at a local television station to seize a news film of the incident. CIRPA members brought several of the citizens involved to the police commission meeting and some of them related their experiences. However, CIRPA's documentation of the events became redundant, as police commission members and a deputy chief of police also focused on the Scarborough party incident to the virtual exclusion of the other five incidents, asking for CIRPA's assistance in identifying abusive officers.

CIRPA also embraced the official discourse of reports on the Toronto police force organization prepared by the management consultant firm Hickling-Johnston. This was even perceived by a member of the police commission, who remarked in an interview that CIRPA "in a lot of ways . . . were on the same track as Hickling-Johnston."

CIRPA responded to the police commission's request for public comment on the Hickling-Johnston reports with written submissions dated June and August 1982. The June submission identified "Positive features of the Study," including the need for changes in organizational structure; better planning through ongoing reviews; better mechanisms of public accountability; decentralization at district and divisional levels; alteration of the constable's role in criminal investigation and community relations; and administrative support improvements, including a greater use of civilians. Criticisms were largely directed at what had been omitted, and even in detailing omissions CIRPA remained largely within the management-oriented discourse of the reports.

CIRPA pointed to the failure of Hickling-Johnston to analyze the police commission as a "key element in the management structure." However, unlike its resolution at the February 1982 inaugural meeting, in which the resignation of current police commission members was called for, in this context the areas for reform were simply enumerated. Suggestions largely pertained to the method of appointment, types of citizens represented, opportunities for citizen input, and the need to discontinue the practice of mischief charges, law suits, and malicious prosecution actions against citizens who initiate complaints against the police. Apart from this, CIRPA took on both the administrative-technocratic discourse of the Hickling-Johnston reports and their recommendations regarding goal-setting and review programmes, recruitment, training, promotion, hiring of senior management, supervision, control of special squads, staffing, unit size, building form, use of vehicles, team policing, reducing paramilitary aspects, community involvement, and restructuring at the divisional level.

CIRPA presented this first response to the Hickling-Johnston reports at a meeting of the police commission on 12 August 1982. In addition to its written submission, CIRPA commented on the heavy emphasis given to data processing and "high profile" policing strategy underlying the Hickling-Johnston recommendations. The police commission, who released a second set of Hickling-Johnston reports at a press conference immediately prior to this meeting, stated that they would deal with community group responses to all the reports at their meeting scheduled for 7 October 1982.

In its second response, CIRPA shifted from its position in the first submission, attacking the Hickling-Johnston recommendations on "the nitty-gritty of policing," which were generally characterized as "less sound and in some cases downright dangerous." For example, in the first response praise is given to "professional services" including "data processing," but in the second response there is an attack on the costs of purchasing data processing equipment and "preoccupation with technological 'solutions' to what are, in essence, very human problems." In the first response the professionalization of "public affairs" is praised, but in the second response this too is criticized. In the first response "team policing" and "community based policing" are lauded as able to provide better community relations, better officer morale, more effective law enforcement, and cheaper service, while in the final response these directions are condemned on the belief that they would increase aggressive proactive policing and attendant harassment of citizens and ultimately "breed further discontent between the public and police." CIRPA's desire for a community- and service-oriented approach came to be seen as undesirable in its potential for surveillance, intelligence-gathering, and exercises of police authority outside of special legal authority. In practice, CIRPA members came to appreciate that this policing strategy could be used to target and harass particular sections of the citizenry.

Both the first and second responses indicate the transformation which was occurring in CIRPA's approach to the police commission. The organization again showed itself to be more concerned with making suggestions relating to policing structures, policies, and procedures than with criticizing or dealing with allegations of police misconduct. It increasingly drew upon professional expertise rather than complainants. In CIRPA's original submissions to the police commission, the criticisms, allegations, and recommendations emerged directly from complainants' cases. In contrast, in the second submission regarding the Hickling-Johnston reports the basis for many of CIRPA's observations was a "recent and authoritative study" by Richard Ericson (1982).

Another sign of CIRPA's movement inside the framework and discourse of the state was the manner in which the 7 October 1982 submission was made. The brief was submitted in advance to the police commission and CIRPA was duly scheduled to appear. At the meeting there was much joviality between the police commission chairman and CIRPA representatives, in contrast to the representatives from the Right to Privacy Committee who were treated much as CIRPA had been a year before, that is, shouted at, interrupted, and cut short. The CIRPA presentation was prefaced by stating areas of agreement with Hickling-Johnston recommendations, and critical points were made in a conciliatory tone, such as, "we do not contend that 'high profile policing' is necessarily a bad thing." In response to CIRPA's contention that police proactive harassment was directed primarily at disadvantaged minorities, the chairman offered anecdotes suggesting it was also a problem for white and higher status youths, including his own son. CIRPA had no aggregate data to support its contentions, and anecdotes were exchanged indicating that everyone perceived a level of proactive harassment. When CIRPA quoted a passage from Richard Ericson's (1982) book, the chairman undercut it in a jocular manner by stating, "You could have said it better yourself." The entire transaction between CIRPA representatives and the police commissioners was amicable. The impact of the presentation can perhaps be judged by the fact that according to the minutes of CIRPA's board meeting three months later, "no response to CIRPA's briefs had been received."

The Hickling-Johnston reports became an integral part of the reform process, framing the discourse of reform and legitimating changes desired by the policing authorities in the name of professional, technical, impartial, expert deliberations. All but two of the one hundred and thirty recommendations in the reports were adopted by the police commission. The Hickling-Johnston consultation process can also be read as a sociodrama for public culture consumption (Gusfield, 1981), a reform ritual continuous with previous inquiries (see Maloney, 1975; Morand, 1976; McDonald, 1981) initiated and managed by state reformers as part of the ongoing task of simultaneously reforming the police and policing reform.

After the reports were completed, the police commission did allow outsiders to make their views known. However, this did not so much grant or deny previous demands for reform as change the definition of what was important and hence what outside reformers could reasonably expect (see Edelman, 1971). The outpouring of concern over racism, sexism, bigotry, use of firearms, the structure and role of the police commission, and the use of entrapment and agent provocateurs evaporated in the technocratic discourse of management consultants. CIRPA, increasingly wishing to appear reasonable as part of its search for legitimacy, picked up the jargon and thus took a giant step inside the state reform process. As Edelman (1977, p.98) observes, jargon serves to "neutralize or win over potential opponents" and "resort to jargon in any organization can be understood as an implicit expression of loyalty to the values that are dominant in that organization.'' In spite of strong statements in its second response—such as in ''a number of critical areas'' CIRPA ''rejects completely the underlying philosophy'' of the consultants—the responses of CIRPA to the Hickling-Johnston reports marked a major transformation in its relationship with the policing authorities.

With one exception (a submission to the police commission in September 1982 regarding drug squad officers improperly drawing their guns as they entered drug raids, which led the metropolitan chairman to ''attack'' CIRPA verbally with a semantical defence arsenal of ''boo words'' such as ''vigilante'') the period from the summer of 1982 through the winter of 1983 was marked by conciliation and co-operation. One CIRPA board member explained that, ''whenever you start dealing, appearing before a body on a regular basis, you inevitably start . . . trimming your positions, in response to their reactions to you, to try and be a little more effective in your presentation and to be reasonable and persuasive . . . and of course it's on their terms.''

CIRPA members began planning strategy and making decisions in terms of the impact upon their legitimacy with the police commission. For example, at a CIRPA meeting in December 1982, a member raised the question of how the organization might convey to the news media information about an administrative change in CIRPA. The suggestion was made that news media interest could be heightened by holding a press conference which would also include recent cases highlighting allegations of abuse. Others at the meeting vehemently opposed this strategy, arguing that it would lead to a loss of credibility with the police. It was decided to send out a press release giving details of the administrative change only and not to hold a press conference or publicize allegations.

There were also shifts in positions concerning what had earlier been considered basic and essential reforms. For example, by the second annual general meeting in February 1983, radical demands such as the resignation of current police commissioners and the restructuring of the organization of the police commission had been dropped. During the same period, there was also a radical shift in attitude and approach to the new Public Complaints Commissioner's office. In its first response to the Hickling-Johnston reports, CIRPA argued that, ''the complaint bureau should be abolished. The police commission should begin discussions with the provincial government for all responsibility for this function to be transferred to the Commissioner of Public Complaints. The current split function seems cumbersome to the point of being almost unworkable.'' This is a great distance from CIRPA's initial opposition to the Public Complaints Commissioner's office. CIRPA had been critical of the Police Complaint

Bureau, which it now recommended be abolished, but it had characterized the Public Complaints Commissioner's office as "even worse," a "farce," and a system under which it was even more difficult to prove a complaint than through the Police Complaints Bureau.

CIRPA members confirmed in interviews with us that they had started to refer some complainants to the Public Complaints Commissioner's office. One board member said, "we decided that in cases where we thought there was a valid complaint, but that it wasn't a grotesquely serious complaint, and if the complainant only wanted an apology from the police officer, that we would recommend they go to [the Public Complaints] operation." The CIRPA leaflet was revised, still recommending that complainants avoid the Public Complaints route, but if complainants nevertheless chose this option they should "not talk to police about the case during the first thirty days after the complaint is filed. After that time, the case is turned over to the commissioner and his civilian investigators." In January 1983, CIRPA and Public Complaint representatives met regarding the Scarborough party incident described earlier. CIRPA gave the Public Complaints representative a list of names of persons who had been at the party (without identifying CIRPA clients), and CIRPA received a list of complainants (but not witnesses). Others also perceived a change in CIRPA's approach to the Public Complaints office. A representative of the Public Complaints office stated in interview that CIRPA "have indicated to us that they're sending their complainants here. They can perform a useful role in a sense. . . . CIRPA can assist people in a very constructive way and I think they are now."

The basis of the decision to accept the new Public Complaints mechanism was not evident. One CIRPA member had said that the "acid test" for the Public Complaints office would be their "handling of allegations surrounding the hold-up squad" (*The Varsity*, 24 March 1982), a matter which had been central to CIRPA's original confrontation with the police commission in October 1981. However, the Police Complaints Commissioner did not release his report on this matter until April 1984 (even though it was substantially completed in November 1982), on the grounds that there was an ongoing, "criminal jury trial involving matters similar to those which were the subject of our investigation" (Public Complaints Commissioner, 1983).

In the first year of operation of the new mechanism, there were 609 cases "closed," of which none resulted in findings of "guilt" and penalty by the Public Complaints Commissioner's office. Indeed only sixteen cases were deemed to warrant "action" after formal resolution, and these actions consisted of counselling, cautioning, advising, or speaking to the officer. As an article in the police association magazine *News and Views* (October 1983) remarked, "the Office of the Public Complaints Commissioner views its role in the discipline of police officers in a very positive and constructive manner. Generally speaking, its function is to lessen the tension in the community and to build respect for the police force. Toronto's pilot project has developed a system which is working extremely well."

CIRPA did seem to react positively to the composition of the twenty-four member civilian board who would hear complaints, commenting only on the failure to include someone who was active in the gay community (*Globe and Mail*, 17 June 1982). This may have been one reason why CIRPA was prepared to step inside this state mechanism, despite earlier disavowals. However, the explanation of their co-operation with the Public Complaints mechanism and with policing authorities generally relate to CIRPA's concerns for achieving legitimacy and, ultimately, organizational survival.

EXPLAINING THE TRANSFORMATION TO CO-OPERATING WITH POLICING AUTHORITIES

Privately, in interview, CIRPA members believed that over this period things had not improved. No one believed the police commission had improved; it continued to be described as "unrepresentative" and "out of touch." Only one person described the Public Complaints Commissioner's office as an improvement, while others described it as a "pacifier" with no impact on the police. Publicly, however, CIRPA members increasingly engaged these official bodies and their criteria of reform. One way to explain this is in terms of CIRPA's need for a public face of legitimacy and credibility. In the process CIRPA necessarily became co-opted by the state system for policing reform.

One reason why this change in strategy was necessary is the fact that the state's policing authorities "own" the public problems and issues in question. Their role in this regard is already legitimated:

> At any time in an historical period there is a recognition that specific issues are the legitimate province of specific persons, roles, and offices that command public attention, trust and influence. They have credibility while others who attempt to capture public opinion do not. . . . Today the state appears more often as the active agent, the owner of problems it seeks to solve. Government officials and agencies operate to define public issues, develop and organize demands on themselves, and control and move public attitudes and expectations. (Gusfield, 1981: 10, 15; see also Christie, 1977)

A second reason is that CIRPA initially failed to comprehend the power of the state in policing reform. It assumed that it could rally support around the "obvious" need to reform problems, and that its organization would provide the necessary power to accomplish the task.

CIRPA immediately faced a fundamental dilemma when it came to taking action to discredit the procedures supported by the police commission. Although CIRPA was very critical of the police commission, initially calling for abolition of its present form, it also felt that the police commission was the best available forum for bringing complaints and criticisms. CIRPA was obviously in a weak position organizationally. If CIRPA had never gone to the police commission, it is doubtful the police commission would have gone to it. If CIRPA limited its criticisms to internal organizational meetings, it would have received little attention. The regular attendance of media representatives at police commission meetings facilitated presentation of CIRPA's criticisms to the public. In order to be seen, and heard, at least under some limiting conditions, CIRPA necessarily gravitated to the policing authorities.

A sign that CIRPA began by taking its legitimacy for granted is seen in its initial confrontational posture. The previously cited correspondence, prior to the first police commission meeting CIRPA attended, indicates its lack of deference to the body before which it wished to appear. Moreover, as indicated by the statement in CIRPA's 22 October 1981 submission that the allegations are "so strong, coming from members of the legal community," CIRPA assumed the involvement of lawyers would raise its credibility.

This air of confidence was quickly reduced to the status of hot air by the police commissioners, who refused to schedule CIRPA for the meeting, hear allegations in public, or initiate a public inquiry. Allegations regarding the hold-up squad were simply fed back into police channels by having the chief of police appoint three senior officers to investigate. Subsequent allegations were either subject to a hostile reaction and then ignored or co-opted into the authorities' ongoing investigation. If issues identified by CIRPA were not in the policing reform agenda of the commissioners, they simply ignored them or side-stepped them by joking. They eventually became amicable when CIRPA began "talking the same language," that is, the technocratic discourse of the Hickling-Johnston reports. In all of this, the police commission effectively responded to CIRPA's "contestatory action" by enforcing their parameters of legitimacy and directing CIRPA into "approved paths of protest" (Elliott et al., 1982, p. 74).

The experience of CIRPA with the police commission illustrates general aspects of how that body is constituted and operates. Of the five people on the police commission, three are appointed by the province of Ontario, one is appointed by the metropolitan council, and the metropolitan chairman is a member via provincial legislation. Thus, only one of the five is chosen via the democratic election process; consequently, the organization is vulnerable to criticism that it is unrepresentative. The police commission employs various devices to appear to be in touch with the public, such as by giving well-publicized commendations to citizens who have assisted the police and by allowing public input at meetings. Even this is limited, however. In our observations of the police commission, the door is only open on certain conditions; the chance to be heard varies with the content of what is offered. Groups making criticisms and related suggestions find they have little impact. Even a police commission member stated in interview that citizens do not perceive the commission as having an open door policy.

In relation to CIRPA, the police commission did keep the door ajar under specified conditions. It seems that CIRPA did have enough legitimacy and organizational power to gain a modicum of attention. As part of maintaining the ideology of policing by consent (Brogden, 1982), the police commission had to be concerned with managing the dissent of CIRPA. Indeed, the commission eventually managed it to the point of lending it credibility and usurping it for their own purposes. Most fundamentally, CIRPA moved from their initial *raison d'etre* of vehement opposition to the Public Complaints Commissioner's operation to public acceptance of the operation, even dealing with them on some matters.

CIRPA had little choice but to show deference and conformity. It had little outside support from potential sources of power, such as the press, being subject to imputations that it had "no authority and even less credibility" (*Toronto Sun*, 21 September 1981). As Piven and Cloward (1977, p. xi) observe, "organizations endure, in short, by abandoning their oppositional politics." CIRPA endured by switching to "status elevation" ceremonies (Schur, 1980), accepting the police commission's hierarchy of credibility and discourse of reform issues, eventually to the exclusion of its original purpose of directly serving complainants' interests.

THE SEARCH FOR LEGITIMACY AMONG CITIZEN CONSITUTENCIES

The problem of accomplishing legitimacy in the eyes of others while maintaining internal legitimacy and cohesion is not just a matter of becoming acceptable to the authorities. It also entails accomplishing credibility and establishing legitimacy with a range of citizen organizations which are relevant constituencies for support in furthering the cause.

The potential constituencies of CIRPA were complainants, citizen minority groups, radical police critics, and general public opinion. CIRPA faced the dilemma that achievement of credibility in relation to any one constituency put constraints on the organization in other areas. In particular, the eventual priority given to the achievement of legitimacy with the police commission meant that CIRPA had little credibility with some other constituencies. This was the case both because organizational energy and resources were directed at accomplishing legitimacy with the police authorities and because the eventual compromises with them were considered compromising by some important citizen constituencies.

In relation to complainants, CIRPA had originally stated that it would "help" complainants, but complainants would "make all the decisions" (CIRPA leaflet, "Information for Complainants"). However, this was no more than an ideal in the face of CIRPA's legalistic approach and its advice that complainants avoid the official structures.

For example, an internal document to guide CIRPA members in processing complaints stated that the "number one priority" was to get a written statement from a complainant. It advised, "you will likely have to provide real encouragement to some complainants to produce written statements," adding that complainants "may be getting weary of the exercise especially when you place demands on them to clean up their statements." This appeared to be a warning that the legalistic priorities of CIRPA would not always accord with the desires of complainants.

CIRPA began with a priority of gathering information about allegations of abuse, because this is necessary for the social construction of "facts" on which to base calls for reform. As the organization evolved this became of increasing significance, given the shift of focus from particular complaints of abuse to policing policies. Consequently, as one board member articulated, a negative effect of CIRPA for complainants is that the organization cannot "follow through" on complaints and complainants might have "hoped otherwise." This board member was of the opinion that CIRPA should stress to complainants that it is not "just the individual case but the overall pattern that's important." Most CIRPA board members acknowledged their main function for complainants was to provide a "listening-board," "comfort," and a "feeling" that they have somewhere to go with their complaints. In short, CIRPA's increasing focus on reform, which no longer highlighted individual allegations of abuse, affected its legitimacy with complainants.

CIRPA also faced a dilemma in relation to complainants who wished to go through official structures. Such actions by complainants conflicted with CIRPA's original advice to avoid the official system. Moreover, CIRPA's "you make all the decisions" statement to complainants had to be reconciled with this advice to avoid the appearance of coercion. Faced with this contradiction, CIRPA eventually made referrals to, and had clients in common with, the Public Complaints Commissioner's office. In turn, CIRPA was limited in criticizing the very office it had set out to oppose, ending by working within the forms and strictures of that office.

CIRPA faced enormous problems of credibility in relation to a range of citizen groups. Assertions were made from the outset that "Black, South Asian and Gay communities" were subject to abuse from police and have "become increasingly disaffected from the police" (Revised draft proposal, Introduction, 8 July 1981), and that CIRPA "consists of representatives of Toronto's main minority groups, all of whom have experienced police abuse in the past and have been frustrated and disillusioned by existing mechanisms for dealing with it" (*Action!* 1, p. 5). However, in terms of board representation and active involvement in CIRPA, visible minority group participation was very minimal while gay community membership was proportionately very high. As one board member commented in interview, "there's not a lot of support from the Black community, there's not a lot of support from the East Indian community, there's not a lot of support from the women's community. The only people who seem to support it are gay men . . . and a few liberal lawyers." Among nine CIRPA members interviewed, all identified the gay community as a major constituency of support for CIRPA, and seven mentioned this constituency first. Although reference was also made to visible minorities, it was often accompanied by such comments as they are "supportive but not active" and they are involved "but not as consistently as desirable."

CIRPA's priorities have not resulted in substantial efforts to build networks among citizen groups. A board member observed in interview that "we've spent a lot more time making briefs and analyzing the cases and going to the Police Commission than we ever thought we would do. And that's chewed up an awful lot of resources." Other board members concurred that this was a major factor in not developing a broad base of citizen group support. One member said that when he visited various groups to invite their involvement in CIRPA, "they kept saying to me, 'why should we be interested in CIRPA? CIRPA is not interested in us. CIRPA is only interested in the gay community.' " Another member said, "I do feel the Board consists of a bunch of white middle-class liberals and a couple of gay men here and there. And they're just going out and doing their own thing in the best way they can figure out to do it. And if other people want to come along for the ride then that's fine with them."

Some board members ascribed the difficulty in obtaining minority citizen group support to the location of CIRPA headquarters in an alderman's office at Toronto City Hall. One expressed the need for an office "in the ethnic communities," while another believed "to be credible you have to be independent and CIRPA is surely not independent as long as it's sharing space in an alderman's office. I think it's terrible, we have to be consistent, because we criticized the Police Commission for wanting people to come down to [police headquarters]. We have criticized the Human Rights Commission for not having offices in the community.'' As this member pointed out, CIRPA had set up a facility for ''nearly the same market'' which still had to travel substantial distances to get there.

One explanation for the active involvement of gay men in CIRPA is that the organization provided a potential vehicle for obtaining remedies following the bathhouse raids and other law enforcement crackdowns against gay people. In organizing after the bathhouse raids, the gay community became aware that it could ''have an effect'' on the broader community. Apparently, as their commitments diminished, some gay men consciously sought another cause to become involved with and offered their skills to CIRPA. This is a typical pattern among those who seek ongoing involvement in the reform process (see Becker, 1963, p. 53; Street et al., 1970, p. 159).

We learned through various contexts and personal communications that the perception of CIRPA as being largely composed of and working for gay people dissuaded some Black groups which might otherwise have become involved. Furthermore, according to some young complainants from the Scarborough party incident, the perception of CIRPA as a gay organization dissuaded some of the other youths involved from going to CIRPA.

It is perhaps significant that, during the course of the study, gay people did not play a very active role in making CIRPA presentations to the police commission. In CIRPA's second response to the Hickling-Johnston reports, the gay community is not mentioned by name once. Although CIRPA recommended generally that ''higher priority'' be given to ''race relations and minority concerns,'' it focused on *visible* minorities. The Right to Privacy Committee, specifically on behalf of the gay community, presented its response to the Hickling-Johnston reports to the police commission on the same date as CIRPA but had a very negative reception, while CIRPA was favourably received. CIRPA may actually constitute a relatively legitimate channel through which the gay community can articulate its interests to the authorities.

CIRPA made various efforts to reconcile the dilemma of credibility with visible minority groups. For example, the organization tried to find out about allegations of police harassment in two troubled areas of the city where police-minority tensions persist. Visible-minority concerns are consistently presented to the police commission and are published in the organization's documents. CIRPA has also asked visible minority represent-atives to speak to the police commission as well as at CIRPA's annual meetings, which are open to the public. However, although visible minority representatives have participated in this way, their overall participation in the organization remains low. When it comes to organizational decision-making, they hardly participate at all. This was particularly evident at the second annual meeting, during the election of the new board. A person attending the meeting asked why there was not going to be more representation of women and minorities on the board, but the question was not even discussed.

CIRPA also had to deal with more radical police critics in its midst. For example, at the first annual meeting there was a spirited debate over the wording of a flyer headed "Problems with 52 Division," which was to be distributed among residents in the divisional area. Some argued the wording was too complimentary to the police, and it was eventually altered to convey a more critical, radical tone. However, to offset this, the revised flyer contained, in capital letters, the conciliatory statement that "CIRPA IS AGAINST POLICE ABUSE BUT NOT ANTI-POLICE."

CIRPA strived to reconcile the public/private tension by shifting formulations and emphases according to the particular audience and context. Radical and critical statements regularly appeared in CIRPA's internal documentation, but when the same issues were dealt with in a public arena, for example with the Police Commission, the tenor of such statements was modified. Furthermore, when CIRPA negotiated with policing authorities, the full extent of these negotiations was not always revealed in the organization's documentation; for example, in the minutes of a meeting at which a CIRPA representative announced that information had been exchanged with the Public Complaints Commissioner's office, the minutes record only a one-way flow to CIRPA and not the fact that CIRPA also gave information to the Public Complaints office.

Over time, radical and critical statements continued to be made by individual members, but organizationally radical, critical, and antipathic statements were very unusual. Again, the pre-eminence of achieving legitimacy with policing authorities gradually reduced confrontational participation or debate. Organizational survival and maintenance became paramount, as CIRPA pressed ahead without the broad-based support and involvement it had originally sought.

ORGANIZATION MAINTENANCE, GOAL DISPLACEMENT, AND THE DOMINANT ORDER

CIRPA has continuously experienced a shortage of funds, membership subscriptions, donations, volunteers to process complaints, and people to answer a twenty-four hour telephone. In CIRPA's Summer 1982 newsletter, members were asked to give financial assistance and their own time to assist the organization in campaigning for more money and members. This newsletter also identified a "number of factors which have caused this cash squeeze," including overhead for telephone services and a part-time co-ordinator; many more cases than anticipated, and attendant costs for such items as stationery, photographs, medical records, and the volume of briefs and summaries prepared; and a previous fundraising event which actually cost more money to undertake than was taken in. The newsletter justifies the membership campaign by saying, "we need money, therefore, we need people." The newsletter also states the need for more volunteers, saying they are "desperately" needed not only for fundraising but also to work with complainants and answer the telephone because "only about one-third of the fifty-plus volunteers on the line are actually accepting the duty." Significantly, the newsletter did not indicate any need for more people to prepare and present briefs to the police commission. These concerns were reiterated at CIRPA meetings and in materials sent out to members and "friends." However, they proved to be unsuccessful financially. During 1982 CIRPA had an expenditure of $2,256.69 on "fundraisers" but took in only $1,203.54 from such events. An invitation for one fundraising event included the statement that "CIRPA has over four hundred individual members and over forty organizational members." If this was the case, CIRPA income from memberships ($10 for individual members and $25 for organizational memberships) for a twelve-month period would be at least $5,000. However, the figure given for income from memberships at CIRPA's second annual meeting was reported as $2,060.

Organization maintenance had become a major problem and priority. As defined by Zand and Ash (1970, p. 517), "organizational maintenance is a special form of goal transformation, in which the primary activity of the organization becomes the maintenance of membership, funds and other requirements of organizational existence. It . . . is accompanied by conservatism, for the original goals must be accommodated to societal norms in order to avoid conflicts that could threaten the organization's viability."

CIRPA's decision-making reflected an increasingly conservative character into the winter of 1982-83. At a December 1982 meeting of CIRPA, information was presented about a person who wished to take a small claims court action against the police and had asked for CIRPA's help. The opinion was put forward that the person concerned was a bit "weird" and would likely lose the case, which would "look bad for CIRPA." CIRPA departed from its own original mandate to act on the instructions of clients, avoiding involvement with the case in order to sustain organizational credibility and interests. Similar to lawyers acting on behalf of persons before the courts

(Ericson and Baranek, 1982), CIRPA members acted as gatekeepers of cases and information in accordance with the framework of the policing authorities.

The matter of visible minority participation can also be seen in terms of organizational maintenance. In our observations, apart from the salaried co-ordinator of CIRPA, only one visible minority person attended CIRPA meetings on a regular basis and took a consistently active part in the organization's activities between July 1982 and February 1983. Other visible minority people elected to the board of directors in February 1982 have apparently not had active participation in CIRPA. Mrs. Johnson, the widow of Albert Johnson, was elected to the CIRPA board at the second annual meeting in February 1983. However, in the period of our research she was not actively involved in CIRPA. These considerations give rise to the question of whether visible minority participation in CIRPA is primarily symbolic of help "in generating public support and some degree of legitimacy" (Schur, 1980, p. 15) in the context of a perception that visible minorities are subject to disproportionate harassment and abuse by police. Similarly, no young people under twenty years of age were consistently and actively involved in CIRPA, even though they are viewed as disproportionate recipients of police harassment. In this case, however, there was not even a rhetoric of involvement, only the gesture of inviting a Black youth to speak about alleged police harassment in a particular area.

If CIRPA is not accountable to the primary citizen constituencies it purports to represent, then the question that emerges is, to whom is it accountable? In interview, several CIRPA board members said the organization is accountable to "its members." One member said, "I don't think CIRPA is accountable to anybody. . . . There are people in the group who are accountable to the groups they come from—like myself. . . . But we don't run CIRPA. . . . We're on the board in name only and CIRPA doesn't seem to be accountable to anybody."

The involvement of lawyers has entailed an element of their own professional maintenance as well as that of CIRPA's. In the original draft proposal for CIRPA in May 1981, it had been stated that "a rotation of lawyers will be necessary to act as a form of duty counsel" and that "the bulk of staffing would be done on a volunteer basis." Given the proposed structure and strategies of CIRPA, including advice to complainants regarding the options of small claims court actions, civil lawsuits, and criminal charges, lawyer involvement appeared crucial. However, the "duty counsel" concept appears not to have been adhered to strictly, since CIRPA's revised procedures for processing complaints, dated October 1981, state "CIRPA lawyers will provide one session to give advice at no charge. After that the complainant will have to retain a lawyer in the normal way, paying fees or obtaining a legal aid certificate." It is arguable that one legal session with complainants might be necessary for information gathering and thus of importance for organizational maintenance, while subsequent sessions are less useful to the organization but of obvious use to individual lawyer maintenance.

Unable to find enough volunteers to answer its twenty-four hour phoneline for complainants, CIRPA contacted lawyers, some of whom agreed to having their offices take calls during the day. Thus, people calling CIRPA during these hours have their complaint processed initially by a lawyer's office. This again serves CIRPA's organizational interests as well as the professional interests of participating lawyers. In the opinion of one board member, "I think they're involved because they're a bunch of liberals and it's good for their job. I think it's prestigious to be involved in CIRPA in radical legal circles. . . . Not all lawyers think it's prestigious . . . but if you're a radical then its prestigious . . . and it's good for business. . . . I think they do care, they're genuinely concerned. But they can go home and forget about it all. It's not real. It reminds me of the Victorian ladies who did charity work." In sum, complainants are drawn into the professional arena of legal experts and are transformed from complainants to clients. With the staff of lawyers' offices processing complaints initially, it is possible that CIRPA's emphasis on expressing care and concern for complainants will shift toward the typical lawyer-client relation (Ericson and Baranek, 1982).

Within twenty months of inception, CIRPA had displaced its original goals from independent review, particularly of citizen complaints against the police, to accommodation with the official review procedures of the Public Complaints Commissioner's office; from democratizing the police commission to working within its parameters; from bringing allegations of police abuse before the police commission to making standard recommendations regarding policing policies and management; from collaborating with a broad base of citizen groups to representing a very narrow constituency; from "working with" troubled complainants to "trying to serve" and "working on behalf of" them in a typical pattern of professional-client relations. This movement has been clearly in a conservative direction, in accordance with the Weber-Michels model of organizational change: "whatever the form of goal transformation, it is always in the direction of greater conservatism (the accommodation of organizational goals to the dominant societal consensus)" (Zand and Ash, 1970, p. 517). Given the original narrow focus in attacking a particular piece of legislation and the mechanism it was to establish, this movement is also predictable. "Although the danger of being co-opted is always present, when a group has relatively narrow claims to press and is not in direct opposition to the prevailing political order working within the system may make sense and may, at times, even be distinctly advantageous" (Schur, 1980, p. 202).

CIRPA board members interviewed had differing views on co-optation. Three felt there was no "danger" of co-optation, two others perceived a danger that it might happen, and three stated that the process of co-optation was occurring. Those who felt that co-optation was not underway gave as the main indicators the belief that individual members were above co-optation and that CIRPA did not accept government funding. Subsequently, a financial grant was accepted from the Solicitor-General of Canada.

At the second annual meeting, a "Review of CIRPA's First Year" was presented by a member. This review first mentioned an award made to a citizen in a legal suit against two police officers and the criminal conviction of two officers on charges of forcibly confining a citizen. Neither of these were CIRPA cases. The remainder of the account focused on submissions which had been made to the police commission and referred to an article in the Toronto Police Association magazine. While not providing tangible evidence of CIRPA's impact, the presenter asserted that "we have had an impact on the police in this city. They know that we're here. The Police Commission knows we're here and even though nobody will admit that we've had an effect, I think we have." A document circulated at the meeting stated that after CIRPA had identified the problems within the hold-up squad, "CIRPA has not received any further complaints against this squad. This would tend to give credence to the original complaints and would tend to demonstrate that community pressure can, in fact, achieve improvements in police operations." CIRPA also claimed some credit for mobilizing community pressure in one police divisional area where complaints had been frequent and stated that since then the volume of complaints had been less and the divisional commanding officer had retired.

In interview, board members were typically discreet and vague about CIRPA's effects. There was some consensus that CIRPA had increased "public awareness" and provided a sounding board for complainants. Otherwise, there was little agreement, although two members mentioned CIRPA's influence on Hickling-Johnston and two referred to the hold-up squad stopping their previous interrogation tactics. One member thought it positive that CIRPA "exists."

CONCLUSION

CIRPA is effectively an "add-on" to the system. CIRPA saw as "cumbersome" the "split function" between the Police Complaints Bureau and the Public Complaints Commissioner's office, but CIRPA splits that function further. How, one wonders, does a potential complainant decide whether to go to a police station, to the Police Complaints Bureau, to the Public Complaints Commissioner's office, or to CIRPA? Through which of these channels are the complainant's interests best served? Overall procedures for processing complaints against the police have become more complex, if not more satisfactory. If CIRPA had pursued and accomplished its original objective of working closely with complainants themselves and with a broad range of community and minority groups, the group could at least have attempted to delineate the criteria for "successful" reforms and strategies for attaining them, from the perspective of those whose interests were supposed to be served by the organization.

In practice, police reform issues are blurred as CIRPA works through the police commission, the Public Complaints Commissioner's office, and legal channels. Structural problems of policing are transformed into policy and management problems, into misunderstandings or individual reflections of "bad apples," and into tinkering with legal technicalities. While individuals in CIRPA perceived these processes, the organization as a whole did not reflect upon them. An organizational commitment to action accompanied by consistent, systematic, and critical examination of the nature, purposes, and effects of their endeavours could have helped to bring these complexities and their implications more clearly into CIRPA's view.

As it operates, CIRPA has implications for state control, albeit not in the manner intended. Rather than loosening state control, CIRPA may contribute to its solidification. In the eyes of a board member, CIRPA's existence means the police "have to be a bit more careful about what they say. It doesn't mean they have to be a bit more careful about what they do, but at least they have to keep up a façade." In other words, CIRPA assists the police commission in maintaining and refining the surrogate accountability of the police institution. The police commission does its part by hearing CIRPA and other citizen groups, which help construct the image that the police commission is willing to account for its actions not only to those who support it but also to those who come to criticize. In the process the veil of administrative decency is drawn, and the legitimacy of the state's policing reform efforts are secured.

Challenging the legitimacy of the police is a more substantial threat to the dominant order than challenging educational, social welfare, or economic institutions. While these institutions have substantial and pervasive social control effects, they are more implicit than those of the police. The police in Canadian society are elevated to the status of a national symbol and are at the forefront of debates about the relation between the state and citizens. In spite of their virtual monopoly on violent forms of social control and their increasing monopoly on information which makes citizens knowable for control purposes (Ericson and Shearing, 1986), the police remain legitimacy incarnate. They are the very embodiment of all the state stands for, of "peace, order and good government" and its translation into "law and order".

State reformers give credence to outside reformers only to the extent that the latter can be embodied in this policing system. When the police are questioned seriously, the authorities do not hesitate to deem reform to be in order, and they proceed to frame the boundaries of the discourse and the outcome of reform. Thus policing reform serves to "re-form" the police institution, and to "re-order" the system of domination it is established to serve.

* We are particularly grateful to the Citizen's Independent Review of Police Activities Organization for the access they granted. We also received help from representatives of the Toronto Public Complaints Commissioner's Office, the police commission, and the Police Complaints Bureau. For comments on earlier drafts we acknowledge Anthony Doob, Clifford Shearing, and Peter Solomon.

REFERENCES

Becker, H. S. 1963. *Outsiders: Studies in the Sociology of Deviance.* Glencoe: Free Press.

Brodeur, J. P. 1983. "High Policing and Low Policing: Remarks about the Policing of Political Activities." *Social Problems* 30: 507-20.

Brogden, M. 1982. *The Police: Autonomy and Consent.* London: Academic Press.

Bruner, A. 1981. "Study of Relations Between the Homosexual Community and the Police." Report to Mayor Arthur Eggleton and the Council of the City of Toronto. Toronto.

Chambliss, W. J., and R. B. S. Seidman, 1971. *Law, Order and Power.* Reading, Massachussetts: Addison-Wesley.

Christie, N. 1977. "Conflicts as Property." *The British Journal of Criminology* 17: 1-15.

Edelman, M. 1971. *Politics as Symbolic Action: Mass Arousal and Quiescence.* Chicago: Markham.

_____. 1977. *Political Language: Words That Succeed and Policies That Fail.* New York: Academic Press.

Elliott, B., F. Bechofer, D. McCrone, and S. Black. 1982. "Bourgeois Social Movements in Britain: Repertoires and Responses." *The Sociological Review* 30: 71-96.

Ericson, R. V. 1982. *Reproducing Order: A Study of Police Patrol Work.* Toronto: University of Toronto Press.

_____. and P. M. Baranek. 1982. *The Ordering of Justice: A Study of Accused Persons as Dependants in the Criminal Process.* Toronto: University of Toronto Press.

Ericson, R. V., and C. D. Shearing. 1986. "The Scientification of Police Work." In N. Stehr and G. Bohme, eds., *The Knowledge Society.* Sociology of the Sciences Yearbook, vol. 10. Dordrecht: Reidel.

Fleming, T. 1983. "Criminalizing a Marginal Community: The Bawdy House Raids." In T. Fleming and L. Visano, *Deviant Designations: Crime, Law and Deviance in Canada.* Toronto: Butterworths.

Goldstein, H. 1967. "Administrative Problems in Controlling the Exercise of Police Authority." *The Journal of Criminal Law, Criminology and Police Science* 58: 160-72.

Gusfield, J. R. 1981. *The Culture of Public Problems.* Chicago: University of Chicago Press.

Hartford Institute of Criminal and Social Justice. 1980. *Civilian Review of the Police: The Experiences of American Cities.* Connecticut: The Hartford Institute of Criminal and Social Justice.

McDonald, D. C. 1981. "Commission of Inquiry Concerning Certain Activities of the R.C.M.P." *Freedom and Security Under the Law.* 2nd Report, vol. 1. Ottawa: The Commission.

McMahon, M., and R. V. Ericson. 1984. *Policing Reform: A Study of the Reform Process and Police Institution in Toronto.* Toronto: Centre of Criminology, University of Toronto.

Maloney, A. 1975. *The Metropolitian Toronto Review of Citizen-Police Complaint Procedures.* Report to the Metropolitan Board of Commissioners of Police, Toronto.

Morand, D. R. 1976. *The Royal Commission into Metropolitan Toronto Police Practices.* Toronto: The Commission.

Pitman, W. 1977. "Now Is Not Too Late." Report submitted to the Council of Metropolitan Toronto by Task Force on Human Relations. Toronto: The Task Force.

Piven, F. F., and R. A. Cloward. 1977. *Poor People's Movements. Why They Succeed, How They Fail.* New York: Pantheon.

Public Complaints Commissioner. 1983. "First Annual Report of the Public Complaints Commissioner and the Police Complaints Board." Toronto.

Punch, M., ed., 1983. *Control in the Police Organization.* Cambridge, Massachusetts: MIT Press.

Schur, E. 1980. *The Politics of Deviance: Stigma Contests and the Uses of Power.* Englewood Cliffs, New Jersey: Prentice-Hall.

Skolnick, J. 1969. *The Politics of Protest: Violent Aspects of Protest and Confrontation.* A Staff Report to the National Commission on the Causes and Prevention of Violence. Washignton: U.S. Government.

State Research Bulletin. 1981. "Controlling the Police?: Police Accountability in the

U.K.'' *State Research Bulletin* 4, no. 23 (April-May): 110-23.

Street, D., G. T. Martin Jr., and L. J. Gordon. 1970. *The Welfare Industry: Functionaries and Recipients in Public Aid.* Beverly Hills: Sage.

Taylor, I. 1981. *Law and Order: Arguments for Socialism.* London: MacMillan.

Zand, M. and R. Ash. 1970. "Social Movement Organizations: Growth, Decay and Change." In J. R. Gusfield, ed., *Protest, Reform and Revolt.* New York: John Wiley and Sons.

4

Ideological Biases in the Evaluation of Criminal Justice Reform

EZZAT A. FATTAH

WHAT IS CRIMINAL JUSTICE REFORM?

What exactly is criminal justice reform? Literary and dictionary definitions are inadequate for the sociological analysis of reform. In "The State and Criminal Justice Reform" (this volume) and in "Reforming the Police and Policing Reform" (with McMahon, this volume), Ericson argues that reform is making something *better*[1] by changing imperfections, faults, errors, abuse, or malpractice. He sees reform as intimately linked with the idea of progress, in that successive reforms are part of the quest to progress toward a more efficient and humane system. Efficiency in the criminal justice sphere is interpreted, in turn, as the ability of a particular reform to prevent crime by deterrence and to be relatively cost-effective, while humaneness is understood as the reform's conformity with the moral sensibilities of its time.

In both papers, as in other criminological writings on the topic, change in the criminal justice system is often equated with reform. But reform needs to be distinguished from simple change. Although reform involves changing the status quo, not all change would qualify as reform. Change can be objectively observed and measured; reform, on the other hand, implies a subjective judgment. To label a certain change as improvement or as reform is to pass a value judgement that fits our ideological beliefs; thus, reform is not synonymous with change.

Reform is an ideological and a relative concept because adjectives such as good, better, progressive, efficient and humane are not value free and mean different things to different people.[2] What may be seen as progressive reforms by some may be considered as permissiveness by others. Blood transfusion is a life-saving mechanism to some and the work of Satan to others. Moral crusaders are the heroes of the right and the villains of the left, and the changes they advocate are hailed by conservatives and denounced by radicals.

The same ideological biases appear when changes in the criminal justice system are examined. Speedy disposal of cases in criminal courts may be regarded as an indicator of enhanced efficiency by some and condemned by others as the sign of expedient, summary justice. During "the golden age of California prison reform," for example, the combination of diagnosis, evaluation, treatment, and classification was highly praised by Dr. K. Menninger in his book *The Crime of Punishment* (1969), only to be severely criticized by J. Irwin in his book *The Felon* (1970) as "a grand hypocrisy in which custodial concerns, administrative exigencies, and punishment are all disguised as treatment."[3] Humaneness in criminal justice was viewed by some as a desirable goal and denounced by others as molly-coddling criminals. An increase in police autonomy and police power is usually applauded by those on the right end of the ideological scale while regarded by those on the left as an oppressive, tyrannical move. For the former, criminal justice reform is what strengthens the dominant order. For the latter, it is what weakens, destroys, or replaces the existing order.

IS THERE GOOD AND BAD REFORM?

Adjectives such as "good" or "bad" are often encountered in discussions of reform. Good reform, it is claimed, is what makes things better, and bad reform is what makes things worse. Yet, as Henshel (1976) points out, "better" and "worse" are terms not ordinarily used in sociological analysis. There is no such thing as good or bad reform; there is only good and bad *change*, depending on whose side we are on. Before labelling any change in the criminal justice system as reform, it is necessary to define what, in the view of the observer, would constitute "progress" or "improvement." This, needless to say, cannot be done in neutral or value-free terms; it can only be done with reference to a specific ideology.

Change aimed at or resulting in increasing state control over citizens in general and criminals in particular would not qualify as progressive reform but as regressive intervention when viewed in the light of a non-interventionist ideology. The same change would be viewed as a considerable improvement by those who feel that society has become too permissive and who believe that the present nature of crime requires more state intervention and stronger police powers. Furthermore, change that would qualify as reform from the administrator's point of view may not be seen as such by the general public. Quite often, the interests of administrators are at odds with those of the users of the criminal justice system. Most of the time, reducing costs can only be done by cutting down on services. Thus, measures aimed at making the system cost-efficient may be regarded as reform by those who manage the system but may raise the ire of the public. Changes in police, court, and penal practices aimed at rendering the system more humane may have strong appeal to liberal and radical criminologists but may be vehemently opposed by those in the system, by the public, or by victims' organizations. Inversely, measures aimed at preventing crime through the sacrifice of legal safeguards and the imposition of harsher penalties may be welcomed by the general public as sweeping reforms while decried by civil libertarians. Consequently, as long as it is impossible to dissociate the notion of reform from its ideological content, denouncing change in the criminal justice system amounts to nothing more than a criticism of the ideology underlying that change.

WHO IS A REFORMER TODAY?

This problem with regard to the concept and definition of reform needs to be addressed whenever an attempt is made to define who is a reformer. The frequent, indiscriminate use of the label can be confusing with no explanation of who qualifies as a reformer and why. Distinctions between state reformers and non-state reformers or between inside reformers and outside reformers are meaningless unless criteria are provided that would make it possible to determine who does and who does not fit these categories. Does anyone who calls for the reform of the police, the courts, corrections, or the criminal law qualify as a reformer? And if reducing cost or improving effectiveness (or efficiency) are sufficient criteria for reform, then every civil servant, every administrator is a reformer!

Traditionally, the term "reformer" has only been used to describe dedicated, ideologically motivated, and strongly influential individuals. One can easily accept as reformers persons who devoted their lives to what they ideologically believed to be necessary reforms, persons such as Beccaria, Bentham, or Romilly. Their claim to the status of reformer is based on "their assault on the folly, injustice and cruelty of the then existing criminal jurisprudence, in their trenchant criticism of outworn codes, obscurantist traditions, blind superstitions, dogmatic technicalities, oppressive fictions, and useless relics of the past, in their proposal of rational substitutes, in their pointing the way to the light."[4] The absence of such individuals in the recent history of Canadian criminal justice is neither reason nor excuse to extend the label to every zealous, committed, or opportunistic politician or bureaucrat. Reform, as mentioned above, is not merely the modification of any aspect of the status quo. Reform is a deep, thorough, fundamental, comprehensive, ideologically motivated change.

Thus when the solicitor general of Canada advocates and urges the early release of non-violent offenders to relieve the overcrowding in federal institutions, he is not professing reform. Practical considerations are, of course, ideologically grounded, but change based on nothing other than pragmatism cannot be viewed from a sociological point of view as reform. The vast majority of changes in our criminal justice system were not motivated by explicit ideological beliefs or a clear penal philosophy. They were dictated by considerations of expediency, efficiency, or cost-effectiveness, in which ideological awareness functions as an undercurrent rather than as a guiding presence. Many of the changes are simple responses to demands made by an unsophisticated and manipulable public that finds relief in adopting a punitive mood. They are outdated recipes catering to public demands for promises of deliverance from what is perceived as the social evil of crime. As Sieber (1981) points out, the greater the perceived ill, the greater the frustration, and hence the greater the demand for a strong, immediate, definitive, and hence simplistic solution.

Humaneness, still viewed by many as primary criterion for criminal justice reform, has disappeared, not because the system has become overly humane but because humaneness is no longer regarded as a necessary or desirable attribute of criminal justice. Humanity and compassion—which until recently were believed to be the two most essential ingredients of a civilized criminal justice—are giving way to primitive, vengeful, and retaliatory responses. One need only listen to the demands made by those who claim to speak on behalf of victims of crime to witness the open display of vindictive instincts long held in check by the demands of civilization. Surprisingly, radical critics have been conspicuous by their silence about the growing dangers of the so-called victim movements.[5]

Humane justice is seen nowadays as weak and ineffective. No wonder there has not been one single change in recent years that was motivated by or sold to the public on the basis of humanitarian considerations. Whether one looks at the new *Young Offenders Act* (which is one of the major pieces of legislation in the history of Canadian criminal law) or at other implemented or contemplated changes in the field of corrections (such as gating, tightening of mandatory supervision, construction of special handling units, and so forth) the inevitable conclusion is that humaneness is no longer an animating force behind the changes being introduced. Neither legislators nor administrators are trying to appear humane nowadays. Our society has reached the sad state where humaneness is out of fashion and is no longer a desirable quality in politicians or criminal justice practitioners. Toughness and hawkishness are more valued than the traditional attributes of mercy and forgiveness. It is not surprising, then, that despite the economic crisis and the policy of restraint, politicians are willing to propose and implement changes which, although quite expensive, are popular with a public strongly in favour of harsh punishments. Whether at present or in the past the general public has always been unsympathetic to prison reform. And many of the barriers in the way of effective criminal justice reform could be traced directly to the opposition of, or pressure from, the electorate. And yet discussions of criminal justice reform continue to ignore the important and crucial role the general public plays in initiating or hindering such change. The studies of Ranulf (1964) on middle-class punitiveness and of Lipset (1960) on working-class authoritarianism remain isolated pieces in the abundant literature dealing with public attitudes to crime and punishment. Summarizing Lipset's working-class authoritarianism approach, McDonald (1976) points out:

> The lower the status of the group the more there is to gain from policies of punitiveness, hence the greater the support for punitive measures, and the more perceptions of crime and sanctions will support this position. Those at the bottom rung of the social hierarchy have the most to fear by being identified with criminal and other unsavoury elements. It is they, consequently, who have the most to gain by separating off a criminal group, with which they can compare themselves favourably, and which can be seen by others to rank clearly below them. The more marginal the group, the greater the need for a margin.

Radical criminologists have paid inadequate attention to why the public is so often opposed to attempts to reduce the catalogue of criminal offences and to humanize criminal law or the criminal justice system. Nor have they yet explained why it is that an institution badly in need of urgent reform, such as the police, is rated so highly by the public. Before the revelations made by the McDonald Commission in Ottawa and the Keable Commission in Quebec, it could have been argued that the police organization had succeeded in hiding its wrong-doings, in keeping a deceiving façade and in maintaining a positive public image. Surprisingly, this image has not been significantly tarnished by the revelations of recent years. And if the general public served by the police see little need for reform, on whose behalf should reform be preached or undertaken? And who is to define and determine the content of such reform: the intellectual elite?

INTELLECTUALS' PESSIMISM, RESEARCHERS' CYNICISM, AND OFFICIALS' MISONEISM

Academics are generally sceptical of reform and reformers. Sieber (1981) believes, for example, that a plague of pessimism about the chances of rational human improvement has infected many Western intellectuals as well as a large segment of the public. This echoes what Henshel (1976) wrote five years earlier:

> It is difficult to characterize Western intellectuals today other than to say that now, more than ever before, they sense the need for drastic change and yet despair of either bringing it about or seeing it occur naturally. Having long ago lost their faith in God, they are losing faith in themselves and human action. The sense of progress is dead among the intelligentsia, and seems, by both objective polling and impressionistic reporting, to be declining with the man on the street as well.

Henshel observed that popular belief in inevitable progress can lead to a ready acceptance of new innovations as part of the grand pattern of the future. Pessimism about the future, on the other hand, can lead to despair, lethargy, and alienation. Henshel argued that pessimism coupled with a belief in the potency of one's actions can call forth heroic effort, while pessimism coupled with lack of faith in counteractions can lead to passivity. This illustrates the significance of beliefs about the efficacy of intervention.

Ericson's writings reflect both his pessimism and his cynicism about the possibility of criminal justice reform. He concludes that all "reformers" are in reality commited to maintaining the status quo or to increasing state control over the powerless groups in society. McMahon and Ericson express the view that reform itself is constantly in need of reform. Both are convinced that any reform initiated from within and implemented by those in the system can have no other goal but to maintain the status quo, reinforce the existing order, or reproduce more control. They believe that no real reform can be achieved from inside, that "inside reformers" always attempt to co-opt, neutralize, or use "outside reformers" to their own benefit and to achieve their own goals. By making these claims, they are actually dividing the so-called "reformers" into two categories: the noble and the corrupt. Those outside are the real reformers, anxious to initiate change, to improve the system, or to replace it. Those inside are the ones who suffer from misoneism, they are not interested in reform but in strengthening state domination of and control over the powerless and in keeping the latter in their subservient position in the hierarchy of power. In the words of Ericson:

Reformers of the state constantly define sources of potential harm to the "public interest." They construct definitions of who are the "dangerous" and work to stigmatize and exclude them, thereby ensuring that they remain politically powerless. This process has been well documented within criminology in the case of dangerous individuals, showing how the state often drops its assumed standards of formal legal rationality in order to incapacitate dangerous people.

For those whose political ideology opposes Ericson's, the measures he is criticizing are reforms aimed at achieving what they see as the primary goal of criminal justice—the protection of society. Thus these changes could be seen as reform measures or anti-reform measures depending on one's ideology.

Those who claim that it is the powerful who try to expand the definition of the dangerous and increase the stigmatization and exclusion of those fitting that definition in order to ensure "that these groups remain politically powerless" ignore the fact that it is the working classes who are continuously calling for such extension, stigmatization, and exclusion. The general public, not the elite and powerful, are the strongest advocates of the principle of less eligibility. In times of weak governments, like the time in which we live, the public, the voters, and the pressure groups become the major force. They are either the promoters or blockers of change.

By distinguishing between "inside" and "outside" reformers, a demarcation line is drawn, explicitly or implicitly, intentionally or unintentionally, between the purists and the corrupt, between those who are fighting for justice and those who are struggling to maintain and assert their domination. A differentiation between the advocates of change and the defenders of the status quo seems more appropriate than the distinction between inside and outside reformers, because ultimately those who are genuinely interested in seeing reform do not care whether the impetus for change comes from without or from within, whether it is achieved as a result of confrontation or co-operation, militancy or reconciliation.

Officials' hatred of change is likely to pave the way to stagnation and lack of innovation. This, coupled with intellectuals' pessimism and cynicism about reform, could then lead to despair, lethargy, and alienation. It can also lead to social reformist inclinations being "half-frightened and half-persuaded into a do-nothing position on various social problems" (Schneider, 1978). The ultimate result is passivity and inaction.

UNANTICIPATED NEGATIVE CONSEQUENCES OF REFORM

Many social action programmes, many policies of intervention, and many "reforms" intended to change things for the "better" result in effects directly contrary to those intended or expected. Sieber (1981), who talks about "reverse effects of purposive action" and "the maleficent consequences of beneficent intentions," points out that few institutions, programmes, or leaders (one may add reformers) are immune to the vexatious experience of worsening the condition that they set out so nobly to alleviate.

Criminal justice in general, and corrections in particular, provide countless examples of the unanticipated side effects and ill effects of purposive reform. Writing in the *New York Times*, at the height of the rehabilitation crisis, Gaylin (1977) noted that the rehabilitative model, despite its emphasis on understanding and concern, has been more punitive than a frankly punitive model might have been. Under the rehabilitative model it became possible for society to abuse prisoners without disabusing its conscience.

Early reformers who advocated the indeterminate sentence saw it not only as integral to rehabilitation but also as the ultimate means to eliminate the arbitrariness inherent in the fixed, determinate sentence. Little did they know of the negative consequences that would ensue! Before long, prison administrators realized that the indeterminate sentence was a potent instrument for inmate control. What was meant as a correctional and sentencing reform turned into a monstrous tool for tyranny and oppression. Commenting on the outcome, Mitford (1974) points out that changes in procedure, more flexible criteria for inmate release, and new facilities to house those sentenced to prison do not produce fundamental reforms if certain basic policies and attitudes are retained. New changes are often subverted by deeply held attitudes favouring punishment and control.

Examples of the unanticipated reverse effects in the field of law enforcement are given by Sieber (1981). A few years ago in New York City, additional patrolmen were placed on the streets to reduce the cost of overtime. But since the major source of police overtime is not patrol duty but court processing of arrests, the increased number of policemen only meant more arrests, which in turn meant more time spent in court. As a consequence, overtime costs were increased instead of reduced. Sieber also quotes Brecher and colleagues (1972) who claim that the profitability of the entire narcotics black market depends on untiring efforts of the law-enforcement agencies to hold the available supply down to the level of effective demand. Sieber notes that if these assessments are correct, then one major cause of crime is the policy of suppression itself. In effect, the taxpayer pays to have himself robbed!

Despite the abundant literature on the unanticipated negative consequences of social intervention, discussions of criminal justice reform quite often fail to distinguish between the intentions of the reform and its unintended ill or reverse effects. Radical critics, in particular, are prone to ignore the fact that reform may culminate in a state of affairs contrary to its intentions. According to Sieber (1981), "the strong emphasis on ideological consensus among radicals tends to blind them to the occurrence of unanticipated consequences that confound goals, thus impairing their ability to monitor negative effects and to adopt countermeasures."

Blaming the reformers instead of recognizing and admitting the unanticipated consequences of reform can be seen in McMahon and Ericson's statement that "when reformers occasionally take account of failures they are usually presented as reflecting faulty implementation rather than basic theoretical or political problems." To suggest that those who advocated diversion or community corrections as alternatives to incarceration did so because they wanted to increase and extend state control would be to attribute to them Machiavellian intentions they may never have had. In fact, there is no compelling reason to doubt the intentions of the instigators of those new measures nor the professed goals of those programmes. The widening of the net of social control has been an unanticipated negative consequence of the new measures, rather than a latent objective of the reformers. And in many cases it was actually the faulty implementation of the new concepts that frustrated the original intentions of the reformers. The same criticism could be levelled at the similar claim that "the recent ready acceptance and rapid expansion of community service orders relates to the fact that this punishment has features similar to imprisonment: a measurable number of hours of service, the discipline of time and place, and other visible restrictions on liberty." Moreover, the frequent occurrence of unanticipated *negative* consequences does not mean that the unintended results are always negative. Social action programmes and social reforms may also lead to unanticipated *positive* consequences. Henshel (1976) distinguishes four possible types of unintended consequences:

1) Reforms may turn out *better* than expected because there was an unrecognized deleterious feature about the old condition in addition to that which was noticed. When the old arrangement is destroyed, both problems are removed.

2) Reforms may turn out *better* than expected because there was an unnoticed beneficial feature about the reform itself (in addition to taking care of the recognized evil).

3) Reforms may turn out *worse* than expected because there was an

unnoticed or unappreciated good feature about the old arrangement. When it is destroyed to get rid of the problem, the good feature is lost as well.

4) Reforms may also turn out *worse* than expected because there was an unnoticed deleterious feature about the reform itself.

Henshel insists that terms such as better and worse, or good and bad should only be used in full recognition that they refer to the values of specific cultures or possibly to powerful elements within them, not to some universally valid standards. Social critics, needless to say, concentrate on the third and fourth types of consequences while overlooking whatever positive unintended consequences the reform may have had.

EFFECTIVE AND INEFFECTIVE STRATEGIES FOR REFORM: REALISM VS. IDEALISM

One of the stated goals of McMahon and Ericson's paper is "to document the eventual transformation of CIRPA (Citizens Independent Review of Police Activities) in the course of its transactions with the policing authority." They are critical of the fact that CIRPA's strategy was changed as a result of the group's interaction with the police commission and in its attempt to gain legitimacy. The new strategy, a conciliatory one, is taken as evidence that the group was co-opted by the official system for the purpose of "inside state interests and to reproduce order." They are equally critical of inside reformers for their successful attempts to co-opt outside reformers as they are of the latter for letting themselves be co-opted. But their critique of CIRPA's changed strategy reflects a limited understanding of the dynamic nature of the reform process and the various forces that shape and dictate the daily activities of reform and protest movements. Piven and Cloward (1979) cogently state, "it is the daily experience of people that shapes their grievances, establishes the measure of their demands, and points out the targets of their anger." They are moved by the "conditions governing their everyday experience" and not by "some abstract political ideology."

The reform process itself implies, as Schur (1980) points out, continuous interaction between the reformers and opposition groups:

Each action provokes a counterreaction, which in turn produces a modified situation—a new basis from which decisions regarding subsequent action must be taken. . . . At any stage each party is likely to have some degree of freedom to choose among several lines of responses. At the very least, however, we can see that interaction with opposing groups—whether official authorities or private partisans—will condition such choices. The opposition can rarely be ignored.

In the quest for reform, sacrifices and compromises are made, original goals are modified, and strategies are changed. Contempt for those holding the reins of power may change into deference, and militancy may give way to moderation in an attempt to achieve all or some of the original goals. This is particularly true when a group has relatively narrow claims to press and is not in direct opposition to the prevailing political order. In this instance, working within the system may make sense and may at times be distinctly advantageous (see Schur, 1980).

A shift in strategy or in technique does not necessarily imply a change in goals or ideology, yet even practical considerations and a concern for effectiveness may dictate such change. What should be borne in mind is that there is nothing static about reform movements. They are called movements because they are in constant motion. In the struggle for reform, any actively engaged group will inevitably undergo several changes. The nature, direction, and extent of the change will depend on a host of factors, including the structure and membership of the group, the power it commands, the resources it can mobilize, and the support it gets from influential forces in society, such as the media. To view or interpret the changes taking place as the outcome of sell-out, co-optation, or compromise is both incorrect and unfair. The changes are typical of the passage from idealism to realism which most reform movements go through in the course of the reform process, and they may explain why in many instances grass-roots reform movements achieve much greater success than do academics or radical critics. Still, it would be naive to think that the reform process goes on without the sacrifice of some of the initial goals or without some compromise on the means and strategies. Even terrorist groups, which are the extreme form of reform movements, do compromise on their demands as a result of negotiation and assessment of the situation.

Reform movements are usually born out of a deeply felt need for change. The formative stage is generally a period of effervescence characterized by strong motivation, extreme dedication, burning enthusiasm, and unshakeable idealism. In the early stages a number of characteristic difficulties must be overcome. In the process, many reform movements come to realize how sterile and harmful a militant, confrontational strategy can be to their cause. They quickly discover that a change in attitude and approach can substantially enhance their chances of success. Hence the shift from confrontation to negotiation, from militancy to moderation, from intransigence to reconciliation and eventually co-operation. The change in strategy and technique may also be dictated by the search for legitimacy. Legitimacy is a prerequisite for effectiveness; the impact a reform movement will have is largely a function of its perceived legitimacy. It is the lack of legitimacy, from which terrorist groups suffer, for example, that is largely responsible for their ineffectiveness and their limited success in achieving their goals.

EVALUATING REFORM

What is successful reform? How can the success of a reform movement be evaluated or measured? Who is to define success and to establish the criteria against which the reform could be judged a success or failure? Is it the reformers themselves? Is it academic researchers? Since reform is a relative concept and since it is always defined in ideological terms, it is impossible to evaluate it or measure its success objectively. Ideological biases mean that the desirability of the goals of the reform will be taken for granted by those who advocated or instigated the reform. If the goals of the reform happen to be clearly and unambiguously defined, evaluation could consist of measuring the extent to which these goals have been attained and determining both the anticipated and unanticipated consequences of the actions taken. Still some aspects of the reform will not be susceptible to measurement or evaluation. Reform is a continuing and unending process. Reform means that there will always be room for further improvement. Reform prepares and paves the way for more reform, and this intangible function of reform is impossible to measure or to assess. It is a slow gradual process, the results of which may take years and years to appear. This means that the timing for evaluation is both crucial and problematic. A system, an institution, or an organization cannot be changed in a week, a month, or a year. It can change from extremely "bad" to "bad" to slightly "better" to substantially "better" and so forth. It can never be perfect. Reform of the police moves from little or no accountability to some accountability to more accountability to adequate accountability and so on. The process may take decades. Therefore, there is little to support the claim that "policing reform serves to re-form, re-order, and entrench the police institution." Resistance to change and hatred of change should not be confounded with the impossibility of change. The negativism, the skepticism, and the pessimism academics and intellectuals in general exhibit about changes initiated by grass-roots reform movements reflect strong academic and ideological biases and may simply be defensive mechanisms that help ivory tower idealists rationalize and justify their own ineffectiveness as reformers and as agents of change.

The slowness of reform, its unanticipated negative consequences, and its unintended reverse effects do not warrant the extremely pessimistic view that no matter what attempts at reform are undertaken, the institutions will not change, the status quo will be strengthened and reinforced, things will not turn out all right according to whatever standards the critic may happen to cherish.

A pessimistic attitude, coupled with a belief in the impotency of one's actions and the actions of others, could have detrimental effects. Social defeatism is the social scientist's worst enemy in today's skeptical age. Nothing can be more dangerous than the unwarranted belief that nothing can be done, that all reform attempts are doomed to fail, that the so-called reforms do nothing but perpetuate and strengthen the existing order or produce more order. The "nothing can be done" attitude can have negative consequences similar to or even more serious than those which the "nothing works" doctrine has had in the field of corrections. While strong optimism is neither advisable nor justifiable, the "nothing can be done" attitude can spread the message that all is in vain. It can lead to an aura of helplessness, resignation, and passivity detrimental to the cause of reform. Worse still, it can become a self-fulfilling prophecy.

NOTES

1. My emphasis.
2. This is in accord with the general understanding of "ideologies" as sets of ideas serving as "logical and philosophical justifications for a group's pattern of behaviour, as well as its attitudes, goals, and general life situation." The ideology of any population also usually entails a repudiation of alternative ideological frames of reference. (See George A. Theodorson and Achilles G. Theodorson *[1969]*, *Modern Dictionary of Sociology [*New York: Thomas Y. Crowell Company*].*) Marx and Engels (*The German Ideology*, 1846) embedded the concept of ideology in their analysis of "class" interests, an approach elaborated by Karl Mannheim (*Ideology and Utopia*, 1929) to show why it is that the ideas produced by all classes would have to be ideological in nature.
3. See J. Mitford (1974), *Kind and Usual Punishment* (New York: Vintage Books), pp. 107-8.
4. See Coleman Phillipson (1975), *Three Criminal Law Reformers* (Montclair: Patterson Smith), p. viii.
5. For a discussion of the dangers of victim movements, see E. A. Fattah (1985), "On Some Visible and Hidden Dangers of Victim Movements." In E. A. Fattah, ed., *From Crime Policy to Victim Policy: Reorienting the Justice System* (London: Macmillan), pp. 1-14.

REFERENCES

Brecher, E. M., et al. 1972. *Licit and Illicit Drugs*. Boston: Little, Brown.

Ericson, R. 1985. "The State and Criminal Justice Reform." Chapter 2, this volume.

Fattah, E. A. 1986. "On Some Visible and Hidden Dangers of Victim Movements." In E. A. Fattah, ed., *From Crime Policy to Victim Policy: Reorienting the Justice System*. London: Macmillan, pp. 1-14.

Gaylin, W. 1977. "Up the River, But Why?" *The New York Times,* 18 December 1977.

Henshel, R. L. 1976. *Reacting to Social Problems*. Don Mills: Longman.

Irwin, J. 1970. *The Felon*. Englewood Cliffs, New Jersey: Prentice Hall.

Lipset, S. M. 1960. *Political Man: Essays on the Sociology of Democracy*. New York: Doubleday.

McDonald, Lynn. 1976. *The Sociology of Law and Order*. London: Free Press.

McMahon, M. W., and R. Ericson. 1985. "Reforming the Police and Policing Reform." Chapter 3, this volume.

Menninger, K. 1969. *The Crime of Punishment*. New York: Viking Compass Editions.

Mitford, Jessica. 1974. *Kind and Usual Punishment: The Prison Business*. New York: Vintage Books.

Phillipson, C. 1975. *Three Criminal Law Reformers: Beccaria, Bentham, Romilly*. Montclair: Patterson Smith.

Piven, F. F., and R. A. Cloward. 1979. *Poor People's Movements*. New York: Vintage.

Ranulf, S. 1964. *Moral Indignation and Middle Class Psychology*. New York: Schoken Books.

Schneider, L. 1978. "Unanticipated Consequences of Social Action: Beneficent and Maleficent." Paper delivered at the annual meetings of the Society for the Study of Social Problems, San Francisco.

Schur, E. 1980. *The Politics of Deviance*. Englewood Cliffs, New Jersey: Prentice Hall.

Sieber, S. D. 1981. *Fatal Remedies: The Ironies of Social Intervention*. New York: Plenum Press.

PART TWO

State and Criminal Justice

5

The Problem of Relative Autonomy
and Criminal Justice in the Canadian State

R. S. RATNER
JOHN L. McMULLAN
BRIAN E. BURTCH

As the essays in the preceding section illustrate, much of the theorizing about the state has been based either on an instrumentalist reading of Marx's own undeveloped analysis of the state as "a committee for managing the affairs of the whole bourgeoisie" (Marx and Engels, 1967, p. 82) or on the dominant pluralist ideology which asserts the negotiative and disinterested character of state institutions (Mankoff, 1970). While some progress has been made toward formulating a critique of earlier Marxist formulations, there has been very little empirical work specifically addressed to the problem of state autonomy. Miliband's *The State in Capitalist Society* (1969), though decidedly an instrumentalist approach to establishing the class nature of state power, did foreshadow a structuralist account which has been elaborated in the subsequent work of various neo-Marxist state theorists. Moving away from both an economistic dismissal of the state as a passive instrument acting at the behest of the ruling class, and from the pluralists' liberal fiction of the state as neutral arbiter, contemporary neo-Marxists have advanced analysis of the state by tracing its origins and influence to the particular historical societies in which it is structurally located, a locus determined chiefly, but not entirely, by the mode of production.

Paralleling this development, and after a long period of neglect in the application of Marxist ideas to non-Sovietized problematizations of "crime"—with Bonger's rather primitive analysis as a solitary exception[1]—western criminologists have begun to incorporate elements of neo-Marxist theories of the state in their dissections of the "crime problem" (see

Quinney, 1980; Taylor, 1981, 1983). Some resistance to this development has
come from within Marxist quarters, such as by Hirst (1973), who attributes
only an epiphenomenal status to crime and therefore rejects it as a category
suitable to a Marxist problematic. However, this work is progressing to
the point where the field of criminology has become a "radical" conversion
site for some academicians and the potentially vast clientele of those who are
the object of control by the criminal justice system (Garofalo, 1978).[2]

   A salient concept in the recent literature on theories of the state—one
which as yet has had little impact on the study of crime—is the concept of
the "relative autonomy of the state" introduced by Nicos Poulantzas in
Political Power and Social Classes, (1973). Rejecting the simplistic base/
superstructure formulation, Poulantzas sought to explain the qualified
independence of the state from the immediate demands of private capital
accumulation. The state, in his view, is neither completely autonomous in
the sense that it is free from active control by the dominant economic class,
nor is it simply manipulated by members of that class. Rather, it is relatively
autonomous from the interests of particular fractions of capital, thus
allowing it to serve as the "factor of cohesion"[3] in the "determinate social
formation"[4] and to regulate its overall equilibrium. According to Poulantzas,
the state "can only truly serve the ruling class in so far as it is relatively
autonomous from the diverse fractions of this class, precisely in order to be
able to organize the hegemony of the whole of this class" (1972, p. 247). In
explaining how the state accomplishes this integrative function, Poulantzas
disavows a problematic of social actors, instead conceiving the state as an
objective structure of relations within the determinate social formation.

> This means that if the function of the state in a determinate social
> formation and the interests of the dominant class in this formation
> coincide, it is by reason of the system itself: the direct participation of
> members of the ruling class in the state apparatus is not the *cause* but
> the *effect*, and moreover a chance and contingent one, of this objective
> coincidence. (ibid., p. 245)

Miliband, though not an anti-structuralist in articulating the role of the
state, has questioned the absence of a substantive dialectic between the state
and the "system" in Poulantzas's highly abstract and functionalist analysis.
In Miliband's ironic paraphrase, "the state is not 'manipulated' by the
ruling class into doing its bidding: it does so autonomously but totally
because of the 'objective relations' imposed upon it by the system" (1972, p.
259). Other analysts have criticized Poulantzas's theory as too system-
maintenance oriented and not easily open to counterfactual inquiry. Giddens
(1981, pp. 216-17) has taken issue with Poulantzas's version of Althusserian

structuralism, arguing that it precludes consideration of the reflexive character of human action, thus limiting interpretation of the capitalist state to the operation of abstract class forces. And Block (1980, p. 229), challenging what he perceives to be Poulantzas's unwarranted reductionism, belittles the relative autonomy thesis as merely a "cosmetic modification of Marxism's tendency to reduce state power to class power."[5]

Vague and excessively scholastic at points, Poulantzas's formulation begs factual inquiry that would clarify the meaning of relative autonomy and make apparent the basis for the state's claims to autonomy. In part, such investigation has already begun with inquiries into the relative autonomy of the law (see Balbus, 1977; Jessop, 1980; Fine et al., 1979; also see Hastings and Saunders, this volume). Clarification of the concept may also be derived through an examination of the concrete and specific institutional network of the criminal justice system—the so-called "repressive" component of the state apparatus.[6] The importance of directing attention to the repressive component bears, in part, on the question of why members of a class-dominated society continue to live in exploitative and oppressive social conditions. In turn, the relative autonomy of the state formulation suggests that while the criminal justice system functions primarily to repress dissent and to incapacitate persons who threaten capitalist social order, there is also a degree of latitude and discretion available to criminal justice officials, thus undermining the rigorous internal unity attributed by Poulantzas to the repressive state apparatus. More generally, the importance of the state autonomy issue with regard to criminal justice is implicit in the analytic inseparability of the nature of crime control in capitalist societies, the action of the state in non-criminal spheres, and the nature of accommodation or resistance to the imperatives of capital accumulation.

In this paper then, we engage in a preliminary exploration of the internal arrangements of the state specific to criminal justice and their effects upon the external relationship of the state to class power.[7] Jessop argues the significance of this frequently neglected line of inquiry:

> The "relative autonomy" of actual states is the complex resultant of their form(s) of separation from the economic region and civil society (in the sense of the site of "private," non-economic relations), their *sui generis* institutional structure, their social bases of support and resistance, and the effectiveness of their policies in relation to bourgeois reproduction (or some other point of reference). To neglect this complex overdetermination of state power in favour of the essentialization of "relative autonomy" as an abstract principle of explanation is to neglect the deeply problematic functionality of the state apparatus and state power. (1982, p. 227)[8]

Heeding this observation and going against the opaque hyper-functionalism of Poulantzas's account, we attempt to lay bare the range and levels of activity in the criminal justice branch of the state apparatus, formulating an empirical application of the relative autonomy concept that reveals state/class conjunctures. We agree with Panitch (1977, p. 11) that much of the focus of national study so far has been on the accumulation process and has taken an instrumentalist bent in disclosing elitist concentrations of state personnel along with legitimations of class power; however, we argue that within the coercive apparatus there are processes operating toward state autonomy in the criminal justice sector as well as centripetal class-based actions circumscribing that autonomy, resulting in an amalgam of contradictions for state policy and directives.

Our study begins with a general comparison of theoretical perspectives on the state, showing the way in which the idea of state autonomy and the relative autonomy of the law is understood by each perspective. We then examine the specific meaning of the relative autonomy notion, clarifying the state's grounds for its claims to autonomy. This is followed by a discursive analysis of the Canadian criminal justice system in which we identify different levels of state autonomy connecting the operations of the justice sector to class practices. We conclude our study with suggestions for a theoretical reformulation of the relative autonomy thesis capable of synthesizing elements of the major neo-Marxist state theories and which promises to shed further light on the operations of criminal justice in the Canadian State.

We hope to clarify the possibilities for state-initiated changes of the class distribution of power and, ultimately, for changes in the parameters of the wider social formation. The state's role in shaping societal preferences, in formulating public policies, and in enforcing its own directives should command more investigation than it has been accorded thus far (Miliband, 1983). No longer a mere servant of dominant economic interests, the state is now in a position to perform a liberative role in the process of social change. Even its repressive component has become too complex and multi-dimensional to sustain interpretations of the criminal justice system as simple defender of the status quo.

STATE, JUSTICE, AND CLASS

The analysis of the state as a central feature of political economy has generated an array of insights and arguments that challenge conservative and liberal-pluralist conceptions of criminal justice in Canada. Because the role of the state in criminological thinking and in liberal-reformist justice policy making has been neglected or underemphasized, the system of criminal justice has often been studied as an independent apparatus of inter-related components that are said to be separate and rationally organized to achieve specific goals (Connidis, 1982). While there are debates about the degree of system integration and co-ordination of criminal justice institutions (see Baum, 1979; Willett, 1977) there is nevertheless an underlying commitment to a utilitarian perspective which sees legal analysis, reform, administration, and policy in terms of a rational allocation of punishments and interventions deracinated from the wider sources of state power. Indeed, studies and planning of the police, the judiciary, and correctional institutions are often conceived with little reference to adjunctive aspects of the criminal justice system. Thus competing programmes for institutional reform such as greater police powers, more severe sentencing, increased administrative discretion, diversion, treatment, decarceration, and community corrections are formulated and implemented with little understanding of the nature and operations of the Canadian State. Not surprisingly, the mobilization of appeals, conservative as well as liberal, has had the effect of bolstering the legitimacy of the state as the "agent umpire" of penal control, legislation, and judicial review, without considering its real social character.

To understand the major theoretical dimensions of the controversy regarding the evolution of the state, we begin by sketching five key perspectives on the state—pluralist, instrumentalist, structuralist, class conflict, and capital-logic—focusing on the legal problematic and drawing out the importance of the concept of relative autonomy for understanding criminal justice politics. This theoretical outline provides a necessary background for understanding the tensions and contradictions pervading state/class relations as reflected within the criminal justice system.[9]

The Pluralist View

The pluralist perspective asserts that power or influence is dispersed among a range of visible, competing interest groups, none of which has sufficient resources to impose its demands on others consistently. The locus of power is fragmented and partitioned, allegedly in a democratic structure, so that many groups may expect to have their interests represented in the political system. As Dahl observes, "all the active and legitimate groups in the population can make themselves heard at some crucial stage in the process of decision" (1965, pp. 137-38). Alliances among interest groups are unstable and shifting, forming and fracturing as issues change such that no single alliance is homogeneous for all purposes. The claim is that power is distributed amongst different elites who are influential in different issue areas and whose power is non-cumulative. While the existence of elites is acknowledged, there is no acceptance of a power elite that rules society. The state is viewed as a legitimate force that stands above disputing parties, as a neutral forum in which negotiations are arbitrated and policy outcomes are established according to generally agreed upon rules. As Giddens observes:

> the industrial-society theorists mostly take it for granted that the state was a benign instrument for the progressive achievement of goals of social reform: the redistribution of wealth, the spread of welfare programs, the ever-increasing expansion of education and so on . . . these levels were made the focus of attention with the state as the unanalyzed medium of their realization. (1981, p. 203)

Liberal-pluralist theory argues that in advanced capitalist societies, the legal and political systems have been hived off from the direct determination of economic interests. The power to legislate and rule has been delegated to the state, which superimposes the "interests of all" over "the interests of the particular." Laws created by the state are perceived as a condensation of competing interest groups sanctioned by the authority of the state institutions. Similarly the coercive apparatus embodying many criminal justice functions is understood as operating in popular consent. The "rule of law" in this formulation means equal and impartial "justice for all" and is seen as a positive, neutralizing, and countervailing power to the unequal relations operating in the productive system and in the marketplace.

We have, then, a conception of the state as impartial arbiter: the reconcilor of conflict and the mirror which society holds up to itself as the embodiment of social agreement (Miliband, 1969, p. 3). The pluralists remind us that there is a separation to be made between economic processes and the field of action of law and state. But this is not absolute, for the state is ultimately dependent upon the productive wealth of the economy in order to implement its policies and is thus compelled to reproduce the general viability of the economic relations of capitalism. The catalogue of "reproductive" functions of the modern state is legion; but the essential point is clear: the state and the law, including its coercive institutions, are implicated, directly and indirectly, in securing and bolstering the social foundations of vested capitalist interests while claiming universality and impartiality.

The liberal-pluralists also remind us that there are numerous and often conflicting elite groupings in all advanced capitalist societies, but they devalue, marginalize, or misunderstand the importance of class analysis per se. We recognize that a social class is not an homogenous entity and that the state is a condensation of social forces; however in contradistinction to the pluralist view we do insist on the primacy of class as a coherent expression of specific social, legal, and political relations. We are sympathetic to Giddens's view that "the state remains an 'arena' within which class struggles are fought out, but one in which there are influences at work that have a particular character of their own" (1982, p. 216).

The Instrumentalist View

The second perspective is the instrumentalist one. In this conception, the state is regarded as the direct instrument of class rule, and the legal apparatus as a tool of class domination (Quinney, 1980). In contrast to pluralist theory, a correspondence of class power and state power is said to exist because of the overt similarities in class background, interests, and worldview between those who control the economy and the personnel of the state and criminal justice system. Common class position, close educational ties, family and personal networks, shared ideological perspectives, and close working relationships between the dominant class and intermediary institutions (research units, universities, and political organizations and parties) predispose state criminal justice institutions to favour dominant social and economic interests (Miliband, 1969; Domhoff, 1967, 1970; Clement, 1973, 1976).

The instrumentalist position is confirmed by studies of the class composition and social background of those who hold high judicial offices (Olsen, 1980; Zander, 1968; Griffith, 1977) and by the differential formulation and application of justice to various social classes. For example, state and the law are viewed as particularly lax and ineffective when pursuing corporate tax fraud and business crime, while those petty offenders at the bottom who "fiddle" welfare are vigorously pursued and sanctioned (Goff and Reasons, 1978; Scraton, 1982). Similarly, judicial policy varies considerably, as between white collar crimes of the powerful and the crimes of the lower classes (Reasons et al., 1981; Pearce, 1976; Snyder, 1980, 1982). The same is true of the use and application of the court system.

> Different kinds and types of courts does not lead to equality before the law . . . (the courts) tend to be differentially used by different interests and different classes in society: not only that but standards, procedures, and sanctions vary from one court to another. . . . Canada has probably moved a step away from equality before the law, not towards it, in recent years. (Olsen, 1980, p. 63)

A dual system of justice exists, one for the lower classes and one for the

active elites and the institutions they represent. As Olsen notes, class justice
in Canada works on a number of fronts:

> First, there are the mechanisms which screen out cases the courts will
> never hear: then there is the inconsistency of the court's decisions over
> time; next there is the social background of the judges themselves,
> which is insulated from the experiences and problems of the working or
> lower classes; and finally . . . the proliferation and differentiation of
> courts and regulatory boards in Canada . . . is producing even more
> inequality before the law.'' (ibid., p. 64)

The instrumentalist perspective alerts us to an important source of
judicial bias in that it reveals the direct exercise of state power by members
of the capitalist class through the manipulation of the law and the judiciary,
or indirectly through interest group pressure on the state. Explanations,
however, are almost always put in terms of individuals or interest groups
who staff the state justice apparatus, rather than on classes defined by their
relationship to each other and to the productive relations of society as a
whole. Thus, arguments tend to be reduced to the intentions of groups or
agents, and there is little systematic analysis of how the voluntarism of the
powerful is itself shaped and limited by impersonal, invisible structural
relations (Gold, Lo, and Wright, 1975). Moreover, the instrumentalist
argument tends to assume a homogeneity of ruling class interests, with an
unproblematic translation of economic power to the instrumentalization of
state, law, and criminal justice. As Quinney asserts:

> The state is established by those who desire to protect their material
> basis and who have the power to maintain the state. The law in capitalist
> society gives political recognition to powerful private interests. Moreo-
> ver, the legal system is an apparatus created to secure the interests of the
> dominant class. Contrary to conventional belief, the law is the tool of
> the ruling class. (1974, p. 52)

This is a one-sided formulation. Aside from its simplicity, it does not ascribe
a separate role for the state in terms of state/civil society relations or in terms
of its own mode of operation. There are initiatives taken by the state for
interests broader than, or different from, the dominant class, and there are
crucial areas of state actions which are not the result of capitalist class
manoeuvers or accommodations. Indeed, the state itself may be a terrain of
class conflict; law-making and criminal justice policy may possess levels of
autonomy and not only be the result of simple manipulations (Williams,
1978; Sumner, 1981). Thus, the instrumentalist perspective often presents a

thinly veiled conspiracy thesis. Little power or autonomy actually accrues to the state; when it does it is reduced to an implement of the resources controlled by the dominant class (Hall and Scraton, 1981).

Structuralist Marxism

The structuralist perspective argues that the correspondences between state, law, and economy are not a matter of the direct participation of members of the capitalist class in the state criminal justice apparatus. Instead, as noted previously, the state and law in a capitalist society have an *objective* relationship to classes and the productive forces in a society. The functions of the state are determined by the *structures* of social relations which cannot be understood primarily in terms of the class background of those in positions of state power (Poulantzas, 1969, p. 245). The state, then, is not an instrument but a *relation*; it is not a specific network of institutions but a functional inter-relationship, a hidden reality which organizes the power co-ordinates of class domination and conflict as a whole. For structuralists, the state is conceived primarily in terms of its functional utilities (Offe, 1972; O'Connor, 1973; Panitch, 1977). Poulantzas, for example, argues that the capitalist state functions to counteract the threats of working class unity and action and capitalist class fragmentation and disunity (see Cain, 1976, p. 235). These functions are in turn based upon the wider, fundamental economic contradiction between the increasingly social nature of production and the continuing private appropriation of the surplus product. The state is the site where legitimacy for particular policies is fashioned: above all, the acquiescence of the working class and the petit bourgeoisie to the aims of the dominant capitalist class. Thus in this perspective, the state has the major role of atomizing the labouring class, disintegrating its real or political coherence by transforming workers into individualized citizens, while simultaneously presenting itself as promoting the universal interest of the entire society. Not only does the state tend to exclude or incorporate laws and policies which favour the collective interests of subordinate social classes (which may be formulated in terms such as the national or public interest), and discipline directly through the criminal justice apparatus and the military; it also creates, through the institutions of law, government, and justice, a juridicial subject, with individual rights (as opposed to classes with legal statuses or trade union rights) which estranges other forms of capital and labour from their collective class positions. Law and criminal justice are not mere tools or manipulative instruments but rather collective representations which mask class relations, displace class interests into legal individual ones, and remake the person as a citizen with formal political and legal rights (Hall and Scraton, 1981). Thus the concepts of "the public," "due process," "the rule of law," and "equality before the law" are elements of a legal ideology endowing asymmetrical relations of class power with universality and legitimacy. Mystification, displacement, incorporation, and disorganization result for the subordinated classes (Poulantzas, 1969).

Accordingly, the state is also the guarantor of the long-term interests of the dominant class as a whole. Like pluralists, structuralists stress the divided character of the ruling class and the problematic nature of the capital accumulation process, arguing that the class fractions of the capitalist class may become divergent unless they are solidified into a power coalition under the tutelage of a particular hegemonic fraction. Class power groupings are nevertheless frequently precarious and seldom able to produce the means for long-term capital exploitation of labour. Thus the role of the state is pivotal. It transcends internal disputes, parochial capitalist interests, and contradictions within the power coalition, giving protection and direction for the capitalist class as a whole. The mediation of the state then rests on a relatively autonomous plane rather than directly in the hands of one capitalist grouping (ibid., 1973).

In the structuralist account of the state, we are afforded a more complex formulation, albeit at times schematic and abstract. Law and criminal justice are often reduced to a structural necessity, thus overstressing a functionalist argument about the longterm reproduction of capital. Furthermore, by undervaluing the power of other social classes, advantages won from the state by struggles "from below" (that is, welfare programmes, safety and protection laws, union recognition, and so forth) are difficult to explain within the perspective. There is an unwillingness to view resistance and conflict as leading to results contrary to or subversive of the "needs" of capitalist development (Giddens, 1982, pp. 203-29). Nevertheless, the structuralist perspective generally allots a considerably greater role to the state as an independent source of power, while insisting that the autonomy it possesses can never be more than relative and limited.

Class Conflict Theory

Unlike the structuralists, class conflict theorists place the ideas of praxis and struggle at the centre of their conception of the state. The work of Antonio Gramsci exemplifies this perspective. For Gramsci, the role of the state involves the regulation of the economy for private appropriation, but it also has a central function in developing a moral (class-based) consensus that organizes social, civil, and intellectual life around the structural tendencies set by the economy. Furthermore, the economy is not determinant on the state, nor is it considered separate from particular ideological and political contexts. So in the class conflict model, the character of the state cannot be reduced from some general theory of the state's needs and functions given the prerequisites of capitalist development (as is the case for the structuralist perspective). Rather, the functions of the state may be established only by analyzing specific historical places and times and unravelling the conflicts, balances, and alliances of power as they are played out. From this standpoint Gramsci differentiated between two situations: one where classes were stable within their own limited interests and boundaries, in which rule depended on the exercise of force, and where law was essentially repressive and negative; and another where particular class fractions attempted, through the state, to widen their interests across society, incorporating sections of the dominated classes into an "historical bloc" within civil society and the state. Such an "historical bloc" implies an enlarged social authority, and rule is more by leadership than by coercion, with leadership implying the obtaining of support and legitimacy from the subordinated classes in order to develop a unity of economic, political, intellectual, and moral aims, thus creating "not on a corporate but on a 'universal' plane . . . the hegemony of a fundamental social group over a series of subordinate groups" (Gramsci, 1971, p. 58). Thus, the "winning of consent" enlarges the role of the state in reshaping civil society, and according to Gramsci, law and justice are pivotal as "positive civilizing activities," sanctioning, but as well, educating, moralizing, and rewarding conduct which bolsters the ethical principles and directions of the entire society. The state, then, is allied to civil society in attempting to shape a consensus by largely peaceful means, in which the subjected become accepting partners in their own subordination. It is the site and agency where popular consent is shaped and fought out. Central to this process is increasing state control and manipulation of media, press, church, and schools.

Yet for the class conflict writers this process towards hegemony and control does not go unchallenged. It is countered by contrary oppositional social forces (Willams, 1978). Moreover, the dominated classes have their own agents who are engaged in winning over, neutralizing, or detaching from their allegiances vulnerable elements of the ruling power bloc. In this way, according to Gramsci, subaltern populations construct their counter-ideology and weaken the defences of capital as part of the struggle for state control. Successful revolutionary activity presupposes counter-hegemonic organization and practice.

The implications of Gramsci's writing are important in state/law theory. He abandons the division of ideology into "true" and "false," advances an historical approach that undercuts *a priori* arguments, and recognizes the complex interplay between class, law, coercion and the state (Thompson,

1977; Hay et al., 1975; Hall et al., 1978). By stressing the power of class formations other than the dominant one, proponents of the class conflict perspective recognize the contradictory character of the state and direct us to look at the ways in which the state is "pushed" to be more than a mere functional vehicle of the imperatives of the prevailing mode of production. Because it is enmeshed within the contradictions of capitalism, it is subject to mobilizations from below and is not merely a guarantor of order.

One important limitation of this perspective is that, in attempting to rescue an understanding of criminal justice and law from economic reductionism and determinism, the class conflict position underemphasizes the process of capital accumulation and the ways in which economic forces set limits on coercive and ideological practices. Consequently, until an incorporation of structural constraints is achieved, a systematic theory of the state is unlikely to emerge out of this perspective.

The Capital-Logic Approach

The final perspective, the "capital-logic" approach, attempts to integrate the previous three Marxist variants. While supportive of the Gramscian class conflict positions, its proponents nevertheless argue that politics, ideology, and culture must be seen as more directly connected to the process of capital development. Thus, in their view, the ideological character of law and the state derives from the "logic" of the economic relations of capitalism as articulated by Marx in his economic categories in *Capital* (Holloway and Picciotto, 1978; Fine et al., 1979).

The first formulation of the capital-logic perspective concentrated almost exclusively on the monetary and legal apparatus necessary to facilitate the production and exchange of commodities and the accumulation of capital (Altvater, 1973). The capitalist state was seen as a political force promoting economic competition between forms of capital. State intervention could, however, occur against groupings of capital (as well as the working class when competing fractions threatened the interests of capital in general). Recent work has introduced a greater degree of historical detail in order to elaborate the role of class struggle and exploitation in the formation of the capitalist state (see, the "state-derivation" debate in Holloway and Picciotto, 1978). In this latter formulation, the efforts of the state to secure the conditions for capital accumulation are subject not only to changes in economic structure but also to the influence of class dynamics and changes in the balance of political forces.

In either version of the capital-logic perspective, three historical "moments" or periods of the capitalist state are distinguished: the establishment of the preconditions for accumulation; the "liberal" moment when the full separation of politics and economics takes place; and the contemporary moment when the socialization of production generates a declining rate of profit. The nature and function of law and the state change correspondingly over these three periods.

In the phase of primitive accumulation of capital, the capitalist state adopts a relatively laissez-faire role, intervening only to prevent internecine competition between capital and to guarantee the conditions necessary to assure the maximum scope for capital accumulation. The state acts primarily at the behest of the ruling class during this period, exhibiting little autonomy.

In the period of liberal capitalism there is a change in state forms from absolutism to parliamentary democracy, whereby different fractions of capital create a legal code subjecting themselves to the same general rules, yet asserting a domination over labour. Exploitation is codified by disguising it in legal form (such as "fairness" and "equality"), thus masking the real content of unequal economic relations. At the same time, law is not merely a bourgeois artifice since it also reflects the influence of sustained class struggles, notably in the extension of the franchise to dominated classes and later in the establishment of social welfare programmes. Criminal justice thus appears as the outcome of class struggles over the framing, application, and enforcement of the legal fetishisms arising out of the attempted legitimation of bourgeois hegemony. There is an increase in state autonomy during this period as the state assumes a wider role in moderating class tensions and in assuring the longterm conditions favourable to capital accumulation.

In the shift to the third phase of monopoly capitalism, the form of state moves from an emphasis on the rule of law to more powerful state bureaucratic interventions enabling direct relations with individual capitals for the purpose of counteracting the trend toward falling profits during the increased socialization of production. The role of parliament declines as major capitalist interests seek direct access to executive and administrative centres of power; consequently, the state becomes the locale of conflict between competing capitals and organized labour, responding frequently to the political crises of accumulation as well as to the actual needs of capital. In this third stage, the state acquires extra-parliamentary powers in order to ensure ongoing capital accumulation. While state power is contained to some extent by the "rule of law" legacy established during the period of liberal expansion (and by its continued reliance on the revenues stemming from capital), its relative autonomy is now magnified and its resources are sufficient to define and pursue its own interests.

Though impressive in scope, a major difficulty with the capital-logic approach is that efforts to avoid economistic reductionism by theoretical

incorporation of crises and class struggle do not change the fact that the
"needs of capital" remain as the only explanatory principle for state
interventions, and law is reduced to an effect of the logical self-realization of
capital (Gough, 1979). In the attempt to ground analysis of the ideological
superstructure directly in capital relations, the perspective tends to deny law
any autonomy of its own, since law is treated as a form with a hidden
economic content. Its principal function is to mystify.

The following comparison draws attention to differences in the role of
class conflict and the degree of state autonomy posited within the five
theoretical perspectives on the capitalist state.

THEORIES OF THE CAPITALIST STATE

Type of Theory	*Role of Class Conflict in State Formation*	*Degree of State Autonomy*
Pluralist	voluntaristic conflicts between multiple non-homogeneous competing interest groups, rather than between discrete classes; state as a class-neutral political forum in which conflicts are arbitrated.	state and law as independent and above class/ group interests; ostensible high degree of autonomy in the service of all disputing parties.
Instrumental	state power intentionally monopolized by a relatively homogeneous capitalist class; class conflict pre-empted.	state as class-biased structure of manipulation; legal apparatus an instrument of ruling-class domination; little or no autonomy from economic processes.
Structural Marxist	state as an objective structure of relations within a capitalist social formation; an arena for class struggle, but functioning primarily to support the longterm reproduction of capital.	state as relatively autonomous; a "factor of cohesion"; organizing the hegemony of the whole capitalist class by counteracting the threats of working-class unity and capitalist class disunity.
Class Conflict (Gramscian)	state as the site and agency of class struggle, where popular consent is forged in the "historical bloc."	potentially high degree of autonomy as an "alternative force" since the state is responsive to "mobili-

| | | zations from below" as well as to the dominant class formation; no spurious claims to neutrality. |
| Capital-Logic | state and law function to secure the conditions for capital accumulation according to the developing "logic" of capitalist economic relations; state remains partly subject to changes in the balance of class forces. | lack of autonomy in "laissez-faire" capitalism; to relative autonomy in "liberal" capitalism; to strong autonomy in monopoly capitalism in response to the political crises of accumulation. |

THE MEANING OF RELATIVE AUTONOMY

The foregoing examination of variants of state and law theory reveals some important disagreements. The pluralists regard state and law as independent and above class interests in civil society. For them, the state and law reflect a "working consensus" and are independent but benign instruments of social progress, guarding equality where it already exists and compensating for inequalities by political and juridicial reforms.

The instrumentalists, on the other hand, argue that state and law reflect neither consensus nor social good and are inseparable from class structure. In their view, political and legal forms possess virtually no autonomy from economic processes; they correspond to the needs of the dominant class. Justice is viewed as biased and as a tool of ruling class power. Little autonomy accrues to the state since it is regarded as a structure of manipulation and not a site of class conflict.

The structuralist Marxist, class conflict, and capital-logic variants argue against the economism and reductionism of the instrumentalist position and the "classlessness" and neutrality of the pluralists. In Poulantzas's view, the state is relatively autonomous from the interests of particular fractions of capital who are divided and antagonistic. Functionally necessary to protect the general interests of capital, the state ensures the reproduction of capitalism as a whole.

In the class conflict formulation, relative autonomy is also accorded to the capitalist state but it is based on the relations between classes. The state is independent because subaltern class mobilizations dislocate it from its purely capitalist class moorings, making the state more than only a defender of the status quo. The power that the organized working class is able to bring against the state poses problems of legitimation and accumulation, which in turn lead to a mistrust of the state by the powerful and allows the state to be viewed in some measure as an "alternative" force (Giddens, 1982, p. 220).

The capital-logic perspective, in its versions, also argues the case for the relative autonomy of the state. In a manner similar to the commodity-exchange theorists of law (Pashukanis, 1978; Balbus, 1977), they argue that law and politics are moving away from economy, as capitalism changes from an early commercial competitive form to a monopoly type. Arguing by analogy to the process of commodification of labour power and property, in which capital is shown to have a specific logic (by Marx), Holloway and Picciotto (1978) conclude that law and state undergo similar autonomous phases of historical development with their own specific practices, languages, and processes. But these separate forms are seen as "fetishized expressions" of the underlying exploitative economic relations. In the capital-logic approach, therefore, the ideological character of law and the state is discovered, not in the specificity of the political but as the direct product of the economic relations of capitalism and their logic.

Despite their different emphases, these theoretical formulations direct our attention to one crucial question. What are the state's sources of power to be able to achieve relative autonomy in a capitalist society? These sources are three fold. First, in advanced capitalist economies the state maintains far-reaching surveillance activities in that it both accumulates, stores, and distributes vast amounts of information relevant to the control of the conduct of its constituent population and it directly monitors population conduct and control. Second, the capitalist state has virtual monopoly control over the legitimate use of the means of violence domestically as well as within a multinational world military order. This acts as a powerful undergirding medium of state autonomy. Third, as Offe (1972) has noted, the capitalist state is contradictory in character. Caught up in the dilemmas of a capitalist political economy, it is subject not only to the integrative and harmonizing requirements of capital but also to the power of organized resistance. This is well-conceived by C.B. Macpherson's differentiation between the "liberal" and the "liberal-democratic" state. The latter, a metamorphosis of the first, was the creation in good measure of politically organized working-class pressure. It draws attention to the responsibility the capitalist state has had in establishing, ensuring, and reinventing general legal relations, through which the relationships of persons with "rights and freedoms" are endowed and enforced (Macpherson, 1966). There is a real difference between the rule of law and absolute coercive force. The acquisition of civil rights, fought for by women's groups, trade unionists, prisoners, and others, represents gained power that enhances state independence from exclusively ruling class control (Sumner, 1981). Let us examine these claims.

Surveillance and the State

Foucault (1977) observed that surveillance became of major importance with the rise of capitalism and the modern state, as the system of gathering and storing information joined with an elaborate, centralized, and permanent supervisory apparatus. The reorganization and expansion of the clinic (Foucault, 1975), the asylum, and the prison in the eighteenth and nineteenth centuries were institutional outgrowths of the needs of state authorities to create new modes of controlling disenfranchised populations in large urban territories where earlier informal methods of control could no longer hold sway. The replacement of punishment as a ritualistic, bloody spectacle with the discipline of anonymous surveillance resulted in massive state efforts in information-gathering and processing (Foucault, 1977). The systematic, centralized collation of statistics on population, birth, death, crime, and many other demographic and fiscal data began in earnest in the late eighteenth century and marks a major medium of power of the state bureaucracy unlike that of earlier centuries. With the growth of state control over more and more information came the possibility of increasingly authoritarian modes of population and political control, implemented through a society-wide system of surveillance. Unlike earlier periods where the techniques available for culling and for holding information were limited by the exclusiveness of literacy and by the fragmented and cumbersome channels of communication, state officials in the late eighteenth century had acquired the power to oversee the social system in both national and global contexts. (Giddens, 1981, pp. 169-70). They thus acquired their own unique basis to autonomous power that has facilitated the long-term assistance, protection, and consolidation of capitalism more so than specific fractions of capital have been able to accomplish. There is nothing particularly enigmatic about this development because the economic survival of the state is dependent upon the continued expansion of the private capitalist sector, which is outside its direct control. It is in this sense that the state "intervenes" through accumulation assistance, regulation, management, coercion, and legitimation; not only to attempt to cohere private capital but also to try to ensure its own stability and expansion. Yet the scope and content of its actions and the power of state officials have shifting but distinct limits. On the one hand, (as Poulantzas has observed), the state must be understood as a capitalist state and so the resources constituting its particular mode of domination operate in a context of various "imperatives", since the state's revenue is dependent upon processes of valorization and accumulation which are removed from its direct supervision. On the other hand, (as Gramsci and Offe have stressed), the state has a contradictory character to it, for it does provide a range of community and welfare services which often reflect the power that the organized working class is able to mobilize (Offe, 1972). The state is mistrusted not only because it is sometimes unsuccessful in harmonizing the diverse economic interests that make up the dominant class, but also because it is not a mere protector of the status quo. Enmeshed in the complex contradictions of capitalism, it does, in some part, work against the dominant class and may become an emancipatory force (Giddens, 1982, p. 220).

State, Contract, and the Monopolization of Violence

A second factor relevant to the autonomy of the state is the control of the means of violence by the state, coincident with the emergence of a capitalist labour market. Unlike earlier class-divided agrarian societies where the exploitation of surplus production relied directly on license or military force, the capitalistic labour contract depends upon the appropriation of surplus value by means of an essentially legal-economic relation of dependency established between capital and labour. Control over the means of violence, which in European feudal societies was decentralized and fragmented, became increasingly centralized by the seventeenth century, under the control of absolutist states, as they made their peace with the rising capitalist classes (Anderson, 1979). This had two important results. First, the monopolization of the means of violence in the hands of the modern state went along with "the extrusion of control of violent sanctions from the exploitative class relations involved in emergent capitalism" (Giddens, 1981, p. 80). Under capitalism, the appropriation of surplus value and the reproduction of order do not depend directly upon relations of force. On the contrary, the newly expanding labour market, in marginalizing the sanctions of violence, replaced them with the capitalist labour contract and an adjunct commitment to work, freedom, and private rights. As Hirsch observes of capitalist relations of production:

> The manner in which the social bond is established, in which the social labour is distributed and the surplus product appropriated necessarily requires that the direct producers be deprived of control of physical force and that the latter be localised in a social instance raised above the economic reproduction process: the creation of formal bourgeois freedom and equality and the establishment of a state monopoly of force. (1978, pp. 61-62)

Thus, the nature of domination and rule in advanced capitalist societies is such that the dominant class is reliant upon a state that has a separate existence with immense and expanding surveillance, policing and militaristic powers.

Second, in the wake of uneven, limited, and decentralized surveillance functions in both gathering and using information about given populations (in earlier class-divided societies), there emerged a new system of labour control. While the gathering of tribute, the corvee, and the slave plantation system all made use of close surveillance in the supervisory sense, they lacked a central command and integration of system. By the nineteenth century there was an organization of disciplining labour through *co-ordinated production* rather than by means of forced plunder. The labour process and the wage-labour contract were institutionally removed from public authority with different but related systems of discipline prevailing. The nexus of capital's control of labour power shifted to the legal contract and labour surveillance in the work-place through direct time, space, and task requirements. The main sanctions the employer now possessed were wage limits, dismissals, and paratechnical-management controls. The modern state, for its part, has arrogated increasing amounts of control over the use of violence, centralizing them particularly in military and policing orders, thus acquiring a powerful authoritative resource undergirding its partial autonomy from private sector influence and control.

The State as Contradiction: Class Conflict and Legal Rights

A third claim to the state's ability to achieve relative independence from direct capitalist class domination is to be found in the contradictory character of the capitalist state, which we have already mentioned with regard to the writings of Offe, Gramsci, and Macpherson. This means emphasizing the importance of class dynamics in the internal development of the state. By undervaluing the power of the working class and other class groupings, functionalist Marxists have tended to obscure the relative autonomy of the state (Gough, 1979). On the question of law and legal rights, Poulantzas is certainly right to stress the isolation effect by which the state and law break down class collectivities and relations, reconstituting them as individual ones with atomized personal rights and liberties (Poulantzas, 1973). There is little doubt that a powerful political-juridicial ideology with a theory of the legal individual plays an important hegemonic role in consolidating and maintaining capitalism. Yet it is also important to insist that juridical rights have their origins directly in class conflict—of bourgeoisie against aristocracy in the first instance and of a capitalist dominant class and an organized working class in the second. The rights of equality before the law and the varieties of contractual freedoms that have been analyzed as ideological support to the power of capital over wage-labour were won by the bourgeoisie against the residues of feudalism and in opposition to the legal form of absolutism. Political rights (particularly the extension of the franchise and the right to organize trade unions and political parties), welfare rights, the provision of social services, unemployment insurance, compensation pay, and universal medical care emerged in the context of class conflict between capital and labour (Giddens, 1981, pp. 226-29). They were in large measure achieved by an active effort on the part of labour and farmer's movements: first to realize the notion of the "free universal subject" by achieving the rights to organize and vote; and second by using the result of these victories to construct systems of community and welfare services. The implementation of supposedly bourgeois values by the working class was not only fiercely combated by its very initiators, but it also resulted in the formation of labour and social democratic parties and the transformation of the state from a quintessentially bourgeois to a liberal-welfare state. In the process, freedoms and rights have come to take on a double-edged character: on the one side, they appear as purely formal and ideological—the constitutional guarantor of cohesion and consent; on the other side, their existence has created a specific political terrain through which class conflict has been fought out and in which the capitalist state has become increasingly subject to the contradictory pressures of capitalism. As a result, there are limits to the power of the capitalist state to implement policies that might be resisted by either business or labour interests; while at the same time the state is neither class-neutral nor just a tool of class control. For in the process, and given its already discussed surveillance and violence-sanctioning functions, the state culls an added power and autonomy in terms of its control over the formulation and entrenchment of citizenship rights.

LEVELS OF AUTONOMY IN CRIMINAL JUSTICE

We have argued that the state's claim to relative autonomy rests upon its ability to carry out the above functions of surveillance, control of use of violence, and guarantor of general legal relations. Yet the manner and extent of their fulfillment are not automatic; on the contrary, the process becomes more indeterminate as the locus of the behaviour of state agents shifts from ideological (and mainly symbolic) affirmations of class dominance to the actual implementation of class-differentiated objectives of criminal justice. The range of state activity in the criminal justice sector occurs over the following levels: 1) the general orientation of the criminal justice system to the sway of class dominance within the social order; 2) the relative autonomy of the criminal justice sector vis-à-vis other state sectors (health, welfare, finance); 3) the relative autonomy of organizational components within the criminal justice system (police, courts, corrections); 4) the relative

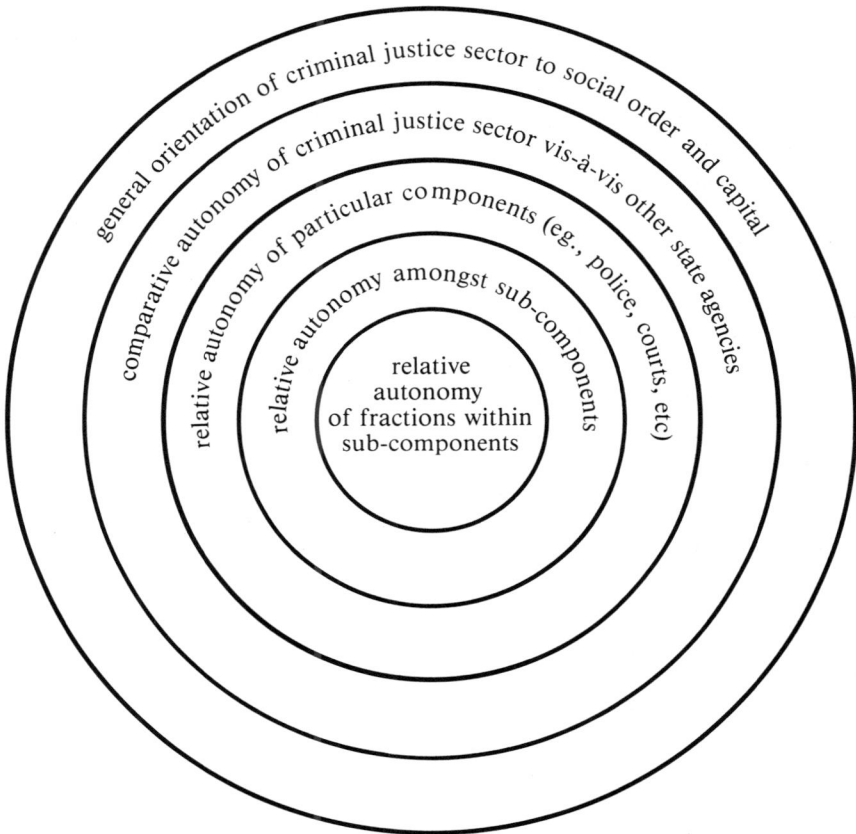

DIAGRAM 1: LEVELS OF RELATIVE AUTONOMY
IN THE CRIMINAL JUSTICE SECTOR

autonomy of internal divisions within each of the organizational components (role of different police forces in the protection of the state and of
private capital); and 5) the relative autonomy of the different specialized
units within and across components of the criminal justice sector (policy
versus praxis units in the organizational division of labour).

Each of the five levels at which state autonomy impacts criminal justice
and modifies the relationship between class and state must now be detailed.

General Orientation of the Criminal Justice Sector to Capital

Although created in the first instance by and for capital, the relative autonomy of the state repressive apparatus is doubly warranted by the crucial services that it performs in the protection of capital and also by the threat of withdrawal of those services. Through the technical capacities required for mass surveillance of exploited sectors of the population, by control over the legitimate exercise of violence, and as chief agent of the ideological hegemony of the legal form, the criminal justice system ensures its virtual indispensability to the ruling fractions of the dominant class. Moreover, in the course of performing these services, the state repressive apparatus develops its own resources, enabling some independence from capital, and assembles powers in civil and administrative realms which extend beyond the sphere of criminal law.[10]

To illustrate the direction and magnitude of growth in the state repressive apparatus, the present era is unprecedented in the extent to which personal data have been gathered by government agencies and the private sector (Rule et al., 1980). Official state surveillance of the population is accomplished through sophisticated technological devices and legislative enactments such as the federal Protection of Privacy Act (Bill C-50, 1974; Bill C-53, 1977) that legalize state intrusions into privacy in the interests of crime control and national security. The purported emphasis on combatting organized crime and thwarting foreign intelligence operations, however, has been debunked by evidence that petty criminals and domestic dissidents are often the targets of state electronic eavesdropping and surveillance (Burtch, 1979). Although Canadian police officials do not have *carte blanche* in their use of surveillance powers—the courts will dismiss evidence gathered improperly (see Watt, 1979)—these surveillance capacities do consolidate overall police strength. Moreover, the recent passage of legislation creating a Civilian Security Intelligence Service, (Bill C-9, 1984) has magnified state surveillance powers.

Regarding the state's legal monopoly on violence, the traditional use of police forces, the courts, and corrections against organized labour in Canada signifies state mobilization of its repressive apparatus against workers (see Morton, 1980).[11] Yet, while Gosselin (1982), and Quinney (1974), and others adopt an instrumentalist interpretation of the criminal justice system (that is as a weapon used against subaltern classes in the interests of the bourgeoisie), the criticism of state violence (such as the "deadly force" employed by police) and the limits set on such violence by statute or popular resistance imply countervailing class pressures; they cannot be dismissed as inconsequential.[12]

With respect to legal relations, the consolidation of state power rests on the wage-contract, labour discipline, and juridical rights, a combination sustained through ideological hegemony and reproduced through the general cultural legitimation of state authority, patriotism, and nationalism. This confers a considerable degree of legitimacy on the criminal justice sector, noticeable in the absence of sustained challenges to general police powers, especially the RCMP (see Mann and Lee, 1979), the courts, or corrections. As Chan and Ericson (1981, pp. 82-83) note, the increase in criminal justice personnel and expenditures in Canada has been dramatic in recent years, a trend bolstered by an ideology of "law and order," perhaps most discussed in the British context (Hall et al., 1978) but surfacing in Canadian politics as well (Ratner and McMullan, 1983; Taylor, 1980, 1983).

While the general orientation of the criminal justice sector in the protection of capital is evident in most of the above developments, analyses that portray the criminal justice system as merely responsive to bourgeoise interests are incomplete. Unremitting pressures are placed on legislative and executive bodies to curtail state powers, pressures that instigate counter-ideologies or reformist forces that partially check the concerted powers of state and hegemonic class fractions. Challenges by civil liberties groups to various aspects of state action, ongoing public controversies over provisions set out in the Criminal Code, (such as abortion, prostitution, or sexual assault), attempts to provide legal services to the poor or to abolish prisons, and widespread resistance to proposals for extensive security and intelligence operations all illustrate the debate over the parameters of state authority, including criminal justice.

Further undermining ruling-class confidence in the state are such portents of betrayal as a threatened defaulting of the vital services necessary to maintain capitalist order (such as in the instance of police strikes or job actions by correctional officers), or an over-extension of the repressive apparatus which would disrupt the equilibrium of class forces by redirecting coercive powers against those previously immune from them.[13] Conversely,the state's claims to relative autonomy in the criminal justice sector are weakened by the fact that the criminal justice system is not directly involved in capital accumulation. In this respect it depends largely on externally generated revenues for its own survival, consequently assuming a subordinate character. Moreover, it services a largely discredited clientele, the unrelieved excrescence of capitalist social disorder judged worthy of little more than punishment and constraint. So, the criminal justice sector's warrant for autonomy is strong but paradoxical. Its bourgeois patrons are indebted to the disciplining powers of the state coercive apparatus, although this is experienced as a grudging concession to a necessarily invented and mistrusted ally. Should the repressive apparatus fail in its delegated mission, whether through inefficiency or recklessness, a frustrated bourgeoisie can resort to its own penultimate sanction—staunching the flow of revenues which underwrite the coercive apparatus. This counter-threat serves as a brake on the relative autonomy and possible renegade orientation of the criminal justice sector.

Comparative Autonomy of Institutionally Differentiated Regions of the State

Connections between the criminal justice sector and other state agencies clarify the comparative autonomy of the criminal justice apparatus. While the key ministries of the state are those which are directly tied to the processes of capital accumulation—that is, those which collect and allocate revenues—the relative autonomy of the criminal justice system is established by the fact that other state agencies rely on it to ensure conditions essential to the fulfillment of their objectives. Every ministry or department faces the prospect of enforcing regulations over a potentially fractious clientele. As noted in the previous section, police, judicial, and correctional intervention is available to maintain a code of discipline that largely facilitates the goals of capital against their opponents. For example, peace officers are used to eject or arrest dissident groups occupying government offices or blocking highways, while civil and criminal prosecution and detention are generally available to the state in dealing with troublesome clients (such as welfare abusers, tax evaders, maintenance defaulters, and political dissidents).

In this respect, all state institutions are symbiotically linked to the repressive apparatus of criminal justice, the ultimate guarantor of state legitimacy. Invocation of the War Measures Act in 1970 illustrates an instance in which the government executive responded to pressures from the state repressive apparatus. A political struggle was redefined as the conspiratorial action of terrorists and thus used ideologically to recoup faltering state institutions. While this does not suggest the primacy of the coercive apparatus (nor its comparatively greater relative autonomy) in the state institutional network, it does emphasize the strategic enforcement capabilities which make it the regulator of the social relations essential to the reproduction of capitalist order.

Comparative autonomy of the criminal justice sector is also manifested structurally in the extent to which state agencies are barred from investigating and criticizing such operations as policing, decisions of the court, and penal policies. Although government policies affecting immigration, housing, education, and the like are occasionally scrutinized by the criminal justice sector, that sector is seldom monitored by other branches of the state. [14] On more routine grounds, the relative autonomy of the criminal justice system vis-à-vis other state institutions is apparent in the wide discretionary powers of police officers, the general tradition of internal discipline and scrutiny within particular police forces, the gatekeeping function of the courts on fundamental conflicts referred to them[15] (such as the specificity of division of powers among the federal, provincial, and municipal governments), and the largely unfettered disciplinary powers exercised by penal officials (Culhane, 1985; Jackson, 1983). Not to be overlooked, however, is the potential of the criminal justice system for serving as other than simply a repressive instrument, given its capacity to constrain excesses by state officials in other departments. The prosecution of officials for violations such as influence peddling, conflict of interest, and interference with the courts is proof of a remedial function; it demonstrates a measure of equity operative in criminal justice.

Relative Autonomy of Organizational Components within the Criminal Justice System

The difficulties in sustaining a social formation prone to class struggle and hegemonic discord become more palpable at the operational level of the organizational components of the criminal justice system. In responding to the social frictions generated by class inequalities, the police, courts, and corrections typically act to protect the interests of capital with constitutional restraints. Relative autonomy is especially visible when legal norms are periodically violated by these authorities in order to safeguard bourgeois interests jeopardized by changing trajectories in the class distribution of power.

The Police. The relative autonomy of the police includes the powers of prosecution and arrest. Clearly, the ambit of criminal law is so broad that many citizens could be charged with violations; nevertheless, the tendency is for police officers to concentrate on the working class (Snider, 1982) and minority groupings (Lee, 1981), with relatively little attention to corporate criminals (Goff and Reasons, 1978). The trend is for police crime control activities to centre on highly visible crimes (Tepperman, 1977; Hagan, 1984) characteristic of the working class—break and enter, theft, assault—along with more serious personal crimes such as murder and rape. Within this framework the police retain considerable autonomy in dealing with suspects, paying informants, and diverting suspects out of the criminal justice system.

The autonomy of the police force is not divorced from state/class hegemony; indeed, police ideology tends to be supportive of political authority. This ideology emphasizes the need to expand police powers, reinstate the death penalty, and oppose prisoners' rights and early release programmes, which may clash with more lenient state policies. In sum, the police serve in theory and in deed as reinforcers of state power and class dominance.

The foregoing should not imply, however, that the police are always successful in merging their particular concerns with dominant interests. Their opposition to government abolition of the death penalty, instances of police strikes in various Canadian jurisdictions, and efforts by RCMP officials to pressure ministers away from certain probes into police operations (Mann and Lee, 1979) exemplify conflicts between the police components and the government of the day. But these instances are dramatic exceptions to the day-to-day operations of the police at the federal, provincial, and municipal levels.[16]

One measure of establishing police autonomy—the level of secrecy—was perhaps most pronounced for the security service within the RCMP. Mann and Lee (1979) noted the strength of the "national security" explanation against attempts to delve into the workings of the security service. Even when instances of illegal action were documented, RCMP officers were unlikely to be convicted or imprisoned. As Brodeur (1981, p. 131) suggests, the law serves to legitimate deviant police behaviour. The RCMP, at least until the advent of the Civilian Security Intelligence Agency, have been almost unfailingly successful in preserving their superordinate powers in intelligence work within Canada. The municipal and provincial police forces have likewise relied upon agency secrecy and internal probes to offset the potential for wider scrutiny by the press or community groupings.

In sum, the police have engaged in violations of due process, the general intimidation of labour, infiltration, and agent provocateurism within dissident political groups, while showing much less persistence in their surveillance and enforcement of organized and corporate crime. Contrarily, the immediacy of police encounters with class pressures "from below" may encourage periodic abstinence from class-biased enforcement (such as the instances of lax and discretionary non-enforcement when racial minorities mobilize against discriminatory policing practice). The drift is nevertheless toward enforcement of capitalist discipline and increased crime control.

The Courts. The court is commonly presented as the most autonomous component of the criminal justice system, especially in terms of judical independence.[17] This independence is, however, limited by the appointment procedures for Canadian judges, their somewhat dependent relationship with police and prosecutors, the social origins of the judiciary, and the content of criminal law. The position of prosecutors is likewise constrained.

The prosecutor has substantial discretion whether or not to proceed with criminal charges. There are instances where prosecutors decline to lay charges despite police recommendations and protests by senior police officials (Grosman, 1974, p. 192). The provincial Attorneys-General may also withdraw charges against defendants despite police recommendations (Snider, 1980, p. 361). In these instances the discretion not to lay charges appears to fall to the benefit of "respectable" persons, a process that corresponds with our earlier comments on the incorporation of class and justice. The conservative nature of the prosecutor's office is, of course, partly related to the middle- or upper-class origins of most prosecutors, mediated by the requirement that most prosecutors have completed law school and are in good standing with their provincial law society (Grosman, 1974). It is not clear, however, that this class conjuncture is so compelling; instead, there appears to be considerable pressure on prosecutors to reduce charges and not to press ahead with minor offences (see Ericson and Baranek, 1982).

The formal separation of powers of the prosecution from those of the police and the judiciary must be placed in the context of power. The prosecutor's knowledge of pre-trial procedures and people in the other criminal justice components gives him a substantial advantage over an accused without legal representation (Grosman, 1974, p. 196). Others have concluded that criminal justice authorities retain extensive control over the destiny of accuseds in pre-trial and trial situations (Ericson and Baranek, 1982), just as the disposition of cases in other jurisdictions is appropriated by officers of the court (see Carlen, 1976). Part of the interactive process among the justice sector's sub-components, therefore, reflects their separate degrees of autonomy in managing "cases," refuting the image of a wholesale apparatus directed instrumentally against the working class and away from the bourgeoisie.

Of all elements within the criminal justice system, the Canadian judiciary is most closely aligned with the ideology of independent justice. In contrast, police officers are expected to press for crime control rather than due process protections (Packer, 1964), the prosecutor is sometimes cast as a major figure in the "war against crime" (Stone, 1979), and correctional officers are well downstream from the formal pre-trial deliberations of suspected criminals. The independence of the Canadian judiciary, however, is presumably reinforced by their salaried, tenured status (Olsen, 1980, p. 45). Judges are not easily dismissed, thus they enjoy a limited measure of autonomy from the public and politicians (since judges are not elected in Canada). Judges also have the power to hold others (including government ministers) in contempt of court should judicial decisions be criticized.

But this motif of judicial independence is qualified by the social origins of judges. Wylie (1982, p. 10) notes that superior court judges in Upper Canada in the late eighteenth century were drawn from the wealthier classes; these courts functioned to stabilize economic transactions, thus promoting the legitimacy of early capitalist development and state authority. Canadian judges continue to be drawn disproportionately from middle- or upper-class origins (Hogarth, 1971, pp. 52-54; Olsen, 1980).

The judicial independence motif is further qualified since judges are appointed by the party in power, thereby eliminating the likelihood of lawyers with a radical orientation receiving an appointment to the bench. These factors of social origins and political appointment are congruent with Miliband's (1973, pp. 61, 125) assertion that British judges tend to be ideologically disposed toward capitalism and the conservation of state power. So in spite of the relative political insulation of the judiciary, judicial politics is inclined to reproduce general patterns of authority and class. This is apparent, for example, in the comparatively lenient sentencing of persons convicted of white-collar crimes. Prison terms are rarely meted out for such convictions in Canada, with fines attached to the "person" of the corporation rather than individual owners or managers; indeed, the content of and administration of criminal law are structured to divert white-collar offences to regulatory bodies rather than the criminal justice system (Goff and Reasons, 1978; Card, 1979). The net result is that wealthier offenders in Canada are rarely sentenced to penal institutions. Judical dispositions for working-class offenders tend to contrast sharply with this motif. Greenaway (1980, p. 258) notes that working-class juvenile offenders in Canada are most likely to receive "major dispositions," and the composition of Canadian penal institutions attests to the largely working-class profile of those incarcerated. The courts' occasionally liberal interpretation of due process safeguards and the intermittent prosecution of white-collar criminals indicates some responsiveness to competing class agendas. However, these are exceptional gestures, the principal effect of which is to legitimate and reinforce bourgeois hegemony through the criminal courts.

Corrections. The corrections component—jails, prisons, penitentiaries, the parole board—retains a substantial degree of autonomy from other criminal justice components. Clearly, prison officials are not empowered to refuse admission to persons sentenced to penal confinement; nevertheless, these officials enjoy a wide latitude in determining the conditions of that confinement. The prerogatives of correctional authorities to make decisions about prisoners—transfers, disciplinary proceedings, use of solitary confinement, eavesdropping of conversations in visiting areas, and so forth—have been largely unfettered by the Canadian courts. As with most other actions encroaching on fundamental freedoms (see Tarnopolsky, 1975), the tradition of the courts is to avoid interference with the administrative discretion of public officials. This latitude is largely unchallenged in actions involving prisoners' rights in Canada (Conroy, 1980; Price, 1974) and has been extended in instances of the power of correctional authorities to revoke visiting privileges of civilians (Culhane, 1979, 1980, 1985).

The "hands off" position of courts legitimizes the power of correctional officials in meting out punishments and arbitrating disputes within penal institutions. Formal mechanisms for internal review of official decisions have been regarded as largely gratuitous, and Gosselin (1982, p. 41) found that only a tiny percentage of appeals of such disciplinary proceedings resulted in an acquittal or reprieve.

There are other instances in which the administrative powers of correctional officials have been limited. Solitary confinement practices in the British Columbia Penitentiary were held to violate the "cruel and unusual punishment" clause of the Canadian Bill of Rights (McCann et al., 1976; Jackson, 1983). Nevertheless, the conditions of solitary confinement in this institution were not altered substantially following the *McCann* decision, nor did subsequent litigation, stemming in part from a prison hostage-taking incident in the same institution (*Regina v. Bruce, Wilson, and Lucas*, cited in Conroy, 1980; pp. 27-74), uphold a defence based on necessity arising out of conditions of solitary confinement.

One encroachment on the powers of correctional officials to control prisoners involves the court's mandate to manage the conduct of trials. In a recent case, federal penitentiary officials were obliged to return prisoner-witnesses (who had been transferred) back to the province in which the trial was being heard and also to transfer defendants closer to the trial site to facilitate consultation with their lawyers (see Conroy, 1980; pp. 69-71). The point remains, however, that the vast majority of official decisions in correctional settings are not scrutinized by the courts, and when they are reviewed the decision almost invariably favours administrative discretion over fundamental freedoms and rights.

The penetration of the courts into the discretionary powers of the parole board is also quite limited. The general trend has been for the courts to take a "hands off" position regarding parole decisions (Burtch and Ericson, 1979; p. 69), with limited reform of the traditionally secretive hearing of the parole board. Although the courts did declare that the "gating" practices of parole board officials concerning persons eligible for release on mandatory supervision were illegal, this check on the autonomy of the parole board was largely removed by amendments to the Parole Act (Bills, C-67, C-68, 1986).

The class composition of corrections is similar to that identified generally within the criminal justice system in Canada. The majority of convicted offenders are drawn from the working-class (Friedenberg, 1980), with considerable over-representation of native offenders within the corrections system, most notably in western Canada (Hagan, 1976; p. 16; Verdun-Jones and Muirhead, 1980). Custodial officers tend to be working class or lower middle class (Ellis, 1979; Willett, 1977a), while upper echelon administrators in corrections are drawn from the more solidly middle-class origins. The net result of these overlaps of class and corrections is not only the jobs that are created for thousands of Canadian workers, but also the object lesson that it provides in punishment. The corresponding emphasis on the moral culpability of individual offenders further obscures the direction of disciplinary activities by the state (see Foucault, 1977, 1980).

Correctional practices, then, similar to those of the police and judiciary, give evidence of relative autonomy functioning within and circumscribed by the social formation of advanced capitalist society. As with other components of the criminal justice sector, there is some official deference to the demands arising in subordinated classes (if sufficiently strident), but the overall momentum is toward a model of crime control congruent with the ideological hegemony of class-dominated social order. In theory, the criminal justice system addresses consensual concerns and is revised according to pluralistic input and debate. In practice, a variety of formal mechanisms are used to reinforce spheres of autonomy among legal components while achieving the substantive goal of applying repressive law primarily against persons of lower-class origins.

Internal Divisions of Organizational Components

Relative autonomy of the state repressive apparatus can be observed to function within organizational sub-components of the criminal justice system. A characteristic manifestation is the obliteration of consensually approved jurisdictional boundaries between organizational components of the criminal justice system, as when particular police divisions (federal, provincial, municipal) map out territorial jurisdictions in ways that produce both overlap and gaps. These jurisdictions then establish claims to police areas without interference from other forces. With uncertain jurisdictional boundaries, accountability is weakened, enabling the commission of excesses and improprieties by those entrusted with coercive powers. Efforts to monitor abuses (as in the Quebec Keable Commission's attempt to bring the RCMP to brook) are generally squelched.[18]

As noted earlier, while the Canadian courts tend to be conservative, they have considerable discretionary power which may be applied "on the merits" of particular cases rather than in accord with other interests. The recent eighteen-month jail sentence meted out to a British Columbia lawyer for fraud, the million-dollar fine levied against Simpson-Sears for false advertising, and the occasional incarceration of white-collar offenders suggest that in some instances the ideology of judical independence is not simply chimerical; indeed, the power of superior courts in establishing jurisdiction over "inferior" courts, the reversal of lower court decisions through appeal courts, and a host of judicial decisions bearing on the inadmissability of Crown evidence (with consequent acquittals) attest to the considerable autonomy that may be exercised by court personnel. In emphasizing these anomalies in law we are not omitting counter-arguments that highlight the ways in which court actors facilitate the production of guilty pleas in criminal prosecutions (Ericson and Baranek, 1982) or the overall conservatism inherent in the court apparatus. But we do insist that the analysis of the courts must also clarify the grounds for decisions which at least temporarily, push aside class allegiances. While such exercises of relative autonomy within judicial sub-components may signify little more than the ideological use of law to obtain greater state control (via "tokenism"), they may also indicate the use of law to promote democratization, a not inconceivable objective of semi-autonomous units of the judiciary.

The corrections component is also vested with considerable autonomy, albeit less autonomy than the police or the court. This lessened autonomy stems structurally from the position of penal authorities downstream from the filtering agencies of the police, prosecutor, and the judiciary wherein the nature of policing, charging, prosecution, and disposition have already channelled state power against a primarily working-class population (Friedenberg, 1980; Gosselin, 1982; Snider, 1982; Trubeck, 1977).

The autonomy of the correctional sub-components, then, is largely directed at the control of those sentenced to prison institutions. It is achieved through jurisdictional autonomy, since various prison authorities rarely infringe on decisions and policies of one another. This intra-component autonomy, coupled with the inter-component autonomy (whereby the courts and police generally do not involve themselves in prison law or prison discipline), contributes to the considerable autonomy of penal officials in dealing with their prisoners.

Organizational Division of Labour within Specialized Components

There are fractions of personnel within the criminal justice system sub-components. Shearing (1981) has identified four types of police officers—good, real, wise, and cautious—in his study of an Ontario police department, and there are starker polarizations of outlook within particular police forces, especially in relation to the policing of minorities (Darnton, 1976). Similar variations in philosophy and practice occur within the judiciary (Hogarth, 1971; Olsen, 1980, pp. 59-60), variations that are either actual or potential sources of tensions within particular sub-components. The right of police officers to take job-actions (strikes, working-to-rule, and so on) and the propriety of judicial commentaries on public policy— exemplified by official criticism of Justice Tom Berger's comments on constitutional negotiations in Canada—likewise represent instances of dissent within particular sub-components.

Fractions within the correctional component are readily apparent. Conflicts between treatment personnel and custodial staff in penal settings are well-documented (see Zald, 1969), episodic "mutinies" by custodial staff against prison directors have been verified (Vance and McNeil, 1978), and the recommendation by the Sub-Committee on the Canadian Penitentiary System (1977) to remodel unionized custodial staff along the lines of the non-unionized RCMP illustrates the non-monolithic character of the correctional component. As well, there are potential conflicts between the policies developed through research divisions within correctional agencies and frontline personnel who carry out the daily work. At another level, tensions may emerge between regulations promulgated by centralized headquarters and those issued by regional divisions. The point is that the terrain of relative autonomy extends throughout the organizational components of the branches of the state apparatus, acquiring intra-organizational prominence around actual work-place encounters, such as between the "line staff" and "policy units" of each sub-division. "Think-tank" units, for example, work to anticipate and dispel perceived dissonances in the criminal justice system, but a perhaps unintended consequence of their inquiries into aspects of class struggle may be the edification of previously ignored accounts. Yet, if the balance of class forces is to remain unaltered, incipient critiques of bourgeois hegemony must be curbed. Consider, for example, the experience of the Law Reform Commission of Canada (LRCC), which shifted its research orientation from exploratory and critical reassessments of criminal law to a legalistic modernization of the criminal code. This change was made largely at the behest of ministry of justice personnel who felt unable to translate LRCC recommendations into legislative proposals acceptable to Parliament.

Clearly, the merits of including hegemonically untrammeled think tanks inside the organizational departments of the criminal justice system will evaporate in the context of an ideologically constituted state apparatus poised to reject their recommendations.[19] Therefore, the claims of ideologically defused research units to relative autonomy under state institutional aegis lie in their credibility as a legitimation device. But if state functionaries are to be genuinely effective as agents of social change, they will depend on the state's ability to fashion its own agenda and to deviate from the co-ordinates of social control established for it by the bourgeoisie. Where particular sub-components of the criminal justice system become real terrains of class conflict, the state may grasp initiatives that represent interests broader than, or different from the hegemonic interests of the dominant class.

We have tried to explore how relative autonomy is manifested across five levels of criminal justice in Canada. Neither the dominant correctionalist approach to crime control nor the instrumentalist critique of criminal justice (which reduces state power to class power) are sufficient to account for the complex dialectical forces that shape criminal justice policies within advanced capitalist society. The strength of the relative autonomy thesis stems from its analytic utility in incorporating the diversity and ironies of the dialectics of social control both within the state and between the state and civil society. While the repressive apparatus of the state cannot fashion an agenda indifferent to the needs of capital (that is, inimical to the "system"), its monopolization of surveillance powers, official violence, and formal legality insulates it to some extent from direct manipulation by the bourgeoisie. This leaves unclear the relations between state, class, and capital, which are compounded by the various internal subdivisions within and between organizational components of the repressive apparatus and by the disharmonious demands of their respective clienteles. The complex mixture of the interpretative powers of the courts, the surveillance and definitional powers of the police, and the disciplining powers of corrections is one that operates toward state autonomy but which is also encountered by hegemonic class interests intent on circumscribing that autonomy. The relative autonomy thesis, then, directs us to understand the state (and its repressive component in particular) as pragmatically tied to the agenda of the class in control of the dominant mode of production but not unable to take initiatives for interests which may diverge from those of the dominant class. Precisely *how* divergent is difficult to specify, given the abstract nature of the relative autonomy formulation, though we may assume that hegemonic interests will seek to curb state power when they perceive that their domination is threatened from that source. Yet it is not implausible that the massive powers acquired by the state (especially through its repressive apparatus) will enable it to present itself as an alternative force, eventually taking control of the reins of the dominant mode of production with, perhaps, a re-ordering of social and economic priorities. At such a point the state will obviously have moved beyond the limitations implicit in the notion of relative autonomy.

CONCLUSION

We are led to conclude that even our rudimentary observations of the autonomy of the Canadian state signal the promise of structuralist inquiries when they are unhinged from overly functionalist theoretical moorings. In our view, much can be understood about the ironies, contradictions, and attempted resolutions of state/class hegemonic discord if the activities of the criminal justice sector are studied along the proposed lines. We take issue with instrumentalist readings of the relationship between state and class, since they overlook the workings of relative autonomy, which we take to be vital to the understanding of state/class conjunctures in relation to criminal justice. For the same reason, we also reject the remedial and simplistic systems-oriented perspectives preoccupied with harmonizing criminal justice operations. Their advocates seem oblivious to the fact that the contradictions generated within and between the various organizational components of the criminal justice system by the operation of relative autonomy can be crucially relevant to maintaining the very social order to which they themselves are committed.

In all of the above considerations, we have emphasized the importance of furthering the sociological study of state institutions through exploration of the concept of the relative autonomy of the state, focusing here on the state repressive apparatus. In this endeavour, Poulantzian structuralism is seminal but ultimately cuts off factual inquiry. Going beyond the structural limits on state activity insisted upon by Poultanzas, relative autonomy implies the possiblility of reconstructing the state and civil society along the lines of popular justice. The state, hidden in the pluralist ideology of correctionalism and miscast in orthodox neo-Marxist interpretations as inherently repressive, instead becomes an arena in which its very autonomy can serve to promote democratization and reverse the class bias still evident throughout criminal justice.[20] Denying neither the relevance of class interests nor the logic of capital accumulation, it is essential to regard the capitalist state as more than the abstract operation of economic forces and to recognize that it may be able to acquire a logic and interests of its own (Block, 1977, 1980; Miliband, 1983). Acknowledgement of the state's emancipatory potential and its vulnerability to class practices underscores the theoretical value of the capital-logic, structuralist, and class-conflict perspectives, as against purely economistic approaches or the pluralist view. At this stage, it appears to us that a synthesis of these three more analytically sophisticated perspectives, ideally enabling an account of structural constraints and human agency in complex dialectical interplay, offers the best prospect for further theoretical explorations of "criminal justice" in the advanced capitalist state.

NOTES

1. See Willem Bonger, (1916), *Criminality and Economic Conditions* (Boston: Little, Brown).
2. It remains true, however, that radical accounts of criminal law and its enforcement are a minority contribution to criminological discussion, just as Marxist interpretations of political and economic relations have been dismissed or ignored in western scholarship for the most part (Gurney, 1981).
3. The political structures (that is, the state) function as a "cohesive factor" in that they prevent internecine conflict between and within social classes, keeping society from bursting asunder.
4. "Social formations" are the concrete objects to be understood—particular historical societies at specified times. For Poulantzas, a social formation is dominated by one mode of production which generates a fundamental contradiction (such as bourgeois versus proletariat) around which all other forces are polarized.
5. It should be noted, however, that the divergence in their views is not so marked, as when Block concedes that the activities of the state are ultimately structured around the interests of capital (Block, 1977).
6. The terms "criminal justice system," "criminal justice sector," "state repressive apparatus," and "state coercive apparatus," are used interchangeably throughout the paper. In fact, they are not wholly synonomous, since the latter terms also encompass civil law and courts, domestic and foreign security agencies, and the military, none of which is included in our empirical focus on the criminal justice system. Nor should our use of the term "criminal justice system" be taken to imply our acceptance of the view that the justice sector does, indeed, function as a *system*.
7. For a discussion of some contemporary work focusing on internal mechanisms of the state apparatus in managing contradictions between accumulation and legitimation functions (though not addressed directly to problems of criminal justice), see Gold, Lo, and Wright, 1975.
8. Despite drawing attention to the problem, Jessop (1983) devotes only a few pages of his own text to discussion of the relative autonomy thesis.
9. Our classification of state theories is roughly similar to those presented by Gold, Lo, and Wright (1975, 1975a), Jessop (1977), and Hall and Scraton (1981).
10. The traditional ideology of criminal law as the expression of common interests and its substantive role in ensuring class justice is also invoked in non-criminal courts. Small claims courts, for example, though ostensibly designed for the average person to redress private wrongs, tend to yield decisions favouring those with greater power (see Yngvesson and Hennessey, 1975). There is evidence from Canadian sources that small claims courts are widely used by crown corporations and other organizations against less powerful defendants (see Olsen, 1980, p. 63).
11. Kellough and her associates (1980) find *qualified* support for the instrumental-

ist approach in their study of incarceration in Manitoba between 1918 and 1939. We argue that such qualified findings point to the relative autonomy thesis for understanding the role and effects of criminal justice in Canada.

12. This is so even though the police effectively minimize potential charges of official brutality by charging suspects with assault against arresting officers (Brodeur, 1981, p. 129), or "overcharging," both instances of the enabling rules available to Canadian criminal justice officials (Ericson and Baranek, 1982).

13. Fears that this may come about are made more acute by awareness that the logic of capital accumulation involves contradictions which may dictate that end.

14. Scrutiny of the state repressive apparatus depends more on informal calls for inquiries into criminal justice policies and practices by politicians and various non-state organizations (such as concerned citizens' groups, civil liberties associations, and organized labour).

15. The workload of the Supreme Court of Canada, for example, centres on business and professional litigation; as Olsen (1980, p. 56) observes, "the higher courts generally serve the higher classes, as the lower courts 'serve' the lower classes."

16. Moreover, the state apparatus is ideally arranged so that extra-organizational control of police tasks is afforded by legislation prohibiting police walkouts (see Essential Services Legislation) and substitution of military and RCMP personnel for police and penal officers during labour disputes.

17. Young (1979, p. 14) distinguishes the universalistic patina of the courts from the "direct coercion" exercised by the police and the prisons.

18. This development further illustrates the tendency for internal departments of the state apparatus to localize power in the pursuit of "emergent interests," irrespective of its coincidence with the needs of capital. Bourgeois mistrust of fragmented state policing, therefore, is not without foundation and impels periodic recourse to private policing.

19. For example, the Association of Police Chiefs recently attacked the Law Reform Commission of Canada recommendations on the grounds that it sided with criminals and was aiming to control police. Such recommendations were regarded by the police chiefs as "an intrusion in their territory." The president of the association was quoted as saying that interfering with police autonomy "is a most insidious thing" (*Globe and Mail*, 29 August 1985).

20. Paradoxical as this may seem, we find some recent evidence for our supposition in the advertising campaign of the 1,700 member British Columbia Federation of Police Officers which was directed against the proposed "restraint" legislation of the provincial government—legislation which included a provision for "dismissal without cause" for any public sector employee. The half-page police newspaper ads read: "how will I investigate criminal allegations against politicians when I can be fired without cause? Think about Bill 3."

REFERENCES

Altvater, E. 1973. "Some Problems of State Intervention." *Kapitalistate*, nos. 1, 2.

Anderson, P. 1979. *Lineages of the Absolutist State*. London: Verso.

Balbus, I. 1977. "Commodity Form and Legal Form: An Essay on the 'Relative Autonomy of Law.' " *Law and Society Review* 2: 571-88.

Baum, D. J. 1979. *Discount Justice: The Canadian Criminal Justice System* Don Mills, Ontario: Burns and MacEachern.

Block, F. 1977. "The Ruling Class Does Not Rule: Notes on the Marxist Theory of the State." *Socialist Revolution* 33, no. 7: 6-28.

_____. 1980. "Beyond Relative Autonomy: State Managers as Historical Subjects." *The Socialist Register*: 227-42.

Brodeur, J-P. 1981. "Legitimizing Police Deviance." In C. Shearing, ed., *Organizational Police Deviance*. Toronto: Butterworths, pp. 07-60.

Burtch, B. 1979. "Electronic Surveillance and Legal Civil Liberties." *Canadian Criminology Forum* 1, no. 1: 1-0.

_____. and R. V. Ericson. 1979. "The Control of Treatment: Issues in the Use of Prison Clinical Services." *University of Toronto Law Journal* 29, no. 1: 51-73.

Cain, M. 1976. "Necessarily Out of Touch: Thoughts on the Organisation of the Bar." In P. Carlen, ed., *The Sociology of Law*. Keele: University of Keele, pp. 226-50.

Card, D. 1979. "A Critical Analysis of the Formulation of Bill C-13 (1978): An Act to Amend the Combines Investigation Act." *Canadian Criminology Forum* 2: 31-47.

Carlen, P. 1976. "The Staging of Magistrates' Justice." *British Journal of Criminology* 16: 48-55.

Chan, J. B. L., and R. V. Ericson. 1981. *Decarceration and the Economy of Penal Reform*. Toronto: Centre of Criminology.

Clement, W. 1973. *The Canadian Corporate Elite*. Toronto: McClelland and Stewart.

_____. 1976. *Continental Corporate Power: Economic Links Between Canada and the United States*. Toronto: McClelland and Stewart.

Connidis, I. 1982. *Rethinking Criminal Justice Research: A Systems Perspective*. Toronto: Holt, Rinehart and Winston.

Conroy, J. 1980. "An Introduction to Canadian Prison Law." In J. Conroy and E. Kossuth, eds., *Canadian Prison Law*. Vancouver: Butterworths, pp. 1-75.

Culhane, C. 1979. *Barred From Prison*. Vancouver: Pulp Press.

_____. 1985. *Still Barred From Prison*. Montreal: Black Rose Books.

Culhane v. Attorney-General of British Columbia and Harrison 51. 1980. *Canadian Criminal Case*. 2nd series, pp. 213-37.

Dahl, R. 1965. *A Preface to Democratic Theory*. Chicago: University of Chicago Press.

Darnton, J. 1976. "Color Line a Key Police Problem." In A. Niederhoffer and A. Blumberg, eds., *The Ambivalent Force: Perspectives on the Police*. 2nd ed. Hinsdale, Illinois: The Dryden Press, pp. 96-99.

Domhoff, W. 1967. *Who Rules America?* Englewood Cliffs, New Jersey: Prentice-Hall.
_____. 1970. *The Higher Circles*. Part 2. New York: Vintage.
Ellis, D. 1979. "The Prison Guard as Carceral Luddite: A Critical Review of the MacGuigan Report on the Penitentiary System in Canada." *Canadian Journal of Sociology* 4: 43-64.
Ericson, R. V., and P. M. Baranek. 1982. *The Ordering of Justice: A Study of Accused Persons as Dependants in the Criminal Process*. Toronto: University of Toronto Press.
Fine, B., et al. 1979. *Capitalism and the Rule of Law: From Deviancy Theory to Marxism*. London: Hutchinson.
Foucault, M. 1975. *The Birth of the Clinic*. New York: Vintage.
_____. 1977. *Discipline and Punish*. New York: Vintage.
_____. 1980. "Prison Talk." In Colin Gardon, ed. *Power/Knowledge: Selected Interviews and Other Selected Interviews and Other Writings*. Brighton: The Harvester Press, pp. 37-54.
Friedenberg, E. Z. 1980. "The Punishment Industry in Canada." *Canadian Journal of Sociology* 5: 273-84.
Garofalo, J. 1978. "Radical Criminology and Criminal Justice: Points of Divergence and Contact." *Crime and Social Justice* (Fall-Winter): 17-27.
Giddens, A. 1981. *A Contemporary Critique of Historical Materialism*. Part 1: *Power, Property, and the State*. Berkeley: University of California Press.
Goff, C. H., and C. E. Reasons. 1978. *Corporate Crime in Canada: A Critical Analysis of Anti-Combines Legislation*. Scarborough: Prentice-Hall.
Gold, D., C. Lo, and E. Wright. 1975. "Recent Developments in Marxist Theories of the Capitalist State." *Monthly Review* (October): 29-43.
_____. 1975a. "Recent Developments in Marxist Theories of the Capitalist State." *Monthly Review* (November): 36-51.
Gosselin, L. 1982. *Prisons in Canada*. Montreal: Black Rose Books.
Gough, I. 1979. *The Political Economy of the Welfare State*. London: Macmillan.
Gramsci, A. 1971. *Prison Notebooks*. London: Lawrence and Wishart.
Greenaway, W. K. 1980. "Crime and Class." In J. Harp and J. Hofley, eds. *Structural Inequality in Canada*. Scarborough: Prentice-Hall, pp. 247-65.
Griffith, J. 1977. *The Politics of the Judiciary*. London: Fontana/Collins.
Grosman, B. 1974. "The Prosecutor: Discretion and Pre-Trial Practices." In C. Boydell, P. Whitehead, and C. Grindstaff, eds., *The Administration of Criminal Justice in Canada*. Toronto: Holt, Rinehart and Winston, pp. 186-98.
Gurney, P. 1981. "Historical Origins of Ideological Denial: The Case of Marx in American Sociology." *The American Sociologist* 16: 196-201.
Hagan, J. 1976. "Locking Up the Indians: A Case for Law Reform." *The Canadian Forum* 55: 16-18.
_____. 1984. *The Disreputable Pleasures*. 2d ed. Toronto: McGraw-Hill Ryerson.
Hall, S., et al. 1978. *Policing the Crisis*. London: Macmillan.
_____., and P. Scraton. 1981. "Law, Class, and Control." In Mike Fitzgerald, Gregory McLennan, and Jennie Pawson, eds., *Crime and Society*. London: Routledge and Kegan Paul.

Hay, D., et al. 1975. *Albion's Fatal Tree.* London: Allen Lane.

Hirsch, J. 1978. "The State Apparatus and Social Reproduction: Elements of a Theory of the Bourgeois State." In J. Holloway and S. Picciotto, eds., *State and Capital: a Marxist Debate.* London: Arnold.

Hirst, P. 1973. "The Marxism of the 'New Criminology.' " *British Journal of Criminology* 13: 396-98.

Hogarth, J. 1971. *Sentencing as a Human Process.* Toronto: University Press.

Holloway, J. and S. Picciotto. 1978. *State and Capital.* London: Edward Arnold.

Jackson, M. 1983. *Prisoners of Isolation: Solitary Confinement in Canada.* Toronto: University of Toronto Press.

Jessop, B. 1977. "Recent Theories of the Capitalist State." *Cambridge Journal of Economics* 1: 353-73.

———. 1980. "On Recent Marxist Theories of Law, the State, and Juridico-Political Ideology." *International Journal of the Sociology of Law* 8: 339-68.

———. 1982. *The Capitalist State: Marxist Theories and Methods.* London: Martin Robertson.

Kellough, D. G., S. L. Brickey, and W. K. Greenaway. 1980. "The Politics of Incarceration: Manitoba, 1918-1939." *Canadian Journal of Sociology* 5: 253-72.

Lee, J.A. 1981. "Some Structural Aspects of Police Deviance in Relations with Minority Groups." In C. Shearing, ed., *Organizational Police Deviance.* Toronto: Butterworths, pp. 49-82.

McCann et al. v. The Queen. 1976. *Canadian Criminal Cases.* 2d Series, 29, Agincourt: Canada Law Book Ltd., pp. 337-76

Macpherson, C. B. 1966. *The Real World of Democracy.* Oxford: Clarendon Press.

Mankoff, M. 1970. "Power in Advanced Capitalist Society: A Review Essay on Recent Elitist and Marxist Criticism of Pluralist Theory." *Social Problems* 17, no. 3: 418-32.

Mann, W. E., and J. A. Lee. 1979. *RCMP vs. The People: Inside Canada's Secret Service.* Don Mills, Ontario: General.

Marx, K., and F. Engels. 1967. *The Communist Manifesto.* Harmondsworth: Penguin.

Miliband, R. 1969. *The State in Capitalist Society.* New York: Basic Books.

———. 1972. "Reply to Nicos Poulantzas." In Robin Blackburn, ed., *Ideology in Social Science: Readings in Critical Social Theory.* London: Fontana/Collins, pp. 253-62.

———. 1983. "State Power and Class Interests." *New Left Review,* no. 138 (March/April): 57-68.

Morton, D. 1980. *Working People.* Ottawa: Deneau and Greenberg.

O'Connor, J. 1973. *The Fiscal Crisis of the State.* New York: St. Martin's Press.

Offe, C. 1972. "Political Authority and Class Structure: An Analysis of Late Capitalist Societies." *International Journal of Sociology* (Spring): 73-108.

Olsen, D. 1980. "The Judicial Elite and Class Justice." In *The State Elite.* Toronto: McClelland and Stewart, pp. 42-64.

Packer, H. 1964. "Two Models of the Criminal Process." *University of Pennsylvania Law Review* 113: 1-68.

Panitch, L., ed., 1977. *The Canadian State: Political Economy and Political Power.* Toronto: University of Toronto Press.

Pashukanis, E. 1978. *Law and Marxism: A General Theory.* London: Ink Links.

Poulantzas, N. 1972. "The Problem of the Capitalist State." In Robin Blackburn, ed., *Ideology in Social Science: Readings in Critical Theory.* London: Fontana/Collins, pp. 238-53.

_____. 1973. *Political Power and Social Classes.* London: New Left Books.

Price, R. 1974. "Bringing the Rule of Law to Corrections." *Canadian Journal of Criminology* 163: 209-55.

Quinney, R. 1974. *Critique of Legal Order.* New York: Little, Brown.

_____. 1980. *Class, State and Crime.* New York: Longmans.

Ratner, R. S., and John L. McMullan, 1983. "Social Control and the Rise of the 'Exceptional State' in Britain, the United States, and Canada." *Crime and Social Justice*, no. 19: 31-43.

Reasons, C., L. Ross. and C. Patterson. 1981. *Assault on the Worker.* Toronto: Butterworths.

Rule, J., et al. 1980. *The Politics of Privacy.* New York: Mentor.

Scraton, P. 1982. "Ideology and the Hidden Economy: Private Justice and Work—Related Crime." Paper presented to the Annual Meetings of the Canadian Sociology and Anthropology Association, Ottawa.

Shearing, C. 1981. "Deviance and Conformity in the Reproduction of Order." In *Organizational Police Deviance.* Toronto: Butterworths, pp. 29-47.

Snider, L. 1980. "Corporate Crime in Canada." In R. Silverman and J. Teevan, eds., *Crime in Canadian Society.* Toronto: Butterworths, pp. 348-68.

_____. 1982. "The Criminal Justice System." In D. Forcese and S. Richer, eds., *Social Issues: Sociological Views of Canada.* Scarborough: Prentice-Hall, pp. 395-439.

Stone, M. 1979. "Review of *The Prosecutor*, by B. Grosman." *Canadian Journal of Criminology* 21: 231-33.

Sub-Committee on the Penitentiary System in Canada. 1977. *Report to Parliament.* Ottawa: Supply and Services Canada.

Sumner, C. 1981. "The Rule of Law and Civil Rights in Contemporary Marxist Theory." *Kapitalistate* 9: 63-90.

Tarnopolsky, W. 1975. *The Canadian Bill of Rights.* 2nd ed. Toronto: McClelland and Stewart.

Taylor, I. 1980. "The Law and Order Issue in the British General Election and Canadian Federal Election of 1979: Crime, Populism and the State." *Canadian Journal of Sociology* 5, no. 3: 285-311.

_____. 1981. *Law and Order: Arguments for Socialism.* London: MacMillan.

_____. 1983. *Crime, Capitalism and Community.* Toronto: Butterworths.

Tepperman, L. 1977. *Crime Control: The Urge Toward Authority.* Toronto: McGraw-Hill Ryerson.

Thompson, E. P. 1977. *Whigs and Hunters: The Origin of the Black Act.* Harmondsworth: Penguin.

Trubeck, D. 1977. "Complexity and Contradiction in the Legal Order: Balbus and the Challenge of Critical Social Thought about the Law." *Law and Society Review* 11: 529-69.

Verdun-Jones, S. N., and G. K. Muirhead. 1982. "The Native in the Criminal Justice System: Canadian Research." In C. Boydell and I. Connidis, eds., *The Canadian Criminal Justice System*, Toronto: Holt, Rinehart and Winston, pp. 266-81.

Watt, D. 1979. *Law of Electronic Surveillance in Canada*. Toronto: Carswell.

Willett, T. C. 1977a. "Editorial." *Canadian Journal of Criminology* 19: 327-30.

_____. 1977. "The 'Fish Screw' in the Canadian Penitentiary Service." *Queen's Law Journal* 3: 424-49.

Williams, R. 1978. *Marxism and Literature*. Oxford: Oxford University Press.

Wylie, W. 1982. "Merchants, Administrators, and the Civil Courts of Upper Canada, 1789-180." Paper presented to the Canadian Historical Association, University of Ottawa.

Yngvesson, B., and P. Hennessey. 1975. "Small Claims, Complex Disputes: A Review of the Small Claims Literature." *Law and Society Review* 9: 219-74.

Young, J. 1979. "Left Idealism, Reformism, and Beyond: From New Criminology to Marxism." In B. Fine et al., eds., *Capitalism and the Rule of Law*. London: Hutchinson, pp. 11-28.

Zald, M. 1969. "Power Balance and Staff Conflict in Institutions." In L. Hazelrigg, *Prison Within Society*. Garden City, New York: Anchor, pp. 397-425.

Zander, M. 1968. *Lawyers and the Public Interest*. London: Weidenfeld and Nicolson.

6

Social Control, State Autonomy and Legal Reform: The Law Reform Commission of Canada

ROSS HASTINGS and R. P. SAUNDERS

There is a general agreement among social scientists that law serves a strategic purpose as a formal expression of the dominant values of a society, as a mechanism for the resolution of conflicts and the coercion of rule-breakers, or as a tool in the education or "civilizing" of the general public. In this sense, it is impossible to study the forms and uses of law apart from the wider social relations and structural arrangements from within which it emerges. However, this notion can be operationalized in very different ways. On the one hand, functionalists are more likely to view law as expressing the outcome of a relatively open negotiation process between competing interest groups and to focus their analysis on the consequences of law for the overall welfare of a given social system. On the other hand, Marxists emphasize the class-based material and ideological interests which are served by the law at a given social and political conjuncture. The common thread in these otherwise incompatible positions is a view of the law as emerging within current social relations and social structures and as contributing to their preservation or transformation.

Once this much has been said, however, we are still no closer to a method for analyzing law or an understanding of the specific forms or uses of the law. The easy answer is that we must study law by trying to understand the complex and interpenetrating factors which determine law in specific societies. But this says everything and yet nothing at all! The notion of law as a strategy will only be useful heuristically if it can direct us to an appreciation of the types of problems the law is attempting to resolve, an awareness of the identity of the groups who control the definition of these problems, and an understanding of how and why certain proposals are selected while others are rejected.

These are precisely the type of theoretical and research problems which the thesis of the relative autonomy of the state is designed to address. As indicated by the authors of the previous paper:

> The strength of the relative autonomy thesis stems from its analytic utility in incorporating the diversity and ironies of the dialectics of social control both within the state and between the state and civil society. . . . [It] directs us to understand the state (and its repressive component in particular) as pragmatically tied to the agenda of the class in control of the dominant mode of production but not unable to take initiatives for interests which may diverge from those of the dominant class. (Ratner, McMullan and Burtch, this volume, pp. 117)

The relative autonomy thesis contains the promise of a model capable of dealing with the dialectical interplay of structure and agency in the creation and transformation of the law and provides an abstract picture of the broad lines of a method of inquiry into actual legal forms and practices.

The present paper focuses on an aspect of the specific case of the reform of criminal law in Canada. The process, content, and consequences of legal reform can only be adequately understood in the context of the wider role of the state in general and of the issues of ideology and social control in particular. Our focus will be on the work of the Law Reform Commission of Canada (LRCC), which is one of the key state agencies involved in the current project of the Canadian government to rewrite the Canadian Criminal Code. We wish to establish the LRCC's contribution to this process and the degree to which this is related to the relative autonomy of the LRCC in particular and the criminal justice system in general.

The movement of the Canadian state towards the creation of a law reform agency began in the late 1960's, culminating in 1971 with the formation of the Law Reform Commission of Canada. The commission was intended to be a response, and in part a solution, to the conflict and social disjunctures which marked the 1960's. According to John Turner, Minister of Justice at the time, this period was an "age of confrontation": "we are witnessing today what has been called a 'crisis of legitimacy' or as some would have it a 'crisis of authority.' All our institutions . . . are being challenged" (1971, p. 2). In the face of this crisis, Turner nevertheless argued that "revolution" can be made possible through law, and that "law is not just a 'technical body' of rules; it is the organizing principle for the reconfiguration of society. Law is not just an agency of social control; it articulates the values by which men seek to live" (ibid.).

The LRCC was thus designed to contribute to the challenge of coming to grips with social conflict and social change. There was a recognition that the old order was giving way to a new, more heterogeneous and more fragmented society, one in which the law would be called upon to provide "the means by which multiple sets of values can co-exist and develop" (Burke, 1971; p. 5). The goal was to codify, rationalize, and rethink the law in order to adapt our legal instruments to the task of constructing a more harmonious world.

The formal mandate of the LRCC directed it to engage in both the technical task of systematizing and rationalizing the law and the broader sociopolitical task of reform. More specifically, the LRCC was authorized to make recommendations on:

1) the removal of anachronisms and anomalies in the law;
2) the reflection in and by the law of the distinctive concepts and institutions of the common and civil law systems in Canada and the reconciliation of differences and discrepancies in the expression and application of the law arising out of differences in these concepts and institutions;
3) the elimination of obsolete laws; and
4) the development of new approaches to and new concepts of the law in keeping with and responsive to the changing needs of modern Canadian society and individual members of that society (Law Reform Commission Act, 1970, s. 11).

This mandate, particularly in its directive to develop new orientations to the law, justifies an analysis of the results of over a decade of LRCC work. The notion of relative autonomy, in directing us to the location of the LRCC within the criminal justice system and the Canadian state and to the conflicts which have unravelled over the last twenty years, will help greatly to clarify the consequences and possibilities of legal reform in Canada.

In order to accomplish this analysis, we will discuss the contributions of the LRCC to the current project of revising and rewriting the Canadian Criminal Code, focusing on three major issues. First, we will discuss the internal division of labour and the working process adopted by the LRCC in its attempt to accomplish its mandate. This general description will permit an appreciation of the broad scope of the task assigned to the LRCC, and will allow us to identify some of the main groups who participate in the work of legal reform.

Next, we will discuss the content of the work of the LRCC, focusing specifically on its attempts to specify the aims of criminal law and to translate this general orientation into concrete recommendations for criminal law reform. Our argument is that the LRCC has adopted a pluralist-functionalist perspective on the nature and role of criminal law and now appears content to restrict its responsibility to the task of bringing the law up-to-date with the commonly held values of our modern society.

Finally, we will analyze the consequences of the work of the LRCC in the specific area of criminal law. We contend that the LRCC has developed and adopted a position on the role and functions of criminal law which is ideologically compatible with current social arrangements. It has almost completely abandoned the potential, explicit in its original mandate, for rethinking the law in order to develop new legal approaches more in keeping with the changing needs of contemporary Canadian society. This is a result of a change in the strategic relation of the LRCC to the social and political conflicts of the day. The LRCC is now in a fundamentally different relationship to wider social events, and this has limited its autonomy to propose significant sociolegal reform.

THE LRCC AND THE WORK OF REFORM

Despite its high level of funding and its original intentions to engage in fundamental research and consult broadly during the process of legal reform, the LRCC is relatively little known outside the legal profession. For this reason, a brief description of the organization and working procedures of the LRCC is useful.

In order to fulfill its mandate, the LRCC has structured its tasks so as to best reflect the various potential areas of law reform within the federal jurisdiction.[1] This has led to a division of the work of the LRCC into four major research projects:

1) the Substantive Criminal Law Project, which is responsible for the writing of a new code of substantive criminal law;
2) the Criminal Procedure Project, which is involved in the production of a code of criminal procedure;
3) the Protection of Life Project, which is engaged in the examination of a broad range of medico-legal matters, including issues relating to pollution, the environment, and consumer products; and
4) the Administrative Law Project, which is concerned with research into the general relationship between law and administrative agencies. (LRCC, 1984, pp. 17-18)

Each project is headed by a project co-ordinator and is under the overall direction of an individual commissioner (ibid., p. 5). For the purposes of our study, we have focused our attention solely on the work of the Substantive Criminal Law Project. There are two reasons for this. First, it is this project which is most directly responsible for the production of the *content* of criminal law within the law reform process. As such, its work will best illustrate the positions adopted by the LRCC on both the general aims of criminal law in Canadian society and the process of criminal law reform. Second, the government of Canada is currently engaged in a long-term project of rewriting the Criminal Code.[2] The Department of Justice has placed a high priority on the production of this code; as a result, the work of the LRCC has taken on an increased importance.

During its first years of operation, the LRCC produced its work in several stages:

> First, the publication by a project group of a study paper (which does not express the views of the commission) inviting comments, then, of a commission working paper, written in the light of public reaction to the study paper and again inviting comment, and, finally, publication of a report to the Minister of Justice for his consideration and for tabling in Parliament. (Barnes, 1975, p. 84)

The working procedure of the LRCC changed, however, with more emphasis placed on the working paper itself. Moreover, in practice, the direction and spirit of the criminal law working papers have been substantially the same as those of the reports which followed them.[3]

In the actual preparation and production of its paper and reports, the LRCC and, more particularly, the Criminal Law Project, uses various research techniques. Four methods have been identified: 1) philosophical enquiry; 2) the comparative method; 3) empirical research; and 4) consultation (ibid., p. 72). The first, philosophical enquiry, is a "search for values." We will focus on this issue later in this chapter, for it is the discussions of values and the purpose of criminal law which we find the most illustrative of the orientation of the LRCC. Using the comparative method, the LRCC has focused on the bi-jural nature of the Canadian system and has examined other common law and civil law systems (ibid., p. 76). The goal of the LRCC in its empirical research is to "discover the actual living law, the law that really governs Canadian people." Even from a conventional perspective, however, this research has been found to be sporadic" at best (ibid., pp. 76-77). But a more fundamental criticism can be made of the type of empirical research into criminal law in which the LRCC engages. This criticism relates to the restricted methodology which the LRCC uses and is discussed later in this chapter. The consultation process of the LRCC in the production of its working papers and reports is a relatively narrow one. While the LRCC has at times attempted to involve the wider public in the law reform process, the response has been generally unsatisfying. An early example of the failure of an attempt at broad-based public involvement is the Ottawa Pilot Project (which was basically a series of public information meetings in 1974) which excited little public response (ibid., pp. 85-86). In contrast, the regular consultations in which the LRCC engages are much more important and influential. They involve representatives of five groups: judges, defence lawyers, police chiefs, law teachers, and crown counsel (LRCC, 1984; pp. 19-20). It is evident from this list that the consultation process is a relatively closed one, involving as it does only certain (usually legal) professionals in the criminal justice system. This bias towards the legal profession is evident as well in the background of the majority of the members of the Substantive Criminal Law Project.[4] Not surprisingly, this restricted participation is not without consequence for the findings or recommendations of the LRCC.

THE AIMS OF CRIMINAL LAW

The LRCC has explicitly recognized the need to provide a rationale and coherence for criminal law by articulating the basic premises of its emergence (LRCC, 1982; pp. 156-57; see also 1975A, and 1976). As a result, a great deal of its contribution to the current project of revising the Canadian Criminal Code has focused on the broad issue of the role of criminal law in modern society.

The LRCC has clearly and consistently worked within the broad confines of the functionalist or pluralist paradigm in its attempts to stake out a position on the general aims of criminal law. Its basic argument is that the role of criminal law is to protect the core values of a society, thereby fostering and strengthening the shared trust necessary for the survival of a social system (ibid., pp. 33-35; 1974, pp. 17-19; 1975, pp. 21, 49; 1976, p. 20; and 1981, pp. 171-72).

> In truth, the criminal law is fundamentally a moral system. It may be crude, it may have faults, it may be rough and ready, but basically it is a system of applied morality and justice. It serves to underline those values necessary, or else important to society. When acts occur that transgress essential values, like the sanctity of life, society must speak out and affirm those values. This is the true role of criminal law (ibid., 1976, p. 16).

This protection and affirmation of values is necessary because crime is an "inevitable aspect of social living" (ibid., 1974, p. 6), one which is the predictable outcome of the competition and conflict of values characteristic of our social system.

This is an attractive and even compelling view of the aim of law, especially as an ideal of what law should be. The more immediate issue, however, is the extent to which the theoretical views of the LRCC accurately describe the workings of the criminal law in contemporary Canadian society. In this regard, our contention is that the position of the LRCC is theoretically indefensible. We will focus our discussion on three specific issues:

1) What are the core values which the criminal law must protect?
2) Do these values emerge from a condition of consensus or of value conflict, and who decides which values are worthy enough or important enough to be enshrined in law?
3) How does the criminal law fulfill its stated function?

The LRCC argues that the basic role of criminal law is to reduce the undesired activities which constitute a threat to social welfare. Its position is that there are two broad areas of agreement in any discussion of the aims of law:

> First, criminal law should aim at decreasing certain undesired activities. Whatever the strategy—denunciation, deterrence or reform—surely the only general justifying aim is the reduction of offences. Second, the pursuit of this aim must remain subject to constraints, for the criminal law is not an end in itself but rather a means to an end—to the securing of a society worth living in (ibid., 1982, p. 171).

The constraints in question refer to the limits to the application of the mechanism of law which are required by a commitment to the principles of freedom, justice, and humanity (ibid., 1976, p. 7; also 1982, pp. 171-72). The criminal law must be used with restraint and only against "real crimes" (ibid., 1976, p. 17-20). The LRCC attempts to clarify this approach by proposing "tests of criminality": to determine whether any act should be a real crime, one must ask:

1) Whether it seriously harms other people;
2) Whether it so seriously contravenes social values as to be harmful to society;
3) Whether the necessary enforcement measures will not themselves contravene social values; and
4) Whether the criminal law can make a contribution to dealing with the problem. (ibid., 1976, pp. 33-34)

The problem with this position is that it leaves us with little more than a vague set of standards or references for evaluating and classifying behaviours as criminal. No practical set of criteria for objectively distinguishing criminal from non-criminal behaviour has been offered.[5] For example, it is not at all clear, by these standards, why industrial pollution or accidents in the workplace should not become matters for the criminal law, since they are arguably greater threats to "a society worth living in" than many of the more traditional crimes against the person or property. No valid articulation of the relation of these values to the process of criminalizing certain behaviours is ever offered in the work of the LRCC.[6] Rather, certain vague norms are offered more or less as consensual absolutes. This position requires an almost utopian vision of democracy and fails to come to grips with the realities of structured inequality in social, political, and economic relations. Both of these traits pervade the LRCC's entire body of work on substantive criminal law reform.

The general position of the LRCC will only be acceptable to those who hold rigidly to a consensual and absolutist perspective on the emergence of law. Ironically, the position of the LRCC itself is not consistent with such an approach. At times, the LRCC has at least paid lip-service to the existence of value-conflict (see, for example, LRCC, 1974, pp. 6-9) and has recognized that "we still have one law for the rich and another for the poor" (ibid., 1976, p. 12). Unfortunately, this is as far as the LRCC goes: it does not pursue these ideas to their logical end. There is a failure to deal with the issues of the social origin of values or of who decides which values are to be elevated to the status of law. The unambiguous commitment of the LRCC to a liberal pluralist perspective is presented more as an act of faith than as a position which can be articulated and defended on the basis of scientific criteria. The problem is that the LRCC has focused only on the content of law without dealing with the related issues of the process of moral enterprise whereby this content is formalized in law or of the impact of power and ideology on the decisions that are reached.

An example of this failure can be found in the Working Paper on homicide (1984). The paper presents the "problem" of homicide in Canadian society as legalistic: the relevant laws are poorly and illogically set out, they are repetitive, and they contain too much detail. Having defined the issues as technical or legalistic, the "solution" is to make the homicide provisions in the Criminal Code "simpler, clearer and more straight-forward" (ibid., 1984, p. 26).

The basis of the discussion on homicide is the historical development of the concepts of murder and manslaughter in English common law and, since 1892, the various provisions in the Canadian Criminal Code. Certain aspects of the mental and physical elements of the current provisions are also considered for revision. Unfortunately, there is no examination of the reality of murder in contemporary Canadian society. It is a discussion without reference to the social context of homicide in Canada—who is killing whom, how, and why—and therefore it is a discussion which fails to offer convincing solutions or alternatives. How does society conceptualize murder? How should it? Why, for example, are most non-natural deaths in the workplace viewed as accidents, even though the mental elements of recklessness or deliberateness might have been present?[7] These are just some of the issues which could have usefully served to focus an examination of non-natural deaths and criminal liability in Canada. It may very well be that the recommendations proposed in the paper do address the problems posed by homicide, but because of the failure to examine meaningfully the reality of those problems, it is impossible to make such a determination.

Many of the same problems are evident in the LRCC's Working Paper on Theft and Fraud (1977). The historical discussion found in the paper is extremely narrow and self-serving. While the study accurately states that "law, like other human institutions, can only be fully understood through history" (ibid., 1977, p. 37), that history and the examination of the role of law within it are not what many historians might understand them to be: that is, the changing socioeconomic relationships through time and the law as situated within those relationships. Rather, it is legal history at its worst—a chronicle of the treatment of theft and fraud in English common law and in the Canadian Criminal Code.

The LRCC sets out in the working paper to enshrine the value of "honesty" as the basis for establishing criminal liability in the area of theft and fraud: the law "should clearly prohibit only acts commonly reckoned dishonest and avoid prohibiting any act commonly reckoned legitimate" (ibid., p. 6). A problem with this perspective is that the LRCC sees no need to define the parameters of "honesty"; honesty is "such a basic value that everyone understands its import" (ibid.). It can be argued that perhaps something more is required.

Concepts such as honesty, dishonesty, property, and ownership can be understood only when situated within a particular economic, social, and political framework. To ignore the material dimension of the concepts is to misrepresent the reality of stealing in society. Without the broader analysis, there is no real possibility of addressing the problems presented by theft and fraud nor of seeking viable and effective solutions in legislation. The LRCC recognizes this at the outset of the paper when it states its objective: "to simplify the written law of theft and fraud but leave the substance of that law in essence unchanged" (LRCC, 1977, p. 1). Such recognition, however, cannot replace the broader examination required to arrive at such a conclusion.

In summary, one can find certain important elements of legal fetishism at work in the approach and methodology adopted by the LRCC (see Collins, 1982, pp. 10-14). One of these elements is the centrality of legal rules:

> For those who fetishize law, legal rules are at the centre of social life, forming the basis of social discourse. Like other norms such as the conventions on which linguistic communication is based, legal rules provide the foundation for exchanges, reliance, safety, privacy, and satisfy numerous other perennial human wants. *It can be added that the greater the sophistication of the legal system, the more effective it will be in the satisfaction of those wants.* (ibid., p. 11, emphasis added)

The other important element is the idea that "law is a unique phenomenon which constitutes a discrete focus of study" (ibid.). This notion manifests itself in an unwillingness to explore beyond the traditional confines of legal research and scholarship and a propensity to substitute sterile doctrinal expositions for a broader, more meaningful discussion of the social foundation of the problem at hand.[8]

The LRCC never explains how crime is, in actuality, a form of social interaction which reflects competing social values, yet law can still be regarded as the pluralist ideal of a neutral instrument for achieving compromise and reconciliation (see LRCC, 1974, pp. 1-18; 1976, p. 18). Simply put, why is crime a result or expression of conflict and law a straightforward expression of the "standards of the *whole* community"? (ibid., 1982, p. 184; emphasis added). The failure to address this issue is surprising given the large body of theoretical and empirical work on the critical approaches to law in general and on the criminal law in Canada which has been produced in the last decade. Because of this failure, it is also at this point that one begins to entertain the possibility that the work of the LRCC might have consequences unforeseen in its formal mandate.

This problem is compounded by the inconsistency of the LRCC's model of the individual. At times, the LRCC adopts the functionalist view that crime is "part of our divided human nature" and reflects the darker irrational side of individual consciousness (ibid., 1976: p. 39). Yet functionalists generally adopt an essentially determinist view of behaviour, one which is completely at odds with the LRCC's more general view that "the moral notion of guilt . . . must stay as the basis of our criminal regulatory laws" (ibid., p. 23). This notion of the relative freedom of the individual is only theoretically tenable within the competing Marxist or Interactionist paradigms. Simply put, the LRCC generally favours the position that there is no guilt without moral fault (LRCC, 1982, pp. 172-73). But rather than provide a scientific analysis of the guiding principle of responsibility, the LRCC leaves us with the conclusion that "common sense morality" is the best basis for assessing "guilt, blame and criminal liability" (ibid., 1982, pp. 167, 179).

At this point, the argument comes full circle: if crime is a moral issue, then it is not surprising that the essential role of law would be to affirm and support values by defining the content of those values, socializing members of the society, and reassuring and rewarding law abiding citizens (ibid., 1974, pp. 33-35; 1975, p. 8; 1982, pp. 157, 172). The operation of the trial process is useful because "it is a public demonstration to denounce the crime and reaffirm the values it infringed . . . a sort of morality play" (ibid., 1976, p. 23). By the same logic, criminal sanctions should maximize society's capacity to repair the harm done, to re-establish the breach in human relations and trust caused by crime, and to affirm fundamental values (ibid., 1975, p. ii; see also 1974, and 1976, pp. 24-25).

The problem with this approach is that it reduces the debates on consciousness and liability to a largely unspecified ideal of individual responsibility. Important social, political, and moral dimensions of the explanation of behaviour are left aside. All that we are ultimately offered by the LRCC is a simplistic, unarticulated, and sterile conception of common sense morality. This closes the debate without really addressing the impact of the structural and relational factors which impinge upon interaction and social organization. As a result, there is no theoretical base for the social project of legal reform. This is probably a major reason why the LRCC now argues that the real problems with our criminal code are technical and all that is really needed is better codification or rewriting rather than fundamental reform. In its introduction to and justification of its recent proposals on the revision of the General Part of the Criminal Code, the LRCC argues that:

> it remains faithful in substance to the tradition and thrust of our present law. In other words, the proposed draft is more a codification than a reform of the present law. After all, the shortcomings of our General Part relate less to substance than to form. In substance the rules are well understood, fundamentally accepted and based on general moral propositions. In form, however, they are articulated without sufficient clarity, scattered in a variety of sources and to a large extent left entirely to the common law. (LRCC, 1982, pp. 7-8)

In other words, the conclusion is clearly that the traditional thrust of our law is good enough for the new challenges it must face. This is surprising and disappointing, both in the face of the promise of the original mandate of the LRCC, and in light of its ongoing recognition that we live in a "society undergoing constant change" (ibid., 1982, p. 9). The LRCC has abdicated its responsibility to articulate both its politics and the politics of a new Criminal Code. The law is a part of the wider process of social control, and social control is, by definition, an attempt to preserve a given system or at least to limit and shape the rate and direction of change. In spite of the social, political, and economic inequalities which exist in this country, the LRCC reverts to tradition. The law and common sense which failed the 1960's are, ironically, good enough now. This stand might be defensible, and even acceptable, if the LRCC could:

1) prove the existence of homogeneous community standards across Canada;
2) articulate the relationship of those standards to the wider social, economic, and political context (are they the products of an open democratic process, or do they reflect the workings of an ideology and its constraints?);
3) theorize the role of the law in society (whose law is it? Who benefits from its control?); and
4) theorize its relationship to the reform of law and legal institutions (whose reform is it? Who benefits from this reform?).

The LRCC fails to do any of these. Instead, it offers vague notions of common sense and community standards in lieu of a theory of law and of legal reform, and it foregoes the option of developing new approaches to the law which might be "responsive to the changing needs of modern Canadian society and the individual members of that society" (Law Reform Commission Act, 1971, s. 11 [d]).

THE RELATIVE AUTONOMY OF THE LRCC

Given the original mandate of the LRCC and its recognition of changing social needs and conditions, its failure to address convincingly the basic political and theoretical issues underlying criminal law and legal reform is both disappointing and unsettling. Why has the LRCC adopted the position described in the previous section? The failure to deliver fundamental reform is predictable and probably irreversible.

As suggested in the previous paper by Ratner, McMullan, and Burtch, there are a number of ways to understand the activities of the state or of one of its components (in this case, the LRCC). Moreover, they argue that each of these perspectives highlights certain features of social structure and social relations, but at the cost of downplaying other important considerations or of ignoring specific dimensions of social reality. This is not to suggest that pluralism, instrumentalism, structuralist Marxism, class-conflict theory or the capital-logic approach are of equal value, and that one ought simply to choose according to one's intuition or to some unspecified whim. Our earlier section on the Aims of Criminal Law ought to illustrate the extent to which we feel pluralism, at least as adapted in the work of the LRCC, is a dead end. By the same token, instrumentalism does not provide a satisfactory alternative. Its emphasis on social relations, and on the critical importance of common interests and concerns, of similar backgrounds, and of group or class consciousness and interaction tends to reduce explanations to the level of conspiracies. In the case of the LRCC, the thesis would be that legal reform is simply one more instrument of class domination, one which serves as a placebo for real social change, thereby sustaining the false consciousness of the downtrodden. Such a hypothesis requires that one attribute an exceedingly high level of intelligence, discipline, and organizational ability to the ruling class manipulators of the instrument in question, and that one assume an absurdly naïve and uncritical audience with no access whatsoever to alternative views. Neither of these assumptions seems to us very credible: social reality is not that simple. Legal reform and the LRCC were not prescribed failures, and nothing is gained by the argument that the workers of the LRCC are either pawns or dupes of some hidden hand or are themselves scrupulous Machiavellians tinkering at the machinery of oppression.

It is exactly at this point that the modified structuralist position embodied in the relative autonomy thesis offers such promise. This approach recognizes the importance of structural arrangements and the logic of capital development but is also able to breathe some life into these abstract concepts by connecting them to social relations, class conflicts, and culture and ideology. In the case of the LRCC, the focus is shifted away from the sterile notions of consensus or conspiracy and directed toward the dynamic relationship between a component of the Canadian state and the sifting nature of social structure and social conflicts.

The relative autonomy thesis thus directs us to insert the LRCC within the broad structure and the specific conflicts and transformations which have marked the current conjuncture of Canadian society. In order to perform this task, we need a classification of the different types of conflicts which have emerged in recent years and of the responses or strategies which the Canadian state has adopted in its attempt to resolve them. More simply put, it makes little sense to speak of law and reform as strategic without a sense of where they fit in the larger picture.

Our focus on criminal law and the work of the LRCC directs us primarily to the political, ideological, and juridical complexes of the Canadian social formation: our concern is with the superstructural dimensions rather than with fundamental economic structures and logics. A useful typology for guiding such an analysis is suggested by Stuart Hall and his colleagues (Hall et al., 1978, pp. 218-27; CCCS Mugging Group, 1976, pp. 75-79; and Taylor, 1979, pp. 292-300). Their specific concern is to relate the reaction to "mugging" to a wider and more general "crisis of hegemony" in the British state. Their basic position is that:

> the superstructures provide the "theater" where the relations of class forces, given their fundamental form in the antagonistic relations of capitalist production, appear and work themselves through to a resolution . . . the principal movement to which we relate the "mugging" panic is the shift from a "consensual" to a more "coercive" management of the class struggle by the capitalist state. (Hall et al., 1978, p. 218)

The authors explicitly reject a conspiratorial formulation in favour of a much more complex orientation to the nature and ideological signification of various strategies for manufacturing popular consent or for containing threats to the existence or reproduction of that consent. Their basic point is that hegemony must be won: the reproduction of dominant worldviews is the outcome of a problematic and contradictory process (ibid., pp. 219-20).

The relevance of this perspective for our discussion of legal reform is through its analysis of the dynamics of different types of moral panics (see Cohen, 1980, pp. 9-10). As stated earlier, the LRCC was established with the explicit goal of contributing to the construction of a legal system better able to cope with the crises of legitimacy or authority which were experienced in the late 1960's (see Turner, 1971). In essence, the LRCC was one dimension of the response of the Canadian state to a moral panic; it was an attempt to cope with the perceived crises by mandating legally accredited experts to address the threat to values and interests which was being experienced both popularly and politically. The limitation of the notion of moral panics is that the events tend to be perceived as relatively discrete or disconnected. However, we contend that this was not the case in Canada at that point in time. We hope to show that by 1970 different moral panics were being "mapped together" in a manner that produced a faster sequence. In order to appreciate this convergence and its implications, it is necessary to design a typology of the process of definition or signification of events and contexts. In response to this task, Hall and his colleagues propose the notion of a signification spiral:

> The *signification spiral* is a way of signifying events which also intrinsically escalates their threat. . . . [It] is a *self-amplifying sequence within the area of signification*: the activity or event with which the signification deals is *escalated*—made to seem more threatening—within the course of the signification itself. (Hall, et al., 1978, p. 223, emphasis in text)

This escalation process is not a matter of a simple evolution from discrete and inconsequential events to a general moral panic. Rather, there seem to be definite thresholds which serve to "mark out symbolically the limits to social tolerance. . . . The higher an event can be placed in the hierarchy of thresholds, the greater is its threat to the social order, and the tougher and more automatic is the coercive response" (ibid., p. 225).

Three types of thresholds are discussed in *Policing the Crisis*, each of which is a complex combination of a specific type of perceived threat to social order and of a corollary tendency to respond at the level of the threat in question (ibid., pp. 225-27). The lowest threshold is that of *permissiveness*. The perceived threat in this case is to traditional moral norms and to social authority, and social reaction generally involves moral sanctions and social disapproval. Many of the issues and events identified in the so-called "revolutionary" 1960's were actually at this level. For example, one could argue that the threat of youth in general, and of "hippie" values in particular (for example, the liberalization of attitudes toward sexuality, abortion, or drugs) were threats to conventional moral standards but did not menace the notions of legality in Canadian society. The intermediary threshold is that of *legality*. The law defines the legal boundaries of a system, and illegal behaviour is thus perceived to be a threat to legal order and the social legitimacy it enshrines. The final threshold is that of *violence*, those acts which threaten the basis of social order and the future existence of the state. The events surrounding the "October Crisis" of 1970 are an example of such a threat and illustrate the massive scale of state response in such cases. The hierarchy thus escalates from threats to moral values to assaults on legality and finally to challenges to social control. Conversely, the range of appropriate solutions ranges from moral suasion and education through the use of criminal law and the criminal justice system all the way to the full imposition of the entire ideological and control apparatus of the state. In light of this, a specific control strategy may make more sense if it is connected to such a typology. The question now is how to make sense of the LRCC as just such a strategy.

The abstract notions of thresholds and threats begin to take on some life when we compare the Canada of the 1960's, just prior to the creation of the LRCC, to the Canada of the mid-1980's. For the most part, the conflicts of the 1960's centred on issues of morality and lifestyle; the perceived threat during this period was to the threshold of permissiveness. The battle lines were generally drawn on the basis of age, race, or sex and certainly did not involve anything resembling what a Marxist might call "class warfare." Accordingly, one of the key concerns of the Canadian state was to improve the capacity of the legal system to arbitrate these conflicts. Thus to a certain extent one can argue that the LRCC was intended to be a facilitating device, one that would serve in the pluralist manner of a neutral state instrument. Its function was to resolve or arbitrate moral conflicts and to patrol the twilight zone between morality and law in such a manner that the perceived crisis of moral authority would not degenerate into an assault on the legitimacy of parliament and legal institutions. However, moral and political debates of this type tend to be "luxuries" experienced during periods of relative economic prosperity.

The fiscal crises of the modern state which have been experienced over the last decade have been accompanied by a fundamental shift in the nature and expression of social conflicts. More particularly, there has been a tendency to turn to " bread and butter" issues such as unemployment, mortgage interest rates, and the rising cost of living. The attendant economic instability and uncertainty are usually assumed to be at the root of the conservative blacklash of recent years. However, both these conflicts and the response of the state to them are much more complex than a simple "pendulum" analogy might lead us to believe. The basis of these conflicts has shifted away from lifestyles and morality and the corollary concern to politicize moral issues which characterized the 1960's. In its place are social conflicts rooted in issues of class and power, and which represent a real attempt to alter the social and political cornerstones of our system. The urban riots in Great Britain during the summer of 1981 and the more recent British coal miners' strike are perhaps the most obvious examples of this tendency. There has been no recent direct outbreak of such violence in Canada, in part because the class divisions in Canadian society are less clear and less a part of everyday consciousness than in Great Britain. But extended political and constitutional debates over economic spheres of control have occurred, and there has been a significant level of union-type activity directed at redrawing the lines of economic and political policy. Clearly, though, we are neither in the throes of a Hobbesian nightmare nor on the battle lines of a full blown revolution.

Nevertheless, the threshold has shifted and, as a result, so has the fundamental response of the state. In Great Britain, and to a great extent the United States, the basic strategy has been to control the debate by redirecting it to another terrain. The enthusiasm of Margaret Thatcher for a war over the Falklands, or of Ronald Reagan for the "liberation" of Grenada are good examples of this strategy (it is probably not accidental, nor unintended, that both events were followed within a year by smashing electoral victories). The more general attraction of "law and order" politics has also been explained along these lines (see Taylor, 1980). The so-called "new conservatism" masks a shift in thresholds and responses from arbitrating value debates over permissiveness to controlling fundamental social and class conflicts.

In practice, this means that different demands are made on the law. More specifically, the LRCC as a mechanism for sociopolitical reform is no longer a relevant part of the response of the Canadian state to the current social reality; time has passed this strategy by. The LRCC was an ideal liberal response to the desire to open the political arena and to arbitrate issues of style more effectively. However, its very potential to transform the law makes it a risky proposition once the conflict leads to questioning the fundamental basis of our social organization. In plainer terms, the Canadian state is unlikely to want or tolerate much more from the LRCC than an exercise in technical reform. This contention is confirmed by the failure of the LRCC to get its proposals through parliament or to provide the substantive legal reforms it set out to accomplish (Fortin, 1982, p. 105). The problem is simply that the state is unwilling to risk real debate over issues fundamental to the social structure and class composition of society or to allocate resources to projects of social reconstruction which would redress structural inequality through the creation of collective entitlements and the elimination of social problems.

The LRCC has responded to this development by changing its strategic approach to the process of legal reform. In the view of Francis Muldoon, the current past president of the LRCC, the lack of success is in large part owing to the fact that its work was perceived to be too "radical." As a result, parliament has been scared away from adopting its recommendations. Muldoon argues that a more "evolutionary" approach will be more palatable to legislators and thus more likely to succeed (Muldoon, 1982). Consequently, there has been a shift away from the emphasis on broad public consultation (which was a predictable response to the value conflict of the 1970's), to a more integrated and co-operative process of systematic consultations with the federal department of justice (Muldoon, 1982; and Fortin, 1982, pp. 109-12). The obvious problem here is the risk that this will eliminate what little relative autonomy the LRCC had to set its agenda and to propose significant reforms of the Canadian criminal law.

At this point, it is timely to ask why an agency which has accomplished so little continues to exist. An answer to this question requires that we shift our discussion from actual events to their significance in the ideological arena. In their analysis of the panic over mugging in Great Britain, Hall and his colleagues argued that the British case was characterized by an essentially linear or evolutionary development from the threshold of permissiveness (youth as a metaphor for social change), through that of legality to the threshold of violence. This process was marked by an ever-increasing tendency for events to converge and be mapped together in both ideological representations and popular consciousness.

> The important point is that, as issues and groups are projected across the thresholds, it becomes easier to mount legitimate campaigns against them. When this process becomes a regular and routine part of the way in which conflict is signified in society, it does indeed create its own momentum for measures of "more than usual control." (Hall et al., 1978, p. 226)

At the perceptual level, the Canadian case is quite different. It is our contention that the crises of legitimacy and authority were experienced in both public consiousness and state policy as multi-dimensional. The popular representation included the threat at the thresholds of permissiveness and legality, *and* the threat of violence (the October Crisis) at one and the same time. It was not a case of projecting the possibility of violence as a potential of moral breakdown. Rather, moral, legal, and social breakdown seemed a distinct possibility, one which the Canadian state could not refuse to address.

The situation in Canada was mapped as critical by the end of 1970 and seems to have subsided since that time. Social control has worked, at least in terms of the interests of the dominant groups and of their concern to successfully reproduce a system of class relations. Our argument is that the LRCC is one of the state agencies which have had the ideological consequence of contributing to the de-construction of the general perception of panic and crises at that time.

The contribution of the LRCC has been essentially twofold. First, it represents part of the effort by the Canadian state to limit the perception of the legitimate problem at hand. By turning to parliament and the legal domain, the state could recognize as legitimate the widespread concern over permissiveness and appear to be moving towards a solution. At the same time, this strategy of appearing to open up the law-making process responds to the collective moral panic and the threat of an emerging extra-parliamentary opposition (for example, the NDP Waffle). Moreover, it is a strategy which resonates with the "reasonable" citizen's pluralist conception of the role of the state and of law and delegitimizes violent alternatives. Thus, general crises which were experienced at all three thresholds are responded to by the state only at the level of the threshold of legality. The ideological message is that the pluralist state is flexible enough to adapt its legal system to changing moral values and that crime and violence are unnecessary and counterproductive.

Secondly, and more specifically, the LRCC's work has contributed directly to the successful control of the political dissent of the last two decades. This has been accomplished primarily through the position it has adopted and propagated on the aims and functions of criminal law. In adopting the pluralist (consensus) position we described earlier, the LRCC helps to reaffirm the essential individualistic orientation to legal rights and responsibilities which characterizes the liberal-democratic legitimation of capitalist social relations. It does so in two ways.

The Insistence on Individual Rights

While everyone recognizes the value of enshrining individual rights, we are less likely to appreciate that the hidden ideological cost of such rights is a delegitimation of the conception of collective rights (a notion which was, ironically, basic to feudalism). The LRCC's position on the nature of law, and its methodology, helps to sustain popular consent in this area and thus perpetuate the class fragmentation critical to the reproduction of current class relations. Simply, class relations are atomized and mystified when the juridical object is limited to the individual.

The Insistence on Individual Responsibility

The LRCC's insistence on individual moral culpability as the defining element of crime serves to make it difficult, and usually impossible, to address events or situations where blame cannot easily be apportioned on an individual basis (for example, pollution, organizational deviance, or crime by governmental agencies). As a result, it is next to impossible to seek solutions through the criminal justice system in such cases, or to imagine how collective responsibility can be conceived, much less attributed, within the present framework of legal institutions. The implications for the reproduction of social relations are only too obvious.

The effect of the position of the LRCC is to reaffirm the essential validity and legitimacy of the Canadian criminal system and to support the plausibility of addressing popularly perceived problems within this framework. The result is that the types of social reconstruction which would address the real issues at hand are not attempted. The debate itself is marked ideologically.

CONCLUSION

The form and content of the work of the LRCC can best be understood by relating them to the current social, political, and economic conjuncture of Canadian society. To analyze this, we have related the LRCC to actual events over the last twenty years and to the ideological representations of these same events by the state and in public consciousness. The LRCC was part of the response of the Canadian state to the crises of legitimacy and authority of the late 1960's. This period was marked by public and state concerns over moral permissiveness, law and order, and the threat of violence. The goal of the LRCC was to contribute to a renewed social order by improving the capacity of the law to arbitrate and resolve social conflicts. However, the shift in the fundamental implications of these conflicts from the moral to the economic level has meant an end to the relevance of the LRCC. A Keynesian-like orientation to legal reform has been consigned to the same dustbin as Keynesian economics.

Ideologically, the LRCC has contributed to a specific redefinition of the crises in question and a specific solution to these problems. Our opinion is that in 1970 Canada was perceiving crises at the three thresholds of morality, legality, and violence; the situation was menacing and the crises multi-dimensional. In this context, the LRCC has consistently limited itself to the level of the legal order and, even here, has restricted its view of the law to the pluralist notion of law as an emergent expression of social consensus and a neutral instrument of conflict resolution. Such an approach carries a double ideological message: it focuses the definition of the problem on the level of the threshold of legality, and it restricts the range of legitimate solutions to the levels of moral and legal reform. The view of the LRCC that law expresses core values and that our present legal system is basically sound contributes to the isolation effect through which the state and law fragment class collectivities and relations and reconstitute them as individual citizens with atomized legal rights and personal responsibilities. The LRCC thus helps to defuse the types of crises which most threaten the reproduction of the state and of class relations by serving to depoliticize social issues. The LRCC is an example of the power of the state to control a situation by dictating and legitimating the definition of a problem, the proper terms of public debate, and the allowable repertoire of intervention strategies. Pressure groups operating outside the state are compromised or ignored, and reform is left to serious and responsible professionals (see Ericson, this volume).

In the end, we would argue that the relative autonomy of the LRCC as an agency of the Canadian state is very low. It is largely a case of being "caught between a rock and a hard place": relevance and autonomy seem to co-exist in an inverse relationship. To the extent that it wishes to be relevant, the LRCC must align its work with the political priorities of the party in power and the organizational agenda of the Department of Justice; this, however, means a loss of its autonomy. To the extent that it wishes to be autonomous, it runs the risk of being irrelevant to political and bureaucratic concerns and thus of being ignored.

It would seem that the LRCC has chosen the former option. In an attempt to increase its impact, it has committed itself to a view of law reformers as, in the words of commission president Allen Linden, "smoother-outers, adjusters . . . not revolutionaries" (*Toronto Star*, 20 January, 1985). This approach will increase the impact of LRCC proposals, but only in the areas of procedural or administrative law. In other words, the LRCC will exercise its reform influence in the areas of least political significance. Unfortunately, this may also increase the ideological impact of the LRCC as a symbol of the commitment of the Canadian state to engage in legal reform.

In the long run, however, this may not be too important. The new Canadian Constitution and the emerging tendency for key political and legal issues to be resolved in the courts will probably shift the real axis of legal reform from the LRCC to the Supreme Court. Time goes on—the LRCC probably will not.

NOTES

1. For the structure and personnel of the LRCC, see LRCC, 1984B, pp. 1-5. It should also be noted that there are provincial law reform agencies which focus on areas of law within provincial jurisdiction.
2. See Department of Justice, 1982.
3. For a complete list of the LRCC's working papers and reports, see LRCC, 1984: Appendices A and B.
4. For a complete list of the research personnel and their qualifications, see LRCC, 1984: Appendix I.
5. For a specific discussion of this issue in relation to the recent proposals and recommendations of the LRCC (1982) concerning the revision of the General Part of the Criminal Code, see Hastings and Saunders (1983).
6. The LRCC has attempted in the past to distinguish between "real crimes" and "mere offences," the former being acts which are both prohibited by law *and* repugnant to the basic moral sentiments of society. Mere offences are committed by people acting in specialized roles (for example, drivers parking illegally or merchants selling liquor unlawfully). Also, real crimes are more obvious wrongs

where the harm is direct and readily identifiable (murder), while the harm of mere offences is less obvious and more potential than direct. These distinguishing features, however, suffer from the same deficiencies as those noted in regard to the LRCC's views of the aims of criminal law (see Section 2 of this paper). In conclusion, even the LRCC explicitly recognizes that while the distinction may be "real" in commonsense consciousness, it cannot be pressed too far either theoretically or practically. Ultimately, we are left with the unadorned commonsense notion of crime with which we began.

7. See Glasbeek and Rowland, 1979, and Taylor, 1983, pp. 83-113.
8. See Saunders, 1984.

REFERENCES

Barnes, John, 1975. "The Law Reform Commission of Canada." *Dalhousie Law Journal* 2: 62-90.

Burke, A. 1971. "The Commission and Mr. Hart." *CBA-ABC Journal*: 2, 2.

CCCS Mugging Group. 1976. "Some Notes on the Relationship Between the Societal Culture and the News Media: The Construction of a Law and Order Campaign." In Hall, S., and T. Jefferson, eds. *Resistance Through Rituals.* London: Hutchinson.

Cohen, Stan. 1980. *Folk Devils and Moral Panics.* 2d Ed. London: Martin Robertson.

Collins, Hugh. 1982. *Marxism and Law.* London: Oxford University Press.

Department of Justice, Canada. 1982. *Criminal Law in Canadian Society.* Ottawa: Government of Canada.

Fortin, Jacques. 1982. "La Commission de Reforme du Droit du Canada: Un bilan succinct." *Criminologie* 15: 105-12.

Glasbeek, H. J., and S. Rowlands. 1979. "Are Injuring and Killing at Work Crimes?" *Osgoode Hall Law Journal* 17: 506-94.

Goode, M. 1976. "Law Reform Commission of Canada: Political Ideology of Criminal Process Reform." *Canadian Bar Review* 54: 653-74.

_____. 1978. "The Law Reform Commission of Canada, Barnes and Marlin, and the Value-Consensus Model: More about Ideology." *Dalhousie Law Journal* 4: 793-812.

Hall, S., C. Critcher, T. Jefferson, J. Clarke, B. Roberts. 1978. *Policing the Crisis.* London: MacMillan.

Hastings, Ross, and R. P. Saunders. 1983. "Ideology in the Work of the Law Reform Commission of Canada: The Case of the Working Paper on the General Part." *Criminal Law Quarterly* 25: 206-22.

Hogarth, G. 1976. "The Law Reform Commission as a Powerful Agent of Change: Fact or Fantasy." *Crime et/and Justice* 4: 24-31.

Law Reform Commission Act. 1970. R.S.C., 1st Supp., c. 23, s. 11.

Law Reform Commission of Canada. 1974a. *Working Paper no. 3: The Principles of Sentencing and Dispositions*. Ottawa: Supply and Services Canada.

_____. 1974. *Working Paper no. 5: Restitution and Compensation*. Ottawa: Supply and Services Canada.

_____. 1975. *Working Paper no. 10: The Limits of Criminal Law—Obscenity: A Test Case*. Ottawa: Supply and Services Canada.

_____. 1975. *Working Paper no. 11: Imprisonment and Release*. Ottawa: Supply and Services Canada.

_____. 1976. *Report no. 3: Our Criminal Law*. Ottawa: Supply and Services Canada.

_____. 1977. *Working Paper no. 19: Theft and Fraud*. Ottawa: Supply and Services Canada.

_____. 1982. *Working Paper no. 29: Criminal Law—The General Part: Liability and Defences*. Ottawa: Supply and Services Canada.

_____. 1984. *Working Paper no. 33: Homicide*. Ottawa: Supply and Services Canada.

_____. 1984. *Thirteenth Annual Report, 1983-84*. Ottawa: Supply and Services Canada.

Muldoon, Francis. 1982. Conversation with R. Hastings, 1 June 1982.

Saunders, R. P. 1984. "Review of Law and Learning: Report to the Social Sciences and Humanities Research Council of Canada." *Ottawa Law Review* 16: 218-23.

Snow, G. 1979. "A Note on the Law Reform Commission of Canada's Theoretical Approach to Legal Reform." *University of New Brunswick Law Journal* 28: 225-30.

Taylor, Ian. 1980. "The Law and Order Issue in the British General Election and the Canadian Federal Election of 1979: Crime, Populism and the State." *Canadian Journal of Sociology* 5: 285-311.

_____. 1983. *Crime, Capitalism and Community*. Toronto: Butterworths.

Turner, J. 1971. "Law for the Seventies: A Manifesto for Law Reform." *McGill Law Journal* 17: 1-10.

7

"Relative Autonomy" and the Criminal Justice Apparatus

MICHAEL MANDEL

Is "relative autonomy" a useful concept in understanding the Canadian criminal justice apparatus or elements within it? That is the essential question posed by the two major papers in this section. Of course, one of the difficulties with answering it is that the meaning of relative autonomy is somewhat less plain than the nose on one's face. One sometimes suspects that its appeal lies precisely in its lack of precision. For example, if we stress the term "relative" it can serve to underline the lack of freedom of the state or legal authorities. On the other hand, if we emphasize "autonomy" it can mean the opposite. Then there is the question of "autonomy from what?" Sometimes it signifies only freedom from the *direct* manipulation by individual members of the ruling class or from specific fractions thereof, almost a logical requirement if the state is to serve "the ruling class" considered as a unit. Poulantzas used the phrase "the field of the class struggle" to designate what the state was supposed to be relatively autonomous from (Poulantzas, 1973, p. 256). But this too is ambiguous, for class struggle has both what might crudely be termed a "political" sense and an "economic" one. We might designate this latter sense as the question of autonomy from "class relations" or, to be more orthodox, the "relations of production." Although Poulantzas did not intend, by the notion of "relative autonomy," autonomy from class relations, this is the sense which requires the most attention, if only because it is in this sense that Marx himself was most unequivocally *not* a relative autonomist:

In the social production of their life, men enter into definite relations that are indispensable and independent of their will, relations of production which correspond to a definite stage of development of their material productive forces. The sum total of these relations of production constitutes the economic structure of society, the real foundation, on which rises a legal and political superstructure and to which correspond definite forms of social consciousness. The mode of production of material life conditions the social, political, and intellectual life process in general. It is not the consciousness of men that determines their being, but, on the contrary, their social being that determines their consciousness. (Marx, 1859, p. 389)

This famous passage from the *Preface to a Critique of Political Economy* has its Marxist detractors (in a later work, Poulantzas called it "disastrous" [1978, p. 16]; see also Levine and Wright, 1981) as well as its Marxist admirers (see Cohen, 1978, 1983); however, there seems to be no doubt, even among detractors, that it represents Marx's own theory. Marx himself reaffirmed his adherence to it throughout his life, for example devoting a footnote to its defence eight years later in *Capital: Volume 1* (Marx, 1976, p. 175n) and asking rhetorically in the "Critique of the Gotha Programme," written in the last decade of his life: "are economic relations regulated by legal conceptions or do not, on the contrary, legal relations arise from economic ones?" And supplying the answer: "Right can never be higher than the economic structure of society and its cultural development conditioned thereby" (Marx, 1875, pp. 566-69).

The only Marxist pedigree for the notion of relative autonomy seems to be the use of it by Engels in a well known letter to C. Schmidt well after Marx's death, in which he seems to conceive of it as being entailed by the division of labour:

> Society gives rise to certain common functions which it cannot dispense with. The persons appointed for this purpose form a new branch of the division of labour *within society.* This gives them particular interests, distinct, too from the interests of those who empowered them; they make themselves independent of the latter and—the state is in being . . . the new independent power, while having in the main to follow the movement of production, reacts in its turn, by virtue of its inherent relative independence . . . upon the conditions and course of production. It is the interaction of two unequal forces: on the one hand, the economic movement, on the other, the new political power, which strives for as much independence as possible, and which, having once been established, is endowed with a movement of its own. On the whole, the economic movement gets its way, but it has also to suffer reactions

from the political movement which it itself established and endowed with relative independence. . . . Similarly with law. As soon as the new division of labour which creates professional lawyers becomes necessary, another new and independent sphere is opened up which, for all its general dependence on production and trade, has also a special capacity for reacting upon these spheres. In a modern state, law must not only correspond to the general economic condition and be its expression, but must also be an *internally coherent* expression which does not, owing to inner contradictions, reduce itself to nought. And in order to achieve this, the faithful reflection of economic conditions suffers increasingly. All the more so the more rarely it happens that a code of law is the blunt, unmitigated, unadulterated expression of the domination of a class—this in itself would offend the "conception of right". . . .

The reflection of economic relations as legal principles is necessarily also a topsy-turvy one: it goes on without the person who is acting being conscious of it; the jurist imagines he is operating with *a priori* propositions, whereas they are really only economic reflexes; so everything is upside down. And it seems to me obvious that this inversion, which, so long as it remains unrecognised, forms what we call *ideological outlook*, reacts in its turn upon the economic basis and may, within certain limits, modify it. (1890, pp. 695-97)

This rather clumsy attempt to explain the base/superstructure relationship gives substantially more freedom to the state than was granted by the formulation used by Marx and Engels in *The German Ideology* a half century before:

The division of labour is expressed also in the ruling class as the division of mental and material labour, so that within this class one part appears as the thinkers of the class (its active, conceptive ideologists, who make perfecting the illusion of this class about itself their main source of livelihood), while the others' attitude toward these ideas and illusions is more passive and receptive because they are really the active members of this class and have less time to make up illusions and ideas about themselves. Within this class this split can even develop into opposition and hostility between the two parts which disappears, however, in the case of a practical collision where the class itself is in danger. In this case the appearance that the ruling ideas were not the ideas of the ruling class with a power distinct from the power of this class also vanishes. (1846, pp. 438-39)

Of course to show Marx's own commitment to the base/superstructure metaphor is not to defend it, but neither can its summary dismissal as "simplistic" by Ratner, McMullan, and Burtch do it justice. Of course, the idea must be handled with great care. It is intended not to separate the state and law from the economy but to demonstrate the organic unity behind their formal separation. Furthermore, we must resist the suggestion in the notion of superstructure that the law and state do not matter—that they are epiphenomenal. This seems to have been Engels' main point in his letter to Schmidt ("Or why do we fight for the political dictatorship of the proletariat if political power is economically impotent?" (1890, p. 699). And this also seems to be part of the objection recently raised by E.P. Thompson to the metaphor: "It is because law *matters* that we have bothered with this story at all" (Thompson, 1975, p. 268). But as Cohen has so forcefully argued, it is not the point of the metaphor to make law irrelevant. On the contrary, it only makes sense if we understand that "bases need superstructures, and they get the superstructures they need because they need them" (1978, p. 233): that is, capitalist relations need the law and that is why the law exists and takes the form it does. Finally, we should not confuse a determined or non-autonomous state with an all-powerful one. The state may be a tool of capitalism even if it is imperfect. This also seems to be what E.P. Thompson was getting at when he accounted for the occasional ruling-class loss in the English courts of the eighteenth century as follows:

> and the rulers were, in serious senses, whether willingly or unwillingly, the prisoners of their own rhetoric; they played the games of power according to rules which suited them, but they could not break those rules or the whole game would be thrown away. (1975, p. 263)

With these preliminary remarks in mind I want now to turn to the paper by Ratner, McMullan, and Burtch and to examine those elements of the paper which stress the real and potential autonomy of the state in general and in regard to the specific issue of crime and punishment. It seems to be the view of the authors, and they are certainly not alone in this, that the state has developed in modern times into an entity with increasing freedom to act against ruling class interests (even though it generally does not do so):

> No longer a mere servant of dominant economic interests, the state is now in a position to perform a liberative role in the process of social change. Even its "repressive" component has become too complex and multi-dimensional to sustain interpretations of the criminal justice system as simple defender of the status quo (p. 88) . . . .
> . . . .
> Enmeshed in the complex contradictions of capitalism "the state" does,

in some part, work against the dominant class, and may become an emancipatory force. (p. 102)

The problems I have with these passages, as must any Marxist, do not stem from the notion of the state as a potential emancipatory force in itself but from the notion of its assuming this role while the structure of social power is left intact. In other words, how can there be democracy in the state when there is despotism in the private sphere? This is what the base/superstructure metaphor emphatically denies and what the relative autonomy thesis seems to affirm. Now if one thing is clear, it is that the private sphere remains as despotic as ever. In fact, we are living in a period of declining living standards for workers and increasing profits for the bourgeoisie. Canada's unemployment rate is at an all-time high and the gaps between rich and poor are growing. The basic character of capital has not changed, nor is it in the process of changing, at least for the better. When factories are closing and unionization is fought tooth and nail, even in Canada, there is no sign that the rapacity of capital for profits is decreasing, nor are the demands on the state by capital. Ratner, McMullan, and Burtch do not deny this, of course, but they argue that the state, primarily because of its large growth in terms of the persons and resources at its command, and because of the essential services it performs for capital, has become substantially less dependent on capital and more able to resist its pressures.

In my opinion, this general theoretical outlook, leaving the criminal justice sector apart for the moment, makes far too much of formalities, especially of the formal separation between the state and the economy. Naturally, it is a feature of the capitalist state that it is formally separate from the private sphere. This, in fact, distinguishes it from feudal authority (Wood, 1981). But as pointed out earlier, it is the singular Marxist contribution to our understanding of these matters to have laid bare the organic unity underlying the appearance of separation. Consequently, many theorists have chosen to characterize the growth of the capitalist state as a different way of performing the same basic functions for capital (though no one denies the importance of this difference). In fact, instead of stressing the state's greater autonomy in these circumstances, what is stressed is the greater formal integration of the state with the relations of production as more and more accumulation takes place through the state (O'Connor, 1973; Habermas, 1976; Wright, 1978; Wood, 1981).

But apart from this, while the state has grown larger, capital has not been standing still. As well as inexorably centralizing and concentrating, it has, of course, internationalized. The nation state, even if it is bigger, has increasingly to go on its knees to international capital, either in the old forms or in the new forms, such as the multinational corporation, to beg for investment. Tax giveaways to corporations and the rich in general, at the same time as wages are being controlled by legislation and attempts made to de-index old-age pensions, are much more easily explained by the overwhelming power of capital than by the autonomy of the state. This is altogether apart from the non-economic expressions of capital's power to influence the action of even the biggest and most powerful states in its interests: for example, the current imperialist wars fought on behalf of capital by the United States either directly or through proxies in Central America and the Middle East at enormous human and material cost. And, as the Canadian state inches us more closely to a global holocaust by helping the U.S. test its cruise missile or by encouraging participation in Star Wars against mass wishes, can anyone see in this the growing autonomy of the modern state? The lack of state autonomy is highlighted by the mounting anti-capitalist critique taking place *outside* of the state, for instance in certain Christian organizations and in the labour movement (Canadian Conference of Catholic Bishops, 1983; Hartman, 1983).

What about the criminal justice sector? As the authors point out, the actual practice of each of the components in the criminal justice system is strongly leavened by class bias. At every stage (police, prosecution, courts, corrections), a clear distinction exists between the enforcement practices governing crimes typically committed by the bourgeoisie ("regulatory offences") or on their behalf (the "technical" offences of the RCMP against the left) and those committed by working-class and poor people ("true crimes") or on their behalf (the "ordinary" or "defiant" criminality of peace activists and union leaders). Even within the latter category, further distinctions are made between people, regardless of their offences, who fulfill their roles in the productive apparatus and those who do not. This is why the prisons are not only virtually empty of ruling class elements but are also overfilled with people unemployed at the time of their arrest (Mandel, 1984; 1985a; 1985b).

In this context it is not helpful to talk, as the authors do, of autonomy, either relative or absolute. It seems that here, as with the general issue of the autonomy of the state, there is a danger of mistaking the absence of clear lines of authority between capital and the state and the several institutions of it for autonomy. In fact, Ratner, McMullan, and Burtch seem to use the notion of legal "discretion" almost interchangeably with autonomy. Once again, there is a confusion of appearance with reality. If, in fact, discretion is more or less consistently exercised in a class-biased manner, why should it be considered an instance of autonomy? Indeed, it has long been recognized that the existence of legal discretion enhances the class bias of criminal law. According to *Struggle for Justice*, the "true functions of discretion" are "to increase managerial efficiency," "for political expediency," "to do the publicly unmentionable," "to protect one's own kind," and so on (American Friends' Service Committee, 1971, pp. 134-43). This is why it is an ancient maxim that "deaf and inexorable" laws are "more favourable and advantageous to the weak than to the powerful" (Livy, quoted in Hay, 1975, p. 58). Furthermore, it is increasingly recognized that one of the essential functions of the penal system and its related institutions is "discipline," or the production of "docile and capable bodies" through a process of "perpetual assessment" and "permanent observation" (Foucault, 1977, pp. 294-95) and "the preparation of people . . . so that they would accept an order and discipline which would render them docile instruments of exploitation" (Melossi and Pavarini, 1981, pp. 28-29). The democratic institutions of capitalism have been undermined from the start by various disciplinary mechanisms. Where crime and punishment are concerned discretion is central. It is above all a mechanism of despotic authority, and if the goal of disciplinary institutions is to prepare people for subjection to that authority, discretion is indispensable (Mandel, 1985A).

So it cannot be helpful to call this autonomy, if autonomy from capital is meant. Once we recognize a general orientation of the criminal justice sector, as with other sectors of the state, to the interests of capital (for all the reasons that Ratner, McMullan, and Burtch point out), then it seems misleading to use this term to describe such mechanisms as discretion, which actually *enhance* the power of this sector to practise this orientation.

What happens, then, when discretion is exercised in favour of working-class individuals (as in the many cases of a lack of a criminal record or a good employment record operating in favour of leniency in sentencing or early parole: Mandel, 1984; 1985a)? Or when it is exercised against ruling-class individuals as in the cases cited by Ratner, McMullan, and Burtch of the lawyers sent to jail for fraud, or even against a whole sector, as in the large fine against Simpson Sears for false advertising? There is a natural temptation, to which Ratner, McMullan, and Burtch succumb (when they call this "pushing aside class allegiances" if only "temporarily"), of treating this as proof of autonomy. Another example is when the failure of the state to act against individual police officers who commit crimes is advanced as an example of *police* autonomy. The problem here seems to be the conception of the law's superstructural character (lack of autonomy) as having to do with direct relationships between the state and the ruling class or members or segments of it. Such direct, personal relationships do not seem, however, to capture the point Marxists want to make when they say the state and legal institutions are "superstructural." Remember that what Marx said and meant when he used the "base-superstructure" metaphor was that the state and legal institutions protect and enforce the "relations" of production. These, not the "forces" of production nor the actual participants in the relations, constitute the "economic base." Consequently the ruling class is protected according to Marxist theory only indirectly, by protecting the system which is so beneficial to them. This is what Foucault meant when he wrote that "power is exercised rather than possessed; it is not the "privilege," acquired or preserved, of the dominant class, but the overall effect of its strategic positions" (Foucault 1977, p. 26). And this seems also to be the relevance of the passage from E.P. Thompson quoted above about the rules suiting the ruling class in general, even though individuals may have an interest in violating them from time to time.

Only in this way can we account for the fact that when the police break the law in order to line their own pockets at the expense of the rules of property, they go to jail (*R. v. Cusack*, 1978), but they are congratulated and absolutely discharged if they break the law in order to defend the status quo by beating up on drunks (*R. v. Griffin*, 1975) or disrupting left-wing political movements (*R. v. Coutellier, Cobb and Cormier*, 1977). In these cases they are said to have acted from "noble motives," and judicial discretion is exercised in their favour. However, Jean-Claude Parrot received three months in jail for the precise technical offence for which the RCMP were discharged, despite his noble motives, which happened to be in opposition to the status quo (Mandel, 1983). Lawyers will go to jail if their law-breaking threatens the standard of living of the legal profession by diminishing its general level of trustworthiness, and the same even goes for big businessmen when they are caught defrauding the government (*R. v. McNamara, et al.*, 1981). This will happen when the cases are too egregious to allow them to hide behind limited corporate liability, as was the case with Simpson Sears, though when these sterling citizens do wind up in jail they will be paroled as soon as, if not sooner than, legally possible because they are so little in need of "discipline." This will be accomplished by the discretion of the parole board, as when the National Parole Board reduced the sentences of Hamilton Dredging Scandal culprits Sidney Cooper and Harold McNamara by about 80 per cent on the grounds that their "release plans were sustained by excellent community support" (Mandel, 1985a).

All that said, we must be careful not to identify the superstructural nature of law and state with complete political impotence on the part of the working class. Though reforms as a direct result of working-class pressure on a "class for itself" basis are hard to find in Canadian history, nevertheless the reforms mentioned by Ratner, McMullan, and Burtch: "[p]olitical rights (particularly the extension of the franchise and the right to organise trade unions and political parties), welfare rights, the provision of social services, unemployment insurance, compensation pay, and universal medical care" certainly testify to the fact that as far as the

Canadian state is concerned, the working class is a force to be reckoned with, if only electorally (p. 103-4). But the notion of relative autonomy seems to obscure analysis of the actual pressures and interests which influence state behaviour: what Ratner, McMullan, and Burtch call "clarifying the grounds for decisions." A grave danger of obscuring what actually determines state behaviour is that it may lead to the acceptance or pursuit of phoney reforms which rely on the capacity of the state to be moved by abstract reason or notions of right and wrong detached from social power. Such a reform is the *Charter of Rights and Freedoms*, which has channelled real grievances into a forum where they are attenuated in harmless legal debates about abstract rights with the status quo of social power left unscathed or even reinforced (Mandel and Glasbeek, 1984; Mandel, 1985c).

A good modern example of this kind of analysis of state action can be found in the work of Fred Block who argues that the "theory of relative autonomy" is only "a slightly more sophisticated version of instrumentalism" (1977, p. 9). Block prefers the notion of a "division of labour" to the notion of "relative autonomy" to describe the relationship between the state and the ruling class. It will be remembered that Marx and Engels used this notion to distinguish between the members of the class and its ideologists. I think this is also a useful way to think of the relationships between components of the state which Ratner, McMullan, and Burtch also characterize as being "relatively autonomous" from one another. Human agency being what it is, there can never be perfect consistency, but I would argue that there is much more integration among the various components than Ratner, McMullan, and Burtch suggest. In the recent RCMP affair, for example, the exercise of prosecutorial discretion in favour of the police criminals was justified in part on the basis that the courts were not likely to impose severe penalties and in part on the same grounds ("noble motives") that the courts would use to justify their light sentences (Mandel, 1983; Department of Justice of Canada, 1983). Courts, for their part, often reduce sentences on the basis that the offender co-operated with the police by informing or pleading guilty (*R. v. Kirby, Stuart and Cadwell,* 1981). Prison authorities routinely comply with court recommendations for early temporary absence for white-collar offenders (*R. v. Bigham,* 1982; Ministry of Correctional Services of Ontario, 1982, p. 43). And the parole authorities do the same, as well as taking into account co-operation with the police and corrections authorities (National Parole Board Policy and Procedures Manual, section 103-3). Whether the courts declare a "hands-off" doctrine where prison and parole decisions are concerned, or promise to enforce a duty of fairness, in fact they only interfere rarely, and when they do, they almost always do so on grounds that leave basic relations untouched.

The Law Reform Commission of Canada (LRCC), which is the subject of the paper by Hastings and Saunders, is a good example of how formally and apparently separate components of the criminal justice sector can be closely connected. The LRCC has the added importance of being a source of the glue which holds them together.

Put simply, Hastings and Saunders see the creation of the Law Reform Commission of Canada as an instrumental response to the crisis of legitimacy and authority of the 1960's: it was created in order to reform the law to confront these crises. Consequently, when these crises subsided, or were transformed, the commission was reduced to a technical role. That the ferment of the 1960's contributed to the commission's creation is very persuasive. However, there are deeper reasons for the existence of law reform commissions in one form or another throughout the modern period. Certainly the Law Reform Commission of Canada was not unique. It followed upon the creation of such commissions in various provinces, in the United States, and in England. But major official law reform exercises have a much more venerable history, including, of course, Stephen's Draft Criminal Code for England which was adopted by Canada in 1892. It helps to think of law reform rather in the way Foucault assessed reform of the penitentiary, as part of a "simultaneous system" and as "isomorphic, despite its 'idealism' " with the very things considered for reform (1977, p. 271). Carrying the analogy with Foucault even further, looking at law reform in this way may provide a better understanding of both its "success" and "failure." The Law Reform Commission should be examined as a device to provide an ongoing legitimation of both the law and the social status quo. In other words, I want to place it in the category of ideologists of the ruling class following Marx and Engels in *The German Ideology.*

It is impossible to read a mandate for radicalism in the Law reform Commission's original legislation set out by Hastings and Saunders (pp. 127-28). In fact, it is three-quarters technicalities and only one-quarter a recognition that something was wrong. Furthermore, when one looks at the personnel as they appear in the *First Research Program* (1972), one finds nothing but lawyers, judges, and future judges. Its *Thirteenth Annual Report* (1984), which gives a complete roster of past and present commissioners, reveals that of the nineteen members of the LRCC, eighteen were lawyers, and one was a sociologist who taught at a law school. Eleven were judges, six at the time of their appointment and five appointed to the bench after being with the commission, two of them now judges of the Supreme Court of Canada. There were certainly no radicals on this commission.

The concerns of the LRCC from the very beginning were primarily with explaining and thereby defending the system as it exists, rather than undertaking a fundamental reorganization. The commission was concerned with re-establishing a consensus:

> The law depends upon a broad consensus to achieve an effective ordering of social relations in a democratic society. In pursing our objectives we envisage the process of law reform as involving a reciprocal educative function. The dissemination of study and working papers and continuing consultation with the public and with specialized groups should not only improve public understanding of the issues involved, but should also enhance the Commissions's awareness of the expectations and needs of Canadians. (LRCC, 1972, p. 6)

They were concerned that "many" had been "caused . . . to question the efficacy and in some instances the legitimacy of the present legal system." Consequently, they set about to provide a new defence of the basic components of the system which perhaps might require jettisoning minor irritants, at least as they appeared in the early 1970's (for instance the right to view pornography and the right to commit suicide).

This casts some doubt on the view of Hastings and Saunders that the resulting status quo orientation of the commission was "a result of a change in the strategic relation of the LRCC to the social and political conflicts of the day" (p. 129). But it is impossible to disagree with their statement that "the LRCC has developed and adopted a position on the role and functions of criminal law which is fully compatible ideologically with current social arrangements" (ibid.). The evidence for this exists almost anywhere one looks in the work of the commission (not least in the folksy, loving, and admiring terminology it uses to describe existing law: "it may be crude, it may have faults, it may be rough and ready, but basically it is a system of applied morality and justice." Above all else it is *"Our" Criminal Law* even though its "true role is not to be decided but discovered" (LRCC, 1976, p. 16).

However, it is in the general philosophical outlook developed and applied by the commission that lies its most significant and lasting contribution to the legitimation of the status quo. This is the "core values" approach to punishment. A revealing passage appears in the 1976 report *Our Criminal Law:*

> Looking to the future—admittedly our law does try to do this. It tries by means of sentence and punishment. It seeks to deter potential criminals and rehabilitate the actual offender.
>
>   Unfortunately success is doubtful. Deterrence and reform are not wholly effective . . .

> Organizing the future though, is not the major function of the
> criminal law. It has a different, more important role. After all, even if
> the nature of our free society limits criminal law's impact on crime, we
> still need criminal law. Even if we cannot control the future, this does
> not mean we must ignore the present and the past. We still need to do
> something about wrongful acts: to register our social disapproval, to
> publicly denounce them and to re-affirm the values violated by them.
> Criminal law is not geared only to the future: it also serves to throw light
> on the present—by underlining crucial social values. (ibid., 1976, p. 3)

This passage is revealing because it shows both how desperate the
commission was to salvage the existing system and also what theory it was
driven to in order to do so. Since the system does such a poor job of
preventing crime, you might have expected the commission actually to
consider whether it all ought to be abolished, since prevention of crime had
been the usual political justification for punishment. The failure to do so
becomes explicable only when the passage is seen as being aimed at
defending the status quo on whatever grounds are available. One could
almost read "fortunately" before the last paragraph. Then there is the
actual criterion they used: "underlining crucial social values." As Hastings
and Saunders point out, considered as open-ended, the concept of crucial
social values could have provoked a discussion of what our values really are.
As a legitimation of current practices, however, this criterion could only
result in the ratification of the values of the class with social power or at
least the values of its dominance. This is indeed evident in *Our Criminal
Law* itself, where, having found that the law had basically to do with "core
values," the commission ran up against the fact that our "paradigm crime is
theft" even though the commissioners could not bring themselves to ascribe
fundamental importance to the value of "ownership." But did they
recommend, therefore, the abolition of the crime of theft?

> These questions call for fundamental reappraisal, not only of our law
> but of the role of property in our society. Meanwhile we aim to do two
> things. Immediately we plan to improve and simplify the present law on
> property offences. Later we hope to initiate more general consideration
> of the basic problem and so foster debate across the country—in
> schools, colleges and universities, in churches, societies and community
> associations, in police forces, prisons and indeed all contexts where
> there is a concern with social justice. That way we may eventually
> achieve a general consensus on ownership. (ibid., p. 21)

Needless to say, this debate has yet to be even initiated.

However, the question of whose values or what values are imposed as core values does not seem to be the only one. An important element in understanding the Law Reform Commission of Canada is in the very notion of punishment of individuals for the purpose of vindicating social values without regard for whether or not it has any effect in preventing crime. Through this practice, the central value being vindicated is really that of individual responsibility for crime. This is in turn only the logical result of treating crime as a clash of *values* instead of *interests*. To use the punishment of the transgressor against a value as the method by which the value is to be taught is to provide an explanation of crime in the irreducible failure of some malefactors to accept these values. That is why the commission can make these extraordinary statements:

> Fear of crime is natural. Of all the things that frighten us—accidents, diseases, natural disasters—crime has a particular place. It wears a human face. Other things happen, crime is done deliberately. . . . (ibid., 1)
>
> Criminal law, then primarily has to do with values. Naturally, for crime itself is nothing more nor less than conduct seriously contrary to our values. Crimes are acts not only punishable by law but also *meriting* punishment. As Fitzjames Stephen said, the ordinary citizen views crime as an act "forbidden by law and revolting to the moral sentiments of society." Crimes are not just forbidden, they are also wrong. (ibid., 5)

The basic message the commission wants to put across is the same as that of its favourite author, even though they do not express it as forthrightly as he did: "The criminal law thus proceeds upon the principle that it is morally right to hate criminals, and it confirms and justifies that sentiment by inflicting upon criminals punishments which express it" (Stephen, 1882, p. 81).

The underlining-core-values approach seems eminently suited to defending the continuation and expansion of current punitive practices (note the explosion of the prison population and the large number of individuals on probation in this period) which are demonstrable failures in preventing crime. It also provides a mechanism for defending the exercise of discretion (indeed the existence of discretion) on traditional grounds which faithfully reflect the status quo of social relations. This explains the advocacy of the term "honesty" as the criterion for property crime which allows the court to treat as theft only direct interferences with property relations and not pranks committed by respectable persons (*R. v. Dalzell*, 1982; *R. v. Mitchell*, 1981). It explains why the commission feels it can deal with homicide by redefining the *law* of homicide, and it explains why there can be no scientific analysis of responsibility.

Thus, whatever the fate of the commission's specific recommendations for legislative reform, its general orientation to defending penal practices has been embraced with enthusiasm by courts, politicians, and correctional authorities. (Incidentally, it may be that the judgement of legislative ineffectiveness was premature, given the incorporation of many commission proposals in Bill C-19, the Liberal party's deathbed legislation of February 1984). Sentencing practices which do not seem to prevent crime and merely reward people for their strategic positions in the productive relations can now be defended with citations from the Law Reform Commission of Canada (*R. v. A*, 1974). An all-party House of Commons investigation of the penitentiary system is able to put forward the oldest practices (that is, pay on a piecework basis, earned remission) as new ideas on the basis of this justification (House of Commons, 1977; Mandel, 1979). The Supreme Court of Canada can rely on the notion to defend and entrench the completely preposterous and status quo-oriented distinction between "regulatory offences" (business crime) and "true crime" (working-class crime) (*R. v. City of Sault Ste. Marie*, 1978). In its *Thirteenth Annual Report*, the commission provides an impressive list of cases in which its work figured in justifications for decisions, as well as its generally attentive coverage by the media (LRCC, 1984, pp. 6-8).

At the end of their paper, Hastings and Saunders write "[t]he new Canadian Constitution and the emergent tendency for key political and legal issues to be resolved in the courts will probably shift the real axis of legal reform from the LRCC to the Supreme Court" (p. 146). On the contrary, it seems even more likely that the movement toward court-centred politics will see an ascendency of the commission. This is because of the great similarity between the abstract, status quo-oriented legal philosophy used by courts administering the *Charter of Rights* and the philosophy of punishment adopted by the commission. Certainly the political stock of lawyers and legal philosophers in general has never been higher (Glasbeek and Mandel, 1984; Mandel, 1985c).

The concept of relative autonomy certainly has a place in helping us understand the criminal justice sector or indeed any aspect of state activity. It reminds us that where human agency is involved, action is always contingent to some extent. The danger is in allowing us to forget that though we "make our own history, we do not do so of our own free will or in circumstances of our own choosing" (Marx, 1850, p. 146). Consequently, relative autonomy can only be a way of introducing us to the difficult but crucial task of understanding precisely what it is that makes the system tick in the lopsided way it does.

REFERENCES

American Friends Service Committee. 1971. *Struggle for Justice.* New York: Hill and Wang.

Block, F. 1977. "The Ruling Class Does Not Rule: Notes on the Marxist Theory of the State." *Socialist Revolution* 33, no. 7: 6-28.

Canadian Conference of Catholic Bishops. 1983. "Ethical Reflections on the Economic Crisis." *Canadian Dimension* 17, no. 2: 53.

Cohen, G. A. 1978. *Karl Marx's Theory of History: A Defence.* Princeton: Princeton University Press.

_____. 1983. "Forces and Relations of Production." In Betty Matthews, Ed., *Marx: A Hundred Years On.* London: Lawrence and Wishart.

Department of Justice Canada. 1983. *The Position of the Attorney General of Canada on Certain Recommendations of the McDonald Commission.* Ottawa: Government of Canada.

Engels, Frederick. 1890. "Engels to C. S. Schmidt in Berlin." In *Karl Marx and Frederick Engels: Selected Writings.* Moscow: Progress Publishers, 1968, pp. 694-99.

Foucault, M. 1977. *Discipline and Punish: The Birth of the Prison* Trans. Alan Sheridan. New York: Pantheon Books.

Glasbeek, H. J., and M. Mandel. 1984. "The Legalisation of Politics in Advanced Capitalism: The Canadian Charter of Rights and Freedoms." *Socialist Studies* 2: 84-124.

Habermas, H. 1976. *Legitimation Crisis.* Trans. T. McCarthy. Boston: Beacon Press.

Hartman, G., 1983. "Labour Unions: What Can They Contribute to Economic Recovery." *Canadian Dimension* 17, no. 2: 58.

Hay, D. 1975. "Property, Authority and the Criminal Law." In Hay et al., *Albion's Fatal Tree: Crime and Society in Eighteenth Century England.* London: Allen Lane.

House of Commons. 1977. Standing Committee on Justice and Legal Affairs, Sub-Committee on the Penitentiary System in Canada, *Third Report: The Penitentiary System in Canada.* Ottawa: Queen's Printer for Canada.

Law Reform Commission of Canada. 1972. *First Research Programme.* Ottawa: Information Canada.

_____. 1976. *Report: Our Criminal Law.* Ottawa: Information Canada.

_____. 1984. *Thirteenth Annual Report 1983-1984.* Ottawa: Minister of Supply and Services Canada.

Levine, Andrew, and Erik Olin Wright. 1980. "Rationality and Class Struggle." *New Left Review* 12: 47.

Mandel, M. 1979. "The Ideology of Prison Reform," *Canadian Dimension* 13, no. 7: 6.

_____. 1983. "McDonald and the R.C.M.P." In *Ideas: Law and Social Order:* Pt. 1. Toronto. C.B.C. Transcripts, pp. 1-12.

_____. 1984. "Democracy, Class and Canadian Sentencing Law." *Crime and Social Justice* 21-22: 163-82.

_____. 1985a. "Democracy, Class and the National Parole Board." *Criminal Law Quarterly* 27: 159-81.

_____. 1985b. "Fact Sheet." In "Politics and Sentencing: A Statement on the Squamish Five." *This Magazine* 19, no. 1: 35-38.

_____. 1985c. "The Rule of Law and the Legalisation of Politics in Canada." *International Journal of Sociology of Law* 13, no. 2, pp. 273-87.

Marx, K. 1850. "The Eighteenth Brumaire of Louis Bonaparte." In *Surveys from Exile*. Harmondsworth: Penguin Books, 1973, pp. 142-249.

_____. 1859. "Preface to a Critique of Political Economy." In David McLellan, ed., *Karl Marx: Selected Writings*. Oxford University Press, 1977, pp. 388-91.

_____. [1867]. *Capital: A Critique of Political Economy*. Harmondsworth: Penguin Books, 1976.

_____. [1875]. "Critique of the Gotha Programme." In David McLellan, ed., *Karl Marx: Selected Writings*. Oxford University Press, 1977, pp. 564-70.

_____., and Frederick Engels. 1846. *The German Ideology* in L. B. Easton and K. H. Guddat, trans. and ed., *Writings of the Young Marx on Philosophy and Society*. Garden City: Anchor Books, 1967.

Melossi, D. and Pavarini, P. 1981. *The Prison and the Factory*. London: Macmillan.

Ministry of Correctional Services Ontario. 1982. *Report of the Minister 1982*. Toronto: Government of Ontario.

O'Connor, J. 1973. *The Fiscal Crisis of the State*. New York: St. Martin's Press.

Poulantzas, Nicos. 1973. *Political Power and Social Classes*. London: New Left Books and Shead and Ward.

_____. 1978. *State, Power, Socialism*. London: New Left Books.

Stephen, J. F. 1882. *A History of the Criminal Law in England*. vol. 2. London: Macmillan.

Thompson, E. P. 1975. *Whigs and Hunters: The Origins of the Black Act*. Harmondsworth: Penguin Books.

Wood, E. M. 1981. "The Separation of the Economic and the Political in Capitalism." *New Left Review* 127: 66.

Wright, E. O. 1978. *Class, Crisis and the State*. London: New Left Books.

CASES

R. v. *A.* (1974), 26 C.C.C. (2d) 474.

R. v. *Bigham* (1982), 29 C.C.C. (2d) 221.

R. v. *City of Sault Ste Marie* (1978), 40 C.C.C. (2d) 353.

R. v. *Coutellier, Cobb and Cormier,* quoted in L. Arbour, and L. T. Taman. 1981. *Criminal Procedure. Cases, Texts and Materials*. Toronto: Emond-Montgomery, p. 240.

R. v. *Cusack* (1978), 41 C.C.C. (2d) 289.

R. v. *Dalzell* (1982), 3 C.C.C. (3d) 232; (1983) 6 C.C.C. (3d) 112.

R. v. *Griffin* (1975), 23 C.C.C. (2d) 11.

R. v. *Kirby, Stuart and Cadwell* (1981), 61 C.C.C. (2d) 544.

R. v. *McNamara, et al.* (No. 2) (1981), 56 C.C.C. (2d) 516.

R. v. *Mitchell* (1981), 58 C.C.C. (2d) 232.

PART THREE

The Canadian State

8

Canadian Civil Society, the Canadian State, and Criminal Justice Institutions: Theoretical Considerations

ROBERT GAUCHER

INTRODUCTION: THEORETICAL CONCERNS

As described in the essay by Ratner, McMullan, and Burtch, contemporary Marxist state theory is a formal attempt to study the relationship between the state, capital, and civil society. It may be characterized as an attempt to transcend vulgar Marxist theorization. However, this type of analysis in Canada is problematic in two ways. First, theorizing about the state borrows heavily from the works of European Marxists, and it is not at all clear that their imposition on the analysis of Canadian society does not contradict the Marxist materialist requirement of specificity. In some crucial areas, the analysis does not maintain the vital relationship between theory and the material ground from which it is derived and directed. This transfer of concepts is not dissimilar from the traditional bourgeois analysis in Canadian social science, which relies on the wholesale transfer of analytical models.[1] The result is that the ensuing analysis addresses the "theories" or "models" to a much greater extent than the Canadian terrain to which they are uncomfortably applied.

The second point is that contemporary state theory in this country suffers from the lack of a clear depiction of Canadian civil society. This is a problem of theorizing by Canadian socialists generally, stemming from the absence of detailed, comprehensive works on the nature of Canadian civil society upon which to ground one's theoretical writings. Except for the early works of Stanley Ryerson (1960, 1968), there have been few Marxists attempts to clearly establish the broad historical parameters of the social, political, and economic development of Canadian society, including a characterization of Canadian civil society. Instead, one encounters an array of theoretical and analytical essays which assume much but seldom explicate the assumptions upon which they are based. Formal theoretical discourse is problematic unless it takes into account the material reality of the society analysed, rather than concentrating on existing theories. This position is clearly recognizable in Marx's arguments about the specificity of historical development and his rejection of general theory. The absence of social histories which provide a critical analysis of the form and character of Canadian civil society is a crucial problem for Marxist theorists writing on Canada. Contemporary work on the Canadian State also suffers from this lacuna.

Without comprehensive analyses of Canadian society, the theoretical positions derived from the study of other societies have no link to specific Canadian problems. An example is the use of Gramscian notions of state activities directed towards the achievement of legitimacy and capitalist hegemony. This is not to deny that within Canada the state does not fulfill this function, but it is to question the assumed need for, and level of, such activities. The absence of significant levels of class consciousness and class struggle in the history of Canadian society (which are apparent in some European societies, such as Italy) means that the periodic crises in bourgeois hegemony that European theorists address do not occur regularly here. Furthermore, the Gramscian model can be described as a consensus-coercion framework which assumes the transition from an aristocratic to a capitalist ruling class. It addresses a social formation characterized by a rigid class system. This was not the case for Canada. The ruling class of this county largely arose out of the petit bourgeois base of the social formation; as a consequence, the very nature of the society is different. Rather than simply borrowing European concepts and frameworks addressing bourgeois state-based control, we must rethink our analysis of the state within the specificity of the Canadian conjuncture. What is required is the grounding of theory in Canadian material life—in the real social, political, and economic relations that characterize Canadian civil society. And if we are to ground our theorizing, an analysis of the historical development of this society is necessary.

In arguing for a grounding of the analysis of the state, a complementary problem arises. A common feature of contemporary analyses addressing the historical foundations of the state is the projection into the past of concepts and theoretical positions derived from the study of the modern capitalist state.[2] A prime example is the conception of the state as "ideal" capital. In contemporary state theory, the conflation of the political and the economic is portrayed, at best, as vulgar Marxism or conspiracy theory. While this position is valid relative to the present, to use this modern concept in reference to the era in which a bourgeois nation-state was created is to distort the reality of that historical period. For in that era, there was a virtual correspondence between the economic and the political spheres, with the direct political involvement of the competing ruling-class factions. Finally, and most importantly for the purposes of this essay, contemporary state theory has not yet come to terms with, nor sufficiently elaborated, the relationship of state disciplinary activities to the production of a bourgeois consensus and to the reproduction of the bourgeois social formation. While writers like Panitch (1977, p. 19) have characterized the role of law and the judiciary as central to the legitimation activities of the state, they have focused on the edge of coercion provided by restrictive legislation directed at labour's formal organization and formal struggles with capital. This depiction does not sufficiently grasp the subtlety of how state disciplinary activities contribute to the legitimation function, nor how state coercion is itself legitimized. It ignores the role of criminalization as a means of legitimation. For example, Thomas Mathiesen (1974), in his groundbreaking work, *The Politics of Abolition,* argued that imprisonment fulfills important functions which are integral to bourgeois legitimation activities.[3]

It must be emphasized that the law and criminal-justice apparatus of the state serve as a vehicle for the articulation and realization of ruling-class interests. They operate to create and legitimize in the public mind a distinction within the labouring population which mirrors the needs of capitalist production. Those deemed by this capitalist order to be useless, unproductive, or surplus labour are transformed in the minds of a large portion of labour itself into a criminal class of thieves, drunkards, and idlers: in short, a class of the socially undisciplined. This serves to mask the needs of capital—needs such as surplus labour, a stable social order, and a disciplined work force— particularly in times of high unemployment. By transferring the problem produced by these needs to the terrain of law and order, reflection is shifted away from the its causes.

The formal task of a Marxist or socialist criminology is to locate state disciplinary institutions and their activities within the parameters of the political economy of the society in question.[4] But the intent is to go beyond the location of particular institutions within the state. A detailed analysis should focus on the role of state disciplinary institutions and their activities in relation to the labour requirements of the dominant capitalist class and in relation to the nature and extent of class struggle within the society. While we must characterize ''bourgeois'' law as a principal means of achieving legitimacy and ruling-class hegemony, by focusing on the wider terrain of state disciplinary institutions (for example, prisons or education), the dialectics of our analysis will provide important insights into the very nature of civil society. For example, from a reading of Ignatieff's (1978) *A Just Measure of Pain*, we can conclude that the construction of the repressive apparatus of the state in nineteenth century Britain was pushed forward in times of considerable class struggle, such as the period after the social dislocations caused by the end of the Napoleonic Wars in 1815 and during the great Chartist upheavals of the 1830's. To avoid the type of analysis which either assumes the "progressive" nature of the bourgeoisie's rationalization of social order or argues for some visionary perspective on the part of the leading petit bourgeois ideologues of an era,[5] the analysis of state-based disciplinary institutions must include the material reality of their political economic contexts.

Therefore, it is not enough simply to borrow a line of analysis derived from consideration of other societies, for the conceptualization of the problematic must reflect the material life addressed. For example, one stream within the European literature on the state argues that in order for capitalism to function at the desired level of production, civil society had to be regulated and ordered in a way that best suited that purpose.

> For capitalist production to expand, it was necessary for the whole terrain of social, moral, and cultural activity to be brought, where possible, within its sway, developed and reshaped to its needs. That is what Gramsci meant by the state "creating a new type or level of civilization." The law, he added, "will be its instrument for this purpose". (Hall et al., 1978, p. 203)

They continue:

> In a system based on capitalist reproduction, labour has, *if necessary*, to be disciplined to labour; in bourgeois society the propertyless have to be disciplined to the respect for private property; in a society of "free individuals", men and women have to be disciplined to respect and obey the overarching framework of the nation-state itself. Coercion is one necessary face or aspect of "the order of the state". The law and the legal institutions are the clearest institutional expression of this "reserve" army of enforced social discipline. (ibid., p. 202, my emphasis)

This and other analyses of the emerging European bourgeois state illustrate that the state was constructed in recognition of the "undisciplined" social relations of the pre-capitalist period and, in particular, in terms of the chaos produced during the period of transition to capitalism itself. The new capitalist state structure was largely a response to the chaotic conditions produced by the rise of industrial capitalism and the accumulation of a body of "free labour": the latter a result of land enclosures, the destruction of cottage industries, and the migration to urban areas. While this is not true for all European societies to the same degree, it is generally the case. This does not hold true in Canada, for in Canada capital confronted a much less contradictory heritage. However, by considering the relationship of state disciplinary initiatives to the developing social formation of the embryonic Canadian nation-state in the pre-Confederation era, we may transcend the distortions produced by the straight transfer of externally derived analytic perspectives and gain a clearer picture of the relationship of the state to Canadian civil society.

THE DEVELOPMENT OF CANADIAN CIVIL SOCIETY AND THE CANADIAN NATION-STATE

Most Marxist analysis of European societies starts from the premise of a class-structured society which was transformed by the ruling strata in line with the new requirements of capitalist social organization, including the transition from a manufacturing to an industrialized era. It must be stressed that large segments of the populations of European societies needed to be transformed into capitalist labour. This required the transformation of the state structure, including a new emphasis on those legitimation activities now associated with the state in modern capitalism. In the eighteenth and nineteenth centuries in Europe, labour was transformed into capitalist and industrial labour through the compulsion of the market place (that is, through largescale pauperization and acute want) and through the construction and use of state disciplinary institutions such as work houses and prisons. At this point in capitalism's development, disciplinary and reproductive institutions, such as education, were decidedly secondary to other forms of compulsion and discipline.[6]

As I have indicated, the heritage of pre-Confederation Canada was quite different. At the point of the Rebellion of 1837-38, there were five alternative lines of development possible, as represented by the Native peoples, the Canadiens or habitants, the radical democratic/republicanism of a fraction of the Upper Canada population, the pseudo-aristocratic or loyalist conservatism of the Family Compact,[7] and the bourgeoisie—the dominant fraction of which was centred in Montreal and referred to as the Chateau Clique.[8] The political struggles which occurred between 1820 and 1840 were precisely over what form of social organization the developing Canadian society would take. The locus of these struggles was over the control and operation of the colonial state structures of both Lower and

Upper Canada. The Canadien position coalesced under the leadership of Joseph-Louis Papineau; the radical democrats of Upper Canada organized under William Lyon Mackenzie. It is important to recognize that these two forces challenged the very form of society desired by the politically and economically ascendant Chateau Clique of Montréal and the loyalist conservative alternative supported by the Family Compact of Upper Canada. At this juncture the radicals of both Upper and Lower Canada did not challenge British colonial rule *per se* but rather opposed the internal operation of the colonial state by the dominant Chateau Clique and Family Compact.

By 1835, as their pleas for intervention were ignored by the British colonial office, the movements became more radical. This was in part a product of the split which occurred within their ranks at this point, with the more moderate or petit bourgeois fraction withdrawing from the movement.[9] The support of the moderates in Lower Canada was peripheral, since the political forces under Papineau's leadership were clearly representatives of the rural, Canadien population.[10] In Upper Canada their withdrawal had more serious, though not debilitating, ramifications. However, of central importance was the withdrawal at this time of the official support of the dominant religious organizations—the Catholic Church in Lower Canada and the Ryerson-led Methodist Congregation of Upper Canada.[11]

The historical literature presents two dominant arguments about this period. One is that the lack of popular support for either of these radical movements led to rebellions which were dismal failures. This position is the ideological basis for bourgeois historiography to treat this "class struggle" as nothing more than a footnote in Canadian history.[12] The counter-argument, presented by the Rebellion leaders, was that the oppositional political forces did not actively and violently rebel, but with their political movements and their leaders under attack, they rose in defence of the leadership and their rights as guaranteed under the British constitutional arrangement. In Dr. O'Callaghan's words:

> If you will look carefully through Lord Gosford's dispatches of 1836, as well as those of the colonial secretary of that and preceding and subsequent years, you will find that Gosford recommended the suspension of your constitution more than a year before there was any shadow of an outbreak.
>
> The truth is, the governments here both in Quebec and Downing Street determined on abolishing the Lower Canada assembly, and only sought a pretext to justify its violence. Debartzch, who was Gosford's "confidence man," came to coax and browbeat me in '36 into voting for supplies, and when he found me inébranable, he very plainly told me

that the result would be, that Papineau and I would be hanged! About that time, Gosford recommended that the Lower Canada assembly should be abolished. . . . It was Castlereagh and the Irish Union over again. Goad the people into violence and when they fall victims to the snares, abolish their constitutional rights. Read the history of Ireland and its legislative union with England, and you will see, as in a mirror, the plot of 1836-7 against Canadian liberty.

The movement of '37, as far as I had any knowledge, was the movement of the government against peaceful citizens in order to bring the latter to an indignant resistance of personal violence. . . . We, my friend, were the victims, not the conspirators. (Quoted in DeCelles, 1910, pp. 146-48)

In the Assembly in 1848, Papineau stated:

I defy the government to contradict me when I assert that none of us had ever organized, desired or even anticipated armed resistance . . . not that an insurrection would not have been legitimate, but we had resolved not to resort to it as yet. (Quoted in DeCelles, 1910, p. 156)

The British response, after the violent suppression of this struggle, was to suspend the constitution and send Lord Durham to investigate the situation.

From the point of the Durham Report (1839) and the Union of the Canadas (1841), the trajectory of development in central Canada would be thoroughly bourgeois, and from that juncture we may characterize Canada as a thoroughly bourgeois social formation, a petit bourgeois settler society, with the rural Canadien population remaining the grand exception. The Durham triumvirate (Durham, Charles Buller, and Gibbon Wakefield) recommended that it was a bourgeois social order that would take hold and be the basis for development of the northern half of this continent. [13] After the Rebellion, the wholesale expulsion of the radical democratic opposition of Upper Canada,[14] the repression and then containment of the Canadiens within a reactionary Catholicism, and the eventual transformation of the dominant fraction of the Family Compact into a bourgeois class force (for example, A. MacNab's wholehearted involvement in land acquisition and sale, and railroad construction and its associated economic diversifications in the 1850's) confirm the direction of this movement. What today's nationalists have assumed and articulated as the historical antecedents of Canadian capital—that is, a continuing colonial mentality/subordination—has largely distorted the history of the development of the Canadian social formation.

Durham, or more correctly the unholy triumvirate of Durham, Buller,

and Wakefield—"colonial reformers" arguing for "systematic colonization"—
clearly recommended support for a relatively autonomous political economic situation for the indigenous bourgeoisie of the colony. As well, they
addressed the demand for the containment of alternative lines of political
economic development, represented at this point by the Canadiens and the
fragmented remnants of the radical democrats/republicans of western
Upper Canada.[15] This programme proceeded apace, with the collaboration
of the bourgeois element of Canadien society a necessary precondition for
the collaboration of the Canadien Catholic church—a church moving
swiftly to a reactionary ultramontane position.

To fully grasp the movement which occurred after 1841 we must place the
Durham Report in its British political economic context. It represented a
major policy statement of the ascending Whig political forces (representing
British industrial capital) and their proposals for a new colonial order of
empire. Though it is problematic to refer to the British lines of empire at this
time as still mercantilist, it is clear that, with the rise to political power of the
industrial capitalist fraction,[16] a new laissez-faire[17] economic order of
empire was to be put into place. We can locate the most important formative
years of Canadian capitalist development in this period, an era which Eric
Hobsbawm (1977) has referred to as *The Age of Capital*. This was the age
when international capital, dominated and led by British industrial capital
and its extensions (British colonial entrepreneurs), grew and extended its
lines of operation beyond anything previously experienced. The effects of
these shifts were crucial to the social formation that developed and to the
resulting nature of the nation-state of Canada.

The common wisdom of the day was that the ideas of the Durham Report
were specifically Gibbon Wakefield's and represented his scheme for
"systematic colonization"—"responsible government" and land control.
Charles Buller argued:

> But looking at our colonies properly so called—at the colonies in most
> part inhabited by British settlers or their descendents, and retained for
> pacific purposes alone—it seems that the British interests which require
> to be protected by the Imperial Legislature are very simple, and likely to
> be productive of little necessity for collision. We want colonies in order
> to have customers for our trade and a field for our surplus capital and
> labour. These are the sole objects for which we maintain colonies, and
> for securing which we are obliged to keep our dominion over them. We
> are under the necessity of governing them, and of protecting them by
> our fleets and armies solely in order that we may be sure of trading with
> them, and sending our emigrants to them. We need interfere with them
> solely in order to secure an advantageous trade, and a ready access for

our emigrants, and such a disposal of the lands of the colony as shall promote emigration to it. . . . Our ancient views of colonial trade are now so completely abandoned. (Quoted in Wrong, 1926, pp. 109-10)

The method for securing this situation was "responsible government"[18] for the white settlement colonies. Wakefield defined colonial government as municipal in essence and planned for relative political autonomy for the colonial bourgeoisie, not independence.

> Alteration of the constitution, foreign affairs, defence, regulation of external trade, the Crown Lands—these were to be left to Westminster. In all other things there was to be complete autonomy, and the will of the colony, expressed by its Assembly was to prevail in legislation and administration alike. (Ibid., pp. 69-70)

In short, the Durham Report assigned a place for Canada and the colonial bourgeoisie within the larger supra-national economic order that was developing. Therefore, the British turned towards the moderate "liberal" reformers to gain support for their plan. And it was this conjunction of British and colonial liberal capitalists that was to prove successful. They desired a state structure which would operate in the best interests of the bourgeoisie of each particular colony. The construction of a Canadian nation-state (1864-73) was the ultimate mark of success of this plan.

Responsible government was one aspect of a larger plan aimed at restructuring the economic and political organization of the British white settlement colonies. Central to the plan were the export and investment of British capital and the migration of British labour. With the dramatic rise in the rate of accumulation of capital occurring in Britain, the white settlement colonies were to provide a safe outlet for British investment. There was general agreement with this part of the plan. Arguments for the export of British surplus population as a source of labour in the colonies and as a means of relieving pressures at home were more problematic.[19] Though tight land control was prescribed as a means of maintaining a ratio of capital and labour suitable for reproducing the class structure of Britain—the ultimate goal of the "systematic colonization plan"—other factors intruded. First and foremost was the continuing refusal by the British ruling class to pay the cost of any largescale emigration of the lower orders for surplus labour.[20] This combined with another debilitating feature unique to the Canadian conjuncture which Wakefield had apparently misread.[21] In the Canadas, the largest portion of the accessible land had already been alienated by large grants to loyalists, land speculators, and land companies formed in the 1830's. The importance of the sale and development of land to the profit margins of the internal bourgeoisie compounded the problem.

The cement of this particular conjunction of concerns was the tenuous control of the internal ruling class, as exhibited by the Rebellion and their divisions over the desired lines of development of the colony. Furthermore, British concern since the Conquest in 1760 had been to maintain control of the colony and, since the American War of Independence in 1776, to repress the development of republicanism and other strains of radical democratic ideology within its boundaries.[22] They feared that rapid, unorganized immigration and economic development, without the existence of a suitable class structure to contain it, would jeopardize their control of the colony. Therefore, the systematic colonization plan was aborted, and replaced by the cheaper alternative of encouraging the advance of the internal bourgeoisie via economic and ideological ties, accompanied by a selective immigration policy.

This last point leads to a consideration of the ways in which a focus on class struggle and the discipline and reproduction of labour illuminates the more encompassing developments in political economy. Although the forces of rebellion had been repressed, a large body of oppositional Canadiens in Lower Canada and a smouldering remnant of radical dissent in Upper Canada (located in Canada West) still existed after the Union of 1841. Furthermore, the highly conservative network of the Family Compact, while thoroughly committed to the British monarchical setup, was not inclined toward strictly bourgeois development. It must be understood that in the Durham Report both the Tory Family Compact type of colonial state control and the Canadien community were viewed as impediments to capitalist economic, political and social development. The British Whigs' response to the existing colonial state arrangement in Upper Canada was "responsible government": class democracy providing the bourgeois class with the necessary legal and political conditions for its ascendance. This meant the transformation of a fraction of the Family Compact into a position more amenable to bourgeois development (such as by the Tory leader, A. MacNab). The response (as provided in the Durham report) to Canadien civil society, with its refusal to abandon community for bourgeois "striving," "possessive individualism," and "enterprise," was its destruction and assimilation—in short, its transformation into a bourgeois social formation.[23]

How then, was this thoroughly bourgeois society to be created? In this scheme, which produced a bourgeois nation-state, what was the importance and the nature of the state disciplinary institutions which were constructed?

THE CANADIENS: THEIR CONTAINMENT

From the point of the Conquest, the primary concern of the British was control—maintaining possession of the "booty" that was the land of the dispossessed Native peoples. From the Conquest, the Canadiens posed a threat to British dominance and possession and were also a major obstacle to the economic plans of the Anglo-American merchants who flooded the colony at that time. Rather than unleashing these "passing birds of prey"[24] on the Canadien population, an event which was viewed in the British colonial office as a sure guarantee of Canadien rebellion, the British military administration turned to the only viable locus of control, the Catholic church.[25] Though the administration was reluctant to turn toward the Catholic church, the church was able to establish both its loyalty and its viability as "manager" of the Canadien population through the perilous events of the American War of Independence (1776-83), the French Revolution (1789), the Napoleonic Wars (1793-1813), the Canadian-American War of 1812 (1812-14), and the Rebellion (1837-38). By successfully maintaining its middleman position between the administration and the population, the church established its sway, and ultimately its domination, over the Canadien population.

In a forthright manner, the church functioned as the institution of social control and social discipline for the Canadien population in the latter half of the eighteenth, in the nineteenth, and arguably into the twentieth centuries. However, reliance on the church as the principal agency of social control was an important factor in shielding that society from transformation into a bourgeois social order. It is a strange heritage provided by the Canadien Catholic church, for in its role as manager and disciplinarian, it did safeguard Canadien society from a rapid transformation and assimilation. But at what expense? The reactionary conservatism that the church propagated was surely not the only alternative. What has been lost in the priestly apologetics of Monet (1969) or the nationalist distortions of Rioux (1964, 1971), is that *la nation canadienne* did represent an alternative to bourgeois development,[26] an alternative uniquely Canadian, with its incorporated features of Native cultures.[27] It was that possibility which was contained and ultimately suffocated in a reactionary Catholicism which imposed a regime of discipline that easily matched, though was not identical with, conventional bourgeois state-based disciplinary activities. For the first hundred years after the Conquest, jacobin/republican ideas, the ideals of the French Revolution, and the political consciousness of the Communards of 1848 were part of the political discourse of the Canadien people. What might have been the consequences if that society had not been strangled in incense and excommunications?

But that is only part of the story. The question remains: why did the British administration and the politically dominant bourgeoisie of the colony not actively attempt to transform the Canadiens into a capitalist labour force? Or, if they did, why were they so unsuccessful? The answer lies in the realm of the form of production, the avenues to profit, and the primary interest of the dominant class in establishing a bourgeois social formation and civil society in the largely uninhabited lands of the colony. The Canadiens were contained within an ideology of reactionary Catholicism and within the political and economic domination of the bourgeoisie. This is most apparent in the areas of land control and reliance on the open American border to alleviate problems associated with surplus Canadien population. These aspects will be discussed more fully later, but let it suffice here to point out that no serious attempts were made to transform Canadien society in line with a capitalist mode of production. As the population grew and the settled areas could no longer sustain their numbers, the surplus population flooded into the United States.

> The Townships of Acton, Arthabaska, Drummondville were granted to individuals on the usual [that is, settlement requirements] conditions. The last two, granted in 1810, were still in their primitive waste state in 1860. Acton, surveyed in 1806 into lots of 200 acres . . . fifty-one years later it was still in its original wild state. Adjacent to populous parishes, this fine township remained waste while native sons unable to find suitable land on which to settle were emigrating to the United States. (MacDonald, 1966, pp. 14-15)

Wade (1964) estimates that 90,000 Canadiens emigrated to New England between 1844 and 1849. The settlement and development of Canada was a capitalist enterprise securely tied to the sale of land, and Canadiens could not afford to purchase it; preferred immigrants could.

This discussion of the historical context of the growth of Canadien society exemplifies the problem of borrowing European-based explanations for the role of the state in disciplining and transforming labour. Where within the formal Canadian state structure are the disciplinary institutions directed toward the Canadiens? The degree of success in containing and depoliticizing the Canadien population was such that it was not until after Confederation that a penitentiary and an extensive, though rudimentary, gaol system were constructed in Quebec. Furthermore, the major portion of the reproduction apparatus normally associated with the bourgeois state was given over to the church, often with little or no means of state control. Expulsion from the colony in the form of migration to the United States served to lessen the burden of control, and the surplus population was discouraged from— indeed prevented from—remaining within the boundaries of the colony, for reasons which will be clarified later.

UPPER CANADA: THE REPRODUCTION OF A BOURGEOIS SOCIAL ORDER

The formal creation of state disciplinary and reproduction institutions in Upper Canada, directed towards the primarily British population, followed a more orthodox path. After the Rebellion and subsequent purge, there was no class or class fraction organized in an alternative form and arguing a competing ideology to that of the dominant class forces (that is, the bourgeoisie and the Family Compact). The base of the social formation was involved in petit-bourgeois, "independent commodity" production and was largely in agreement with the British form of bourgeoisie social organization.[28] After a faltering start, the dominant bourgeoisie were able to realize their plans for economic and political development. The major political and economic interests of the internal bourgeoisie in this period were the achievement of a greater degree of economic and political autonomy and the universalization of their interests via the construction of a bourgeois nation-state. However, this was predicated on the possibility of consolidating their hold on the northern portion of the continent. This fell in line with the British Whig government's new plan for a colonial order. In general, the British government and the internal bourgeoisie desired an orderly and peaceful transition to a fully developed bourgeois social order. Their agreement over the use of the Catholic church to contain the Canadien alternative can be understood in light of these over-riding considerations. In short, if successfully contained, the transformation of Canadien civil society could wait until more important goals were achieved. At this stage, the bourgeoisie's hold on the land mass, later to constitute Canada was tenuous, and was still thought to be threatened by American republicanism.

An understanding of this state of affairs is broadened if we examine the dominant lines of economic activity of the internal bourgeoisie, keeping in mind the overarching framework described above. Of central importance to their endeavours was the control and sale of land. First, its sale and the provision of the supplies necessary for settlement and development were a major source of profit. Second, by maintaining tight control of land available for settlement (only through purchase), they could largely determine the type of immigrant who settled. They were able to groom the population by encouraging economically, politically, and socially desired immigrants to settle while for the most part excluding the "others." A major emphasis in terms of maintaining political control was the control of land and immigration.[29]

A problem with much of the historiography of the "left" in Canada has been the general overestimation of the importance and level of industrial growth prior to the end of the "great depression" in the 1890's. This overemphasis can be attributed in part to the reliance on European theorizing and in part to the desire to discover a labour tradition within Canadian history. The more serious distortions have been provided by nationalist writers like Naylor, who impose a "colonial dependency thesis" which denies the very bourgeois nature of the Canadian social formation and civil society. Of central importance to this debate is the characterization of the internal bourgeoisie and their economic interests. They were clearly international in their focus: they were centred in finance and commerce,[30] and land speculation was a major source of profit after the demise of the Montréal-based fur trade. The internal bourgeoisie's involvement in manufacturing and small-scale industry was a product of the diversification of their economic activities and seldom a primary surplus accumulation activity. Within the bounds of the available market, the general degree of diversification of the dominant bourgeois class fraction in the colony (men such as A. MacNab or A. T. Galt) indicates a lack of real conflict among types or forms of internally based capital. While there clearly was competition between fractions of capital within the colony (such as between the Montréal and Toronto based capitalists),[31] they were competitors over markets and state largesse, but not as different forms of capital.

The degree of significance given to industrial activity is crucial to the analysis of the role of the state in the discipline and reproduction of labour within the colony. Without major demands for capitalist labour, the need for an extensive state apparatus directed towards the management and reproduction of labour is greatly reduced. What part of the population, if any, represented problems for this bourgeois development? What were the state initiatives and activities in the realm of social control? What classes or class fractions of the population were problematic in terms of the specific political and economic interests of the dominant class? As Richard Kinsey (1979) has argued, the despotic control of capital assumes different forms at different periods in the development of the capitalist production process. In terms of an embryonic society, such as Canada in this period, it is also necessary to take into account the level of state development.

From this perspective, the rural Canadien population was problematic, but the over-riding concern was their political containment and management. There was no concerted effort to transform them into capitalist labour or petit-bourgeois producers of agricultural commodities. The reliance on the Catholic church as manager attests to this. The radical democrats of Upper Canada, after the Rebellion and the subsequent purge, were submerged within the rapid settlement and economic development of the

1850's, and their political movement was taken over by the liberal bourgeois and petit-bourgeois forces coalescing under the leadership of George Brown. They did not pose a serious threat to the construction of orderly, bourgeois class relations after 1850. The principal threat after 1840 was the Irish surplus labour in the colony, the result of the two major uncontrolled migrations into the colony, in 1832-34 and 1847-50. They were defined as a threat because their sense of social order and social relations was antithetical to the bourgeois social relations desired for the colony.[32]

The first major migration of a strictly labouring class, the Irish pauper migration of 1832-34, coincided with the rising political challenge of the Canadiens and radical democrats of Upper Canada. In 1827, when the need for a penitentiary in Upper Canada was first voiced in the legislature, there was only a very rudimentary structure of criminal-justice institutions. The common gaols that had been constructed in most districts were dilapidated structures, operating as catchalls for community problems and housing everyone from debtors and the mad to vagrants and petty thieves. There was no overall co-ordination and organization of these institutions nor any system of internal discipline. They were decidedly of peripheral significance in the pioneer settlements of this period. Control rested with the military and local militias. It was only with the political challenge to the rule of the Chateau Clique and Family Compact that concern for extending the disciplinary apparatus of the state arose. In his study on the rise of the British penitentiary, Michael Ignatieff (1978) makes the point that there was a sense of immediacy associated with changes in social discipline. Rather than perceiving the elaboration of disciplinary and reproductive institutions as falling on some continuum of linear progress, as liberal writers are prone to do, he indicates the piecemeal nature of ruling class attempts to come to grips with the internal ferment caused by the destruction of the existing social formation during the Industrial Revolution. Reform as a "rationalized progression" was seen by the British ruling class as too costly and beyond their immediate needs. Ignatieff clearly illustrates for the British context that the intensification of class struggle explains the dramatic shifts that occurred and the new forms punishment took under new conditions.

The persistent support for the penitentiary is inexplicable so long as we assume that its appeal rested on its functional capacity to control crime. Instead, its support rested on a larger social need. It had appeal because the reformers succeeded in presenting it as a response, not merely to crime, but to the whole social crisis of a period, and as part of a larger strategy of political, social and legal reform designed to reestablish order on a new foundation. As a result, while criticized for its functional shortcomings, the penitentiary continued to command support because it was seen as an element of a larger vision of order that by the 1840's commanded the reflexive assent of the propertied and powerful. (Ignatieff, 1978, p. 210)

What is relevant here, and appears to be true for western capitalist societies in general, is that internal political ferment and struggle were central to the extension and reorganization of state-based disciplinary institutions. This is seen by the fact that the first major debate and consideration of widening the network of state disciplinary institutions in Canada appeared at a time of political struggle. With the uncontrolled and undesired influx of the Irish paupers in 1832, the plan to construct a penitentiary was put into operation. It should be noted that the literature addressing this historical period abounds with descriptions of the unsuitability of the Irish pauper as labour or as settler. The Catholic Irish paupers' refusal to be transformed into a petit-bourgeois farming class or disciplined into capitalist labour was the basis for moral entrepreneurs to define them as a prime example of the "dangerous class." A ruling-class response was the construction of Kingston Penitentiary, which opened its doors for "business" in 1835.[33]

However, the state structure was in a process of formation at this time and, as is true for the whole pre-Confederation period, the level of bourgeois control associated with a fully developed bourgeois state cannot be considered complete. Criminal justice institutions were also in a formative stage, mirroring the state structure and the level of development of class forces and social organization. At this juncture, in the 1830's, the ruling class relied principally on the street violence of the Church and King mob, and of the "loyal" militia, both strongholds of the Orange Lodges which proliferated during this period.[34] Ultimate control rested with the might of the British military detachments in the colony. There was only minor growth and change in criminal justice and associated disciplinary institutions from this point to Confederation and arguably for the whole of the nineteenth century in Canada. The lateness of penal development in this country, relative to other western capitalist societies, further attests to the uniqueness of the Canadian situation.

In some societies, work houses and houses of correction supplemented the penitentiary and prison as new forms of discipline and punishment. They aimed at forcing the inculcation of work discipline among the surplus labour fraction, usually described as "indigent." However, in Canada, although moral entrepreneurs like Egerton Ryerson[35] continually used the rhetoric of British and American bourgeois reformers who argued for the inculcation of work discipline, there is little evidence of active attempts to construct a system of work houses. The first arguments for their construction occurred shortly after the Irish pauper migration of 1832-34.

In 1834, a House of Industry was opened in Toronto, but it was not a work-discipline establishment, operating instead as a house of refuge for the poor.[36] In 1837, on the eve of the Rebellion, the Tory-dominated Assembly of Upper Canada passed an act to authorize the construction of Houses of Industry in each district of the colony, but implementation was interrupted by the events of 1837-38 and it was not revived after the Rebellion. Arguments in favour of work houses surfaced at other periods in the nineteenth century but no institutions were built. While the ideology underlying the construction of houses of correction/industry in Britain was evident in the arguments of the moral entrepreneurs of the colony, the absence of any concentrated body of labour, or the need for it, reinforced ruling-class reluctance to provide funds for them, and indeed for criminal-justice institutions in general. The cheapest solution— banishment— became a major sentencing practice around 1800; this and its less legalistic variant—expulsion—were the dominant forms of social control in this period. This reliance on banishment and expulsion reflects the aim of controlling and grooming, rather than disciplining, the internal population.

There are a number of reasons for arguing that expulsion formed the bedrock of social control after the Rebellion. Both the British and the internal bourgeoisie desired the orderly creation of a bourgeois social formation. With a small demand for capitalist labour (particularly urban or industrial) expulsion served to reduce the accumulation of surplus labour in the colony. Furthermore, the development of a "proletariat" was viewed by some of the dominant factions in the colony as something to be avoided. Both the Catholic church and the conservative loyalists of the colony proselytized the rural lifestyle and expressed considerable antagonism to urban and industrial growth, which was often characterized as a product of the "morally destitute" democratic republicanism of the United States.[37]

This idea of expulsion needs expansion. In his article "Discipline and Capitalist Development," John Lea (1979) challenges the now prominent view that mechanisms of capitalist control reside solely or predominantly in state institutions. Although he does not deny the central role of these institutions, he does not agree that institutional discipline, whether of the prison or the factory, is identical with the subordination of labour to capital. This is particularly true in the era of transition to a capitalist social order. Lea argues for the disciplinary power of the realm of consumption, independent of a wilful act of capital. His reasoning is that after a population has been separated from the means of production (such as land enclosures and the destruction of cottage industry in Britain) the market place—the realm of saleable labour—constitutes a major means of discipline. An examination of the British context in this period reveals that the constant abundance of surplus labour drove the population to compete for work, adding pure economic need to the compulsion and discipline of the work-place and the apparatus of social control. This understanding is evident in the arguments of Malthus, Bentham, and Wakefield. In short, large portions of the population were forced, because of acute want, to acquiesce to the new mode of production and its attendant disciplinary order. This argument assumes that these populations needed to be, and were, coerced into the new social order of capitalism.

Lea's discussion of the relationship of production and consumption comes to bear most forcibly on an industrializing capitalist economy within a fully formed, though changing, social formation. This stage of development was not evident in the pre-Confederation period of Canadian history. In this context, the disciplining of workers to capitalist (industrial) production was both problematic and secondary to other developmental needs. The size of the internal population and the nature of the economic activity were not such as to promote largescale industrial production. Therefore in this instance the factory as a source of social discipline was also secondary. Production at this stage of economic development in Canada was clearly of a petit-bourgeois character—primarily involving small rural landholders and independent tradesmen. The market played an important role in separating the small capitalist from the strictly labouring population (largely unskilled in terms of capitalist production). The former was the chosen immigrant, the latter a sporadically useful tool: in short, migrant labour. Of particular importance to understanding this situation is the level of settlement and development, and the control and availability of land (that is, land as specifically capitalist property). With the growth of the colony after 1841, a capitalist social order was established, with selective immigration and tight control of land supporting the growth of agricultural surplus production. In this formative state of capitalist development, the disciplining of labour *to production* was largely left to the discipline derived from the market place. The specific interests and associated realizable needs of the colonial bourgeoisie, remembering that the base of surplus production lay with the petit-bourgeois farming class, were such that the disciplining of labour was incidental, except when necessary (in times of rebellion) to maintain the lines of development of the economy in a purely capitalist form and to sustain the drive for the establishment of a bourgeois nation-state.

Control of that body of labour which required disciplining was achieved through excluding them from the land, through the discipline of the market place, and at times through the use of the coercive apparatus of the state (such as the militia). Though labour was desired, the inability of the economy to employ it in any but the most sporadic and peripheral ways designated that labour to disciplining by the market. The possibilities of cheap land or industrial employment in the United States constantly reduced the surplus labour component of the working class by emigration. The entrepreneurial possibilities open to tradesmen moved many to collaborate with the bourgeoisie, thus further delimiting the need to discipline labour in the production sphere. In those periods of considerable pauper immigration—an event to be avoided—discipline was initially instituted via straight coercion and the unmitigated rule of the market place. It must be noted that from its birth, Upper Canada had no legislated Poor Laws and little in the way of sustaining institutions. The harsh physical condition of life in Canada at this time complemented the strength of market control. For the most part, the Irish pauper was largely unwanted, forming a migrant labour force. The market conditions prompted emigration to the United States, while the developing state coercion apparatus (such as Kingston Penitentiary) served notice to the migrants that they must adhere. The ability to refurbish both skilled and unskilled labour requirements via immigration reduced the need to deal specifically with internal labour and its reproduction. As the population of the country increased and the colonizing population expanded, education (as a means of inculcating the morality of the bourgeoisie) and migration (as a means of ridding the colony of its "social problems") formed the cornerstones of social discipline.

Furthermore, the docile worker was often an immigrant who had already been transformed into capitalist labour, with capitalist aspirations for advancement. Such possibilities clearly existed. Therefore, the development of institutions of social discipline was not formally constituted in the relationship of production and consumption, as they were in Britain at that time. The emphasis was clearly on the sphere of consumption, or the rule of the market place.

The economic prosperity and growth of settlement in the 1850's contributed to the amelioration of lingering political problems. The rapidly growing consensus over a bourgeois form of development was evident in the heightened power of the extensive network of reactionary, petit-bourgeois Orange Lodges, in the shift to bourgeois-dominated political debate, and in the absence of class struggle. The dominant bourgeoisie of Montréal and Toronto now competed over the spoils with their petit-bourgeois supporters scrambling for the crumbs. Only L'Parti Démocratique (Rouge) articulated a clear alternative to bourgeois development, but they were soon consumed by their struggles with the ultramontane Catholic church.[38] By Confederation, they were of such minor significance that they were ignored in the final negotiations.

The massive, uncontrolled, and undesired migration of Irish paupers fleeing the famine conditions of Ireland (1847-50) was the major intrusion into this orderly bourgeois development.[39] However, they, along with the

Canadiens, were useful as a migrant labour force in the construction of railroads and in the "capitalist" lumbering operations of the period.[40] Most, perhaps six out of seven, moved on to the republican United States. Those who remained were contained within shanty towns in Montréal (Griffintown) and Toronto (Cabbagetown) serving as a body of cheap surplus labour available for seasonal work. They did not, for the most part, settle on undeveloped land, nor did they take up agricultural commodity production—a result of their inability to purchase land and their rejection in the Orange Lodge-dominated rural regions.[41] The response to this class fraction in terms of state disciplinary activities was minimal. The population of Kingston Penitentiary grew between 1850 and 1857, mirroring the presence of this Irish surplus labour and, more importantly, the general population growth. From that point, however, the penitentiary population declined, not increasing again until after Confederation. Small municipal police forces were created in major urban centres in the late 1850's, but this reflected general expansion and growth of urban areas as much as the presence of the Irish ghettos. The shanty towns and their populations were contained, not actively policed. Of major importance is the relative absence of any arguments in the criminal justice field for the discipline and transformation into capitalist labour of the remaining poverty stricken Irish Catholic population. In short, they were controlled largely by the conditions of the market and the availability of the open American border.

The steady, orderly development of bourgeois society is evidenced in the very lack of concern for problems of internal order and social discipline. Reliance upon a selective immigration policy, land control, and the capitalist market was sufficient. Furthermore, the degree of consensus—the degree to which the bourgeois view of social order was universalized by 1867—is notable. Canada, aside from the church-dominated Canadiens, was a thoroughly bourgeois settler society with little need for the criminal-justice disciplinary institutions evident in other western capitalist societies such as Britain or the United States, with their large labouring class, industrial production, and rapid urban growth. At a time of massive restructuring of the very form of society and state structure, the absence of articulated alternatives which lay outside or in opposition to this type of bourgeois development is also notable.

A state institution which developed rapidly and served to universalize and reproduce bourgeois ideology and consensus was education. Along with expulsion, education formed the bedrock of state institutionalized disciplinary activities in nineteenth-century Canada. Needless to say, for Canadiens and Native Canadians, education was a major disciplinary and reproductive tool of the Catholic church.(Current debate about the relationship of education to the early Canadian state has addressed, almost exclusively, the construction and operation of the education system of Upper Canada/ Ontario, and thus the theoretical points, best illustrated vis-à-vis those discussion, will not be discussed here.) The limited demand for industrial labour, the possibility of importing skilled workmen, and the existing body of surplus labour all combined to reduce the need for reproduction of a disciplined capitalist labour force. Furthermore, the most common immigrants—the small landholding class, petty entrepreneurs, and skilled workmen—were already the products of the transformation of pre-capitalist populations which had occurred in Britain. They already mirrored and supported the reordered social relations of capitalism. These immigrants constituted the largest class in Upper Canada in the pre-Confederation era. In this context, the key to state reproduction activities takes a different form. This was a society primarily concerned with reproducing the petit-bourgeois social order it was then creating. Education was a means of reproducing the "striver ethic," the "possessive individualism" of the petit bourgeois. It was *the means* of inculcating their sense of moral discipline and enterprise. It is noteworthy that the widely accepted proposal for a centralized, free, and general education system in Upper Canada was a departure from the situation in Britain. Commencing with the School Act of 1850, an extensive network of educational institutions was put into place.[42] The major elements of this new system were fully adopted with the School Act of 1871. The argument put forward for general education mirrored the heavy involvement of the Protestant clergy (principally Methodist and Presbyterian) and their sense of morality and industry.

Stephen Schecter's (1977) article, "Capitalism, Class and Educational Reform in Canada," is useful to illustrate this theoretical argument. Schecter argues that education was directed at inculcating (capitalist) social and work discipline among the surplus labour, Irish Catholic population. Why would this be the primary thrust of education in this period? Schecter acknowledges that the dominant bourgeoisie were antagonistic to the programme of general, free education proposed by educational reformers, a fact he attributes to the absence of a factory system. Therefore, the transformation of this surplus labour into a disciplined capitalist labour force was a small selling point. However, the shanty-town Irish did serve as an example of what could occur if the social discipline promoted by these moral entrepreneurs was not constantly reproduced within the existing population. The establishment of shanty towns gave rise to a rhetoric about the criminal or dangerous classes, environmental causes of moral indigence, and the need to countermand these influences through the moral discipline provided by state-controlled education. Schecter's argument that education was to break "pre-industrial work habits, to Canadianize the immigrant worker" is misplaced, since only the Irish surplus labour class fitted this description, and they were largely unwanted in the colony (ibid., p. 375). Furthermore, to attribute some visionary programme to "discipline the nascent labour force for industrial production," which Schecter (p. 379) and Curtis (1980, 1981) both do, simply does not make sense. There are truths buried within the analysis and conclusions of these authors, but their direction is wrong.

The creation of an industrial work force and the disciplining of labour to industrial production were peripheral concerns for the dominant bourgeoisie of Canada at this time. One only need note the containment of that readily available body of surplus labour, the Canadiens, who were trained to subordination by the church. One cannot base an analysis on some conception of the foresight of an ideological fraction of the ruling class in isolation from the material conditions of the society in question. Further-more, Ryerson and his colleagues proselytized a recognizable brand of loyalist conservatism, one which clearly celebrated the rural life of the bourgeois and petit-bourgeois loyalist. The thrust of their remarks was addressed to the petit bourgeoisie and incorporated labour (primarily the skilled, labour aristocracy) of the colony. And this whole segment of society was in general agreement. Industrialization was not a selling point within this base of the social formation. Schecter's argument is distorted by his heavy reliance on European analysis to form the basis of his explanation of educational development in Upper Canada. These specific historical situations were vastly different, and though the development of education in Upper Canada was clearly related to the development of a bourgeois society, the focus of education was not on inculcating industrial discipline in an agricultural, non-industrial society composed primarily of a rural petit bourgeoisie and a largely transient labouring population. If we abandon the orthodox European Marxist paradigm, it becomes apparent that accounts like Schecter's overemphasize the disciplinary role of the state and state institutions in this period in Upper Canada. Certainly education formed an essential part of the whole network of disciplinary institutions (gaols, asylums, Kingston Penitentiary) erected within the colonial bourgeois state, but the very nature of the discipline was determined by the interests and needs of the dominant bourgeois class which in turn were both related to and a product of the existing social formation. In this instance, the establish-ment and maintenance of bourgeois hegemony in Upper Canada were advanced by the moral discipline of education; the creation and reproduc-tion of a working class, in particular an industrial working class, was secondary. Education fulfilled a reinforcement function in a highly transient and insecure society. It was directed at reproducing the petit-bourgeois base of the social formation. The Catholic Irish constituted one pole within the debate on education and served as a symbol of the antithesis of the desired social and moral order that the inculcation of social discipline through education was to achieve.

One final issue must be addressed. What of the "labour movement" or, for example, the struggles of skilled labour in Toronto and Hamilton? What was the class position and relations of this fraction of labour in this nineteenth-century social formation and civil society? The recent spate of social history, which attempts to resurrect or, perhaps, create a working class tradition for Upper Canada/Ontario, while sympathetic to a socialist position, clearly romanticizes the past. From the writings of authors such as Bryan Palmer (1979), it is evident that the small, skilled workman fraction of labour can be described as a labour aristocracy, one which made its own accommodation with bourgeois development.[43] Palmer describes their social and political viewpoint as a "producer ideology." The relative absence of a sense of class identity, both as a class in and for itself, is evident in the lack of political organizations which argued an alternative to bourgeois domination and produced a significant level of class struggle. Surplus labour continued to emigrate until the end of the nineteenth century and posed minimal problems for bourgeois control and legitimacy. The political and social domination of the reactionary Orange Lodges continued, providing a clear example of the ideological temper and the degree of bourgeois hegemony achieved in Ontario during the nineteenth and early twentieth centuries.

The acquisition and capitalist development of the western territories in the late nineteenth and early twentieth centuries were controlled by the bourgeoisie of central Canada. While the Riel and Winnipeg struggles stand out as hallmarks in the history of the Canadian underclasses, they were rare moments of conflict in areas in which bourgeois hegemony was not yet fully established. C. B. MacPherson's (1953) analysis of the nature of the social formation, civil society, and political struggles in Alberta provides the proper sense of balance. MacPherson illustrates that the rise of political challenge there did not represent the struggles of labour as a class, nor did it constitute the rejection of bourgeois development. Rather, it was a political struggle firmly located within a bourgeois social order. In Alberta, a petit-bourgeois-dominated social formation produced a petit-bourgeois political challenge to the economic domination of the grande bourgeoisie of central Canada. In part because of its inherent contradictions this challenge was unsuccessful.[44] It may be argued that the development of western Canada was different from that of central and eastern Canada, but the existing analysis has yet to establish fundamental differences in the form of social organization and civil society. Though the political struggles of the underclasses in the 1920's and 1930's were informed by a radical, socialist, and even communist presence, there is little evidence of a long-lasting impact.[45] The degree to which the trajectory of Canadian development has been seriously affected by the struggles of left-leaning labour or political organizations is open to debate.

CONCLUSION

The disciplinary activities of the state during the nineteenth century exhibited an emphasis on containment and control of political opposition and of other social problems. These activities can be characterized as the management of a basically bourgeois civil society. There are clear indications that the history of the western provinces exhibits a similar pattern. For example, an analysis of the struggles of the Native and Metis peoples in the west indicates that while a rhetoric of discipline, transforma-tion, and assimilation was apparent in state policy and initiatives, exclusion and containment were the major means of dealing with that alternative.[46] (However, this discussion of later developments is beyond the boundaries of this essay.)

The very nature of the Canadian state and state activity must be rethought in light of the thoroughly bourgeois nature of the social formation and civil society created in the nineteenth century, in light of the creation of a bourgeois nation-state which was not constrained by the hegemonic problems associated with the transformation of European post-feudal societies into capitalist social orders,[47] and in light of the relative absence of hegemonic crises since that point. To examine the functions of state disciplinary institutions in Canadian society, one must specify clearly their relationship to this civil society and social formation. An analysis of the role of the state in legitimizing the existing social order must address these specific conjunctions. This is directly relevant to the study of state disciplinary institutions and their role within the state and state processes involved in the reproduction of a bourgeois consensus in Canadian society. What is defined as a social problem and criminalized will reflect the containing civil society, as will the state's approach to social relations and social discipline generally.

NOTES

1. For example, the wholesale reliance on the "dependency model." This model was derived from the analysis of non-industrial, so-called "third world" nations.
2. For example, see S. Schecter (1977) and B. Curtis (1981).
3. Mathiesen (1974, pp. 76-79) describes four "social functions of imprisonment": 1) The expurgatory function; 2) The power-draining function; 3) The diverting function; 4) The symbolic function.
4. See G. Rusche and O. Kirchheimer (1939). Rusche's now famous dictum should be our starting point.

    Punishment as such does not exist: only concrete systems of punishment and specific criminal practices exist. The object of investigation, therefore, is punishment in its specific manifestations, the causes of its changes and developments, the grounds for the choice or rejection of specific penal methods in specific historical periods. (Rusche and Kirchheimer, 1939, p. 5)

    See also R. Gaucher (1983).
5. For example, see S. Schecter (1977) and B. Curtis (1981).
6. In England it was not until the end of the nineteenth century that any state provisions for general education were put into place. In contrast, a state-based education system was put into place in Upper Canada in the 1850's.
7. The "Family Compact" was the title given the ruling class of Upper Canada. They achieved their position through domination of the colonial state and state institutions, including the official state church (Anglican). They represented the loyalist migrants, many of whom established their position of authority in the colonial state on the basis of their staunch loyalist position during the Canadian-American War of 1812-14. They did not constitute a strictly bourgeois class, but their power was centred in their ownership and control of land and their position of dominance in the colonial state as representatives of British imperial interest.
8. "Chateau Clique" was the title given the dominant Anglo-American merchants of Montréal. As entrepreneurs and agents of British capital, they rose to ascendancy by capturing the economic activity of the colony, often at odds with imperial interests. They were a bourgeois class.
9. The moderate, liberal faction was represented by Robert Baldwin and the Bidwells of Upper Canada, and by John Nielson, Etienne Parent, A. Cuvillier and Pierre Debartzch in Lower Canada.
10. The Canadien representatives controlled the Lower Canada Assembly from 1818 to the point of the Rebellion.
11. By "dominant" I am implying widespread support. While the Anglican Church was the official state church in Upper Canada, and its leader, Bishop Strachan, a central member of the Family Compact, the Anglican Church was not the church of the majority of the population.
12. A major criticism of their arguments is their denial of the co-operation and co-ordination of these struggles. By arguing that there were two Rebellions, not one, the importance of this struggle is downplayed. Not acknowledged are the

alliance societies that were organized in both Upper and Lower Canada, as formal organizations aimed at co-ordinating these political struggles, and the clear historical evidence that the radical democrats of Upper Canada rose in support of the repression that was occurring in Lower Canada.

13. In reference to the Durham Report, the common wisdom of the day was that "Wakefield thought it; Buller wrote it; and Durham signed it." For a discussion of the substance and ramifications of the Durham report, see R. Gaucher (1982, pp. 145-62).

14. The extent of the purge of Upper Canada has been downplayed in bourgeois historiography. Keilty (1974, p. 8) estimates that between 1,700 and 1,800 people were charged with high treason and insurrection and were jailed; 32 leaders were hanged, and several hundred were transported; hundreds were exiled or banished; and approximately 25,000 were expelled. Letters to Egerton Ryerson from his brothers capture the tone of the Rebellion purge (quoted in Hodgins, 1883):

That under the pretense of resisting brigand invasion, large militia forces have been raised; violent penniless partisans have been put on pay in preference to respectable and loyal men; and these forces have not been placed on the frontier where invasion might have been expected, but have been scattered in parties over many parts of the interior, in order to exterminate discontent by silencing complaint. (p. 251)

And:

Emigration to the States is the fear of the hour. It is indeed going on to an extent truly alarming and astonishing. A deputation has been sent from this city to Washington to negotiate with the American Government for a tract of land on which to form a settlement or colony. . . . An emigration society has been formed, embracing some of the leading citizens. . . . A very large class are becoming uneasy, and many of the best inhabitants of the country, as to industry and enterprise, are preparing to leave. (p. 184)

These letters were not written by supporters of the radical democratic movement.

15. The Native alternative was largely destroyed in the east with the defeat of Pontiac (1763) and Tecumseh's forces (1814). From that point, the Native peoples were dispersed to the western hinterland or contained on reserves.

16. We can locate their rise to power at the juncture of the Reform Act of 1832, but they did not achieve clear ascendance until 1846.

17. There is considerable confusion over the meaning of a "laissez-faire economic order," particularly in terms of the nineteenth century. The phrase "laissez-faire" when associated with state policy must be understood in its particular historical context and meaning:

It is becoming increasingly clear that the idea of a "pure" version of the non-interventionist *laissez-faire* state in Britain in the mid-nineteenth century is a fiction. . . . As Polanyi argues, for the economic liberals of the mid-century, *laissez-faire* was an end to be realized—if necessary through state intervention— not a description of an existing state of things. (Hall et al., 1978, p. 209)

18. "Responsible government" became the British colonial policy. New South

Wales, Victoria, South Australia and Tasmania were granted it in 1851. In South Africa, the Orange Free State received autonomy in 1852, and Transvaal in 1854.

19. The Chartist agitations reached their final peak in the 1842-43 period, though the European Revolutions of 1848 gave the British a clear indication that serious internal political challenge could still erupt.

20. A common feature of the eighteenth- and nineteenth-century British ruling class position was a reluctance to expend state funds to alleviate internal problems. This applies to funding disciplinary institutions as well as to emigration and colonial settlement. See R. Gaucher (1982, pp. 196-206, 250-66).

21. Note that in New Zealand and parts of Australia the "systematic colonization" plan was put into place in a modified form. Wakefield had worked out his plan during his earlier stay in these colonies. For a discussion of the Durham Report and the colonial reformers, see R. Gaucher (1982, pp. 145-62).

22. Republicanism had been the bane of the British ruling class for over a hundred years. This struggle may be traced from their antagonism to Jacobin ideas in Britain in the eighteenth century through the American and French Revolutions. Radical democratic thought, whether it took a republican or socialist form (such as in 1848), was clearly a major enemy of the British ruling class. For elaboration, see R. Gaucher (1982).

23. What was demanded was the acquiescence of the Canadiens to the capitalist mode of production and its accompanying social relations. Ultimately, the instrumentality of capitalist ideology as expressed in the Protestant Ethic can be conceived of as the capitalist mode of thought. Friederick Sixel (1987) has done some interesting work on "the logic of late capitalism" in which he identifies "instrumentalist thought" as the "theory" of late capitalism.

24. It was the first British military administrator of the colony who referred to the merchants as "passing birds of prey." This phrase was often used in subsequent years.

25. Note that the British administration did attempt to establish the seigneurs remaining in the colony as a dominant force. However, their status amongst the population was such that these attempts were a dismal failure and were soon abandoned. The church was not easily established as a dominant force either.

26. The Durham Report provides excellent characterizations of the society and its alternative form, albeit as part of an argument for its destruction. For discussion of this point, see R. Gaucher (1982, pp. 145-62).

27. Independence from hierarchial control and close community relations were features of Native societies.

28. The use of the phrase "independent commodity production" is problematic. I am following the usage of C. B. Macpherson (1953) when I use petit-bourgeois to signify the political, social, and ideological position of the base of the Upper Canadian social formation and independent commodity production as representing a compatible form of economic activity.

29. A dominant argument within British government circles, reproduced within the loyalist arguments of the Family Compact network, was that the uncontrolled settlement of the pre-Rebellion period (in particular, the period from 1790 to 1812) had led to the establishment of a "Yankee republican" population in

western Upper Canada. This population was viewed as a major source of the Rebellion. This type of uncontrolled settlement was now to be avoided; via control of land and immigration, a suitable class formation (one capable of containing the lower orders) was to be put into place. The fact that control of most of the accessible land lay within the hands of the bourgeoisie, not the state, did not pose insurmountable problems since this land was now a commodity and as such available only to a "superior class of immigrant": in short, the bourgeois and petit-bourgeois immigrant who could afford to purchase it. However, the expedience of the moment often over-rode British policy, as evidenced in the unorganized exodus of the Irish Famine victims in the 1847-50 period. Obviously, in this instance, British concerns at home took precedence over their concerns in a colony which produced little surplus or economic benefit for the mother country. For further discussion, see Gaucher (1982 and 1983).

30. Finance was a central economic activity of the bourgeoisie who constituted the Chateau Clique of Montreal and who dominated the economic activity of Canada after the Union (1841) and responsible government (1848). Hammond writes: "By 1857 or a little later, the Bank of Montreal was larger than any American Bank and probably the largest and most powerful transactor in the New York money market, where it maintained and employed immense sums" (1967, pp. 167-68). Commerce was principally the import/export trade and supporting transportation.

31. See Gaucher (1982, pp. 314-17) for discussion.

32. See Duncan (1974).

33. The construction of Kingston Penitentiary was also in response to the local control of the magistracy and common gaols by the radical democrats. A centrally controlled penal institution would offset this local power base. Kingston Penitentiary was constructed on the basis of the Auburn model, named after the penitentiary in Auburn, New York. By 1826, this model of prison construction and regime was dominant in the United States. Its major selling point was that through the use of convict labour, it promised to be self-sustaining, as Auburn was by 1828, and "Sing Sing" ("the bastille on the Hudson") by 1831. It was a regime of congregate labour, secured by constantly impending punishment and its frequent application.

34. The strength of Orangeism in Canada in the nineteenth century should not be underestimated (see for example Kealey, 1976). The first Grand Lodge in Upper Canada was established in 1830. The Orangemen often fulfilled the role of "Church and King" mob, and were particularly active in the Rebellion period. By 1850, there were 40,000 Orangemen in Canada, and 100,000 by 1860.

    By 1867 Orangemen had found a secure place in Canadian society. There were few villages or urban neighborhoods without an Orange Hall. With its insurance fund, its youth section and its substantial press, the Orange movement had evolved into one of the most powerful popular organizations in the new Dominion. The Conservative Party which held office, with one brief interruption until 1896 normally included two Orangemen in the Cabinet. (Senior, 1972, p. 95)

    It was at the instigation of the Canadian Lodges that the first Grand Masters'

Conference was held in Belfast in July of 1866. Fully one-third of those attending were Canadian members.

35. Ryerson was the leader of the Methodist Congregation in Upper Canada. He is credited with splitting Methodist support of the radical democrats in 1833 and is noted for being the first superintendent and main architect of the education system in Upper Canada/Ontario.

36. By 1840, it was receiving a small subsidy from the state.

37. These arguments for a "rural" lifestyle and the denigration of the American experience are prevalent in the preachings of the Catholic Church and in the position of the Canada First Movement. For discussion see Berger (1970) and Gaucher (1982, pp. 45-20).

38. L'Parti Démocratique, founded to contest the election of 1848, was formed by a nucleus of the young Canadien radicals of L'Institut Canadien in Montréal. When Papineau returned from exile in 1845, he became involved with the Institut, and was thrust into the leadership of the party. The Institut and L'Parti Démocratique, as bearers of the *patriote* tradition, were a focus of attention of church reaction. By 1867, their position had moved toward the centre of the political spectrum. Though achieving some electoral success, they were a spent force by this time.

39. The problems in Britain, produced by the Irish Famine, were considerable. The British provided little in the way of assistance to the victims within Britain and Ireland, which heightened the clamour to escape the starvation and disease of this time. Similarly, no assistance was provided for their emigration. A purely "entrepreneurial" exodus occurred, with the British state turning a blind eye to their own shipping and transportation regulations. Canada was the initial destination of the largest portion of the Irish exodus because it was the cheapest passage. In 1847, New York state tightened shipping regulations, raising the cost of transportation and thus increasing the flow of emigrants to Canada. Though the colonies tightened their immigration regulations in 1848 and 1849, the bulk of the emigrants had already entered.

40. By 1850, a capitalist lumbering industry had emerged with close ties to the American market. As access to coveted stands of timber became increasingly difficult, the process of timber extraction changed. The farmer engaged in land clearing and the small independent woodsman (often Canadien) were replaced by an organized work force, controlled and employed by large companies.

41. Duncan (1974) argues that the Irish chose an alternative lifestyle, rejecting the "striving and enterprise" required to accumulate wealth, for the style of community life they had known in Ireland. His argument amounts to a characterization of the catholic Irish society as an alternative to bourgeois social order, which is similar to my argument concerning the Canadiens. This is an area of considerable interest and requires further investigation. See R. Gaucher (1982, pp. 560-68).

42. The School Act of 1850 was one of the first major pieces of legislation of the new "responsible government" of Canada.

43. For a discussion of the "labour aristocracy," see Eric Hobsbawm (1964).

44. See MacPherson (1953, pp. 220-37).

45. One should note that in the post- Second World War "cold war" years, the left within Canadian unions was under attack. The subsequent move to the right is attributable, in part, to this purge.
46. For a study of western Native movements, see Dobbin (1981) and Sluman and Goodwill (1982).
47. It may be argued that the French-Canadians of Quebec did pose such a problem in the nineteenth and twentieth centuries. An investigation of attempts to transform that society in the twentieth century would be fruitful.

REFERENCES

Berger, Carl. 1970. *The Sense of Power: Studies in the Ideas of Canadian Imperialism 1867-1914*. Toronto: University of Toronto Press.

Curtis, Bruce. 1981. "Preconditions of the Canadian State: Educational Reform and the Construction of A Public in Upper Canada: 1837-1846." Working Paper Series No 24. Toronto: Department of Sociology.

DeCelles, Alfred D. 1910. *The Makers of Canada, Vol. X, Papineau/Cartier*. Toronto: George N. Morang.

Dobbin, Murray. 1981. *The One-And-A-Half Men*. Vancouver: New Star Books.

Duncan, K. 1974. "Irish Famine Immigration and the Social Structure of Canada West." In M. Horn and R. Sabourin, eds. *Studies in Canadian Social History*. Toronto: McClelland and Stewart.

Easterbrook, W. R. and H. G. J. Aitken. 1956. *Canadian Economic History*. Toronto: Macmillan.

Fine, B., R. Kinsey, J. Lea, S. Picciotto, and J. Young., eds. 1979. *Capitalism and the Rule of Law*. London: Hutchinson.

Gaucher, Robert. 1982. *Class and State in Lower and Upper Canada 1760-1873*. Ph.D. Diss., University of Sheffield.

———. 1983. "On the Need for Specificity in Marxist Criminology." *Canadian Criminology Forum* 6., no. 1., 35-46.

Hall, S., C. Critcher, T. Jefferson, J. Clarke, and B. Roberts. 1978. *Policing the Crisis: Mugging, the State and Law and Order*. London: Macmillan.

Hammond, Bray. 1967. "Banking in Canada before Confederation 1792-1867." In W. T. Easterbrook and M. H. Watkins, eds. 1967. *Approaches to Canadian Economic History*. Toronto: McClelland and Stewart.

Hobsbawm, E. 1964. *Labouring Men*. London: Weidenfeld and Nicolson.

———. 1977. *The Age of Capital (1848-1875)*. London: Abacus.

Hodgins, J. G., ed., 1883. *The Story of My Life: Rev. Egerton Ryerson*. Toronto: McClelland and Stewart.

Horn, M., and R. Sabourin, eds. 1974. *Studies in Canadian Social History*. Toronto: McClelland and Stewart.

Ignatieff, Michael. 1978. *A Just Measure of Pain*. London: Macmillan.

Kealey, G. S. 1976. "The Orange Order in Toronto: Religious Riot and the Working Class." In G. S. Kealey and P. Warrian, eds. *Essays in Canadian Working Class History.* Toronto: McClelland and Stewart.

Keilty, G., ed., 1974. *1837: Revolution in the Canadas.* Toronto: NC Press.

Kilbourn, W. 1956. *The Firebrand: William Lyon MacKenzie and the Rebellion in Upper Canada.* Toronto: Clarke, Irwin and Co.

Kinsey, Richard, 1979. "Despotism and Legality," in B. Fine et al., eds., *Capitalism and the Rule of Law.* London: Hutchinson.

Lea, John. 1979. "Discipline and Capitalist Development." In B. Fine et al., eds., *Capitalism and the Rule of Law.* London: Hutchinson.

MacDonald, Norman. 1966. *Canada: Immigration and Colonization 1841-1903.* Toronto: Macmillan.

MacPherson, C. B. 1953. *Democracy in Alberta.* Toronto: University of Toronto Press.

Mathiesen, Thomas. 1974. *The Politics of Abolition.* Oslo: Martin Robinson.

Monet, J. 1969. *The Last Cannon Shot: A Study of French Canadian Nationalism.* Toronto: University of Toronto Press.

Palmer, B. 1979. *A Culture in Conflict: Skilled Workers and Industrial Capitalism in Hamilton Ontario 1860-1914.* Montreal: McGill-Queen's University Press.

Panitch, Leo, ed. 1977. *The Canadian State: Political Economy and Political Power.* Toronto: University of Toronto Press.

Ponting, Rick and Roger Gibbins. 1980. *Out of Irrelevance.* Toronto: Butterworths.

Rioux, M. 1971. *Québec in Question.* Toronto: James Lewis and Samuel.

Rusche, G., and O. Kirchheimer. 1939. *Punishment and Social Structure.* New York: Columbia University Press.

Ryerson, Stanley. 1973. *Unequal Union.* Toronto: Progress Books.

Schecter, S. 1977. "Capitalism, Class and Educational Reform in Canada." In Leo Panitch, ed., *The Canadian State: Political Economy and Political Power.* Toronto: University of Toronto Press.

Senior, H. 1972. *Orangeism: The Canadian Phase.* Toronto: McGraw-Hill.

Sixel, F. *Crisis and Critique: On the 'Logic' of Late Capitalism.* Leiden: Brill. (1987).

Sluman, Norma, and Jean Goodwill. 1982. *John Tootoosis.* Ottawa: Golden Dog Press.

Taylor, Ian. 1981. *Law and Order: Argument for Socialism.* London: Macmillan.

_____. 1983. *Crime, Capitalism and Community.* Toronto: Butterworths.

Wade, M. 1964. *The French Canadian Outlook.* Toronto: McClelland and Stewart.

Wrong, E. M. 1926. *Charles Buller and Responsible Government.* Oxford: Oxford University Press.

9

Theorizing the Crisis in Canada

IAN TAYLOR

THE PRESENT IMPASSE OF SOCIALIST POLITICS IN CANADA

No serious observer could have any doubt about the most important structural change that has occurred in the Canadian economy over the last five years. Overshadowing the continuing speculative chatter in financial circles about the possibility of an economic "recovery" is the brute fact of the massive and sudden increase in unemployment that has occurred throughout the country. The official unemployment rate rose from 6.9 per cent in 1975 to 10 per cent in 1981 and then escalated rapidly to 13 per cent over the twelve months of 1982. In November 1982, the number of unemployed people reached 1,388,000—the highest since 1936. Coming as these figures did at the end of two to three decades of rising expectations, the shock was considerable. Thousands of Canadians found themselves *suddenly* unemployed and unprepared for such an experience. Many others, especially the young, found themselves confronting long periods without work or even the prospect of never being employed at all. The fact that the increase in the official national unemployment rate has slowed, declining to 11.9 per cent by February 1985, has not significantly reduced the widespread anxiety over unemployment that clearly exists amongst Canadians.[1]

The "job crisis" is, of course, very uneven across the different regions and provinces of Canada. In February 1985, the official unemployment rate in Newfoundland totalled 23.4 per cent; in New Brunswick it was 17 per cent, and British Columbia 16 per cent. By contrast, the rates in Ontario, Manitoba, and Saskatchewan were 9.4 per cent, 9.4 per cent and 9.3 per cent respectively. Within the provinces, particular cities and towns were affected much more severely than others, becoming what Massey and Meegan have called "sinks of unemployment" with no real prospect of recovery (1982). Glace Bay, Nova Scotia became one of the best known of such "sink" communities when fires in a coal mine and a fish processing plant pushed its already soaring unemployment rate to some 60 per cent (*Macleans*, 15 April 1985).

Unemployment is also quite unevenly distributed across age groups. In February 1985, the unemployment rate for 15 to 19 year olds in Canada as a whole totalled 20.1 per cent, but only 10 per cent for the over-25 population. In Newfoundland, 37.9 per cent of 15 to 19 year olds and 35.3 per cent of 20 to 24 year olds were officially unemployed, and even in Ontario, Saskatchewan, and Manitoba (where the overall unemployment rate was relatively low) 16.8, 20.3, and 16.5 per cent, respectively, of 15 to 19 year olds, and 14.9, 14.5, and 16.4 per cent of 20 to 24 year olds were out of work.

These marked variations in the impact of unemployment seem to have been largely irrelevant, however, at the political level. One of the striking features of the almost unprecedented collapse in the Canadian labour market during the 1980's is that it has not resulted in any serious challenge in any part of the country to familiar bourgeois politics: it may even have been accompanied by a generalized strengthening of these forms of politics.

This observation has to be made with care. Many commentators have suggested that the worsening of labour market conditions, and the general sense of more difficult economic times, has resulted in an authentic "move to the Right" among the Canadian population. In 1982, the NDP government in Saskatchewan, which in the 1970's had been in many ways the most creative and progressive provincial government in Canada, was overturned; the following year, against many expectations, the NDP in British Columbia failed to unseat the deeply reactionary and apparently widely disliked Social Credit government of William Bennett. Conservative governments were returned to power in 1983 in New Brunswick (with an increased majority) and in Newfoundland and Ontario in 1985 (with some slight loss of overall majority), in defiance of economic problems that would surely have been the downfall of such governments in other times. Most significantly, in its election victory of September 1984, the federal Progressive Conservative Party not only massively increased its share of the popular vote as compared with the previous election of 1980 (50 per cent as against 32 per cent), but it also won the largest share of the popular vote in every province—an achievement that eluded even John Diefenbaker in his "sweep" of 1958. The Progressive Conservatives, under a leader whose succession was supported and partly engineered by the Right of the party, and who has many debts to pay to that section of his party, has an impregnable parliamentary majority over the opposition of 140 seats.

We shall, however, want to argue later that this increased representation of Conservatives in federal and provincial assemblies is not the product of an unambiguous "shift to the Right" in Canadian public opinion and that simple comparisons between the political situation in Canada and those in Britain or the United States are profoundly misleading. The inescapable feature of the present conjuncture in Canada is *the relative absence of political polarization.* Neither during the federal election campaign of the summer of 1984 nor during the first six months of the Mulroney government has there been evidence of the kind of determined shift, at the level of national politics, to right-wing populism and unrevised economic monetarism that has characterized the U.K. and the U.S. What we have witnessed in Canada is a continuing reversion to familiar political forms and, in particular, the ongoing search for a "national consensus." Throughout the early 1980's, such popular and authoritative discussion about politics focused primarily on the need to replace the Trudeau Liberals (defined generally in terms of the need for "new ideas") or on the merits and demerits of individual leaders or candidates for leadership positions at the provincial or federal level. We have not been confronted in rhetoric or in practice with the massive attack on liberal and social democratic policies that has taken place in Britain and the United States.

The absence of such a polarization to the right may be reassuring for some sections of progressive opinion in Canada. But the evidence on the overall political consequences of the new economic circumstances should not be cause for optimism among progressives. The collapse of labour markets seems to have encouraged the growth of individualistic adaptation rather than collective resistance or political radicalization. The mass rally on Parliament Hill in 1981 against the new economic "realism" of the Trudeau Liberals did not give rise to any concerted national campaign: Marc Lalonde's "6 and 5" wages policy was enacted, subsequent to the budget of April 1983, without any real resistance. In the sphere of conventional electoral policies, there is no sign of any major popular shift to the mild social democracy of the NDP. The New Democrats' share of the popular vote in the 1984 election was actually slightly lower than in 1980, although the party was more evenly supported across the country.[2]

Perhaps more significantly, there appears to be little chance of a shift in the politics of the NDP away from their mild, consensual social-democratic moorings, in order to deal with the harsh realities of the economic situation facing working and unemployed people.[3] There is no Canadian equivalent to the left socialism that has emerged in the British Labour Party in and around the person of Tony Benn, or in the women's and peace movements and the miners' strike; nor is there an equivalent to the left liberalism associated with the "Rainbow Coalition" of the Reverend Jesse Jackson in the American Democratic Party.

This is not to say that there is no evidence of working-class or popular resistance to job losses.[4] But the existing social democratic leaderships are very reluctant to give a voice to this resistance, and working-class defensive activity has therefore often taken a primarily sectarian or Luddite form.[5]

The issue here is the relatively unproblematic character of the domination exercised by the bourgeois state over civil society in Canada. In this sense, it is an investigation into the ways in which the bourgeois class appears to have been much more successful in managing social order (if not economic relations) in Canada than have other bourgeois classes in other capitalist societies. The evidence of 1984-85 is of a fairly bloodless transfer of power from one bourgeois political party to another, with very little accompanying ideological or institutional conflict. In this respect, this chapter can be read as an essay on the history and present rearticulation of a secure and successful bourgeois social formation.

Aside from being an essay on the political character of social order in Canada, this chapter is intended as an interrogation of the prospects for the emergence of a socialist alternative in Canada. Presently, the evidence provides unhappy support for commentaries that suggest that "social democracy" is headed "for the scrapheap."[6] There is certainly no evidence to support the optimism with which some socialist activists claim popular support for their programmes and ideas.[7] This chapter is, in this respect, underpinned by the belief that a first move in any thinking about the future of socialist alternatives must be the attempt to clarify our conception of how the economic crisis is being experienced by Canadians, not only in terms of their economic adaptation to changed circumstances but also in terms of their cultural and ideological conceptions of these new, hard times.

THE RECOGNITION OF IDEOLOGY

In Europe over the last few years, analysis of capitalist states by socialists has moved markedly away from a reliance on any form of economic determinism. The rationale behind the search by European scholars for other accounts of capital's relation to the state and "civil society" was, however, rather different from our current concerns. In the 1960's, in what were rather healthier economic circumstances for capital than those of the 1980's—when capital could have been forced to concede wages and indirect social benefits to labour on a massive scale—these concessions were still relatively infrequent and usually involved prolonged strike action by small sections of the trade union movement. Socialist analysis of the relations of capital and labour came increasingly to see the importance of ideology and, in particular, the unequal power of the bourgeoisie to influence popular conceptions of the existing economic conditions and to encourage a mood of "responsibility" or "realism" in the demands which trade unions made on capital. In the tradition of George Lukacs, this kind of analysis focused on the ability of "the bourgeoisie" to inculcate a "false consciousness" among workers even at the height of a capitalist boom.[a] This kind of conspiracy theory is still extremely widespread in some Marxist groups today, especially as an "explanation" of the weakness of labour's resistance in the current recession.

In much more recent socialist analysis in Europe, these conspiracy theories of ideology have finally been more or less jettisoned. Increasingly in their place are the so-called theories of hegemony on the one hand and theories of legitimation on the other.

GRAMSCI AND THE THEORY OF HEGEMONY

The analysis of "hegemony" follows the broad lines of the original prison writings of Antonio Gramsci and emphasizes the need to see the relations of capital and labour as articulated primarily through the state and, in particular, through the agencies of parliamentary democracy. Far from the state being a reflection of the interests of capital (in Lenin's terms, a "nightwatchman"), the state is seen as a "complexly structured totality," within which the longterm interests of capital are quite definitely dominant, but within which there is also evidence of a real responsiveness of the part of the state to the interests of labour and civil society as a whole. The most effective form of domination in a capitalist society is achieved not via coercion but via "the manufacture of consent." The point is put fully in the now classic statement of the Gramscian position forwarded by Hall and his colleagues.

> Gramsci argues [that] the capitalist state functioned best when it operated "normally" through leadership and consent, with coercion held, so to speak, as the "armour of consent", for then the state was free to undertake its more educative, "ethical" and cultural role, drawing the whole edifice of social life progressively into conformity with the productive sphere. The liberal-democratic state, he argued— with its elaborate structure of representation, its organisation of social interests through Parliament and the formation of parties, its representation of economic interests in trade unions and employers' federations,

its space for the articulation of public opinion, its organisational sway over the multitude of private associations in civil life—achieved its *ideal* form, its fullest crystallisation, when rooted in popular consent. These were the essential preconditions for the exercise of what Gramsci called "hegemony." (Hall et al., 1978, p. 203)

Three points about the theory of hegemony advanced by Gramsci and Hall and his colleagues need emphasis here. In the first place, we have to note the absolutely central role given to the state as the site on which the social and economic relations of capitalist society are reproduced ideologically. The role of the capitalist class itself is still of overwhelming significance, but its influence is indirect. The interests of both capital and labour are unevenly represented within the state. The inequality of this representation is of less significance, however, than the fact that "labour" accurately and authentically feels that it does have influence with the state. In this perspective, "labour" consents to the existing forms of domination within a capitalist society not because it is "sold" a "fake" (ideological) account of the relations of power by the ruling class, but because it experiences the forms of the liberal state as democratically responsive or at least open to influence or pressure (especially by comparison with fascist, feudal, or other alternative forms of the state).

The second point follows on from this: working-class and popular acceptance of "bourgeois domination" should be seen, according to the Gramscian perspective, as a reflection of the fact that the state does respond to popular needs and demands. Working-class acquiescence in existing power relations is in part to be explained in terms of the real gains that universal suffrage and the development of the welfare state have involved for the working class. It is important, for example, to recognize that institutions seen in other Marxist writings as integral in the repressive apparatus of the capitalist state (like the police, courts, and the law itself) can be seen, within some of the new Gramscian perspectives, as having key and popular functions in the provision of social peace in working-class communities and fulfilling what may be called "the popular demand for policing" (see Taylor, 1981b). It is not only the involvement of the state in the earlier postwar period in the provision of health, education, and welfare that has had important implications for the manufacture of social consensus within capitalist societies; it is also the state's role in the "coercive" maintenance of social peace: for example via the use of police for the arbitration of local disputes, the surveillance of local drunks and thieves, and the protection of working-class property. The famous distinction in Gramsci between consensual and coercive forms of domination is not an empirical distinction (alluding to the use of social welfare measures for social control purposes, on the one hand, as against heavy state policing on the other); it is more specifically a reference to the specific overall mode of social control in use in particular societies at particular times.

The third and vital feature of the theory of hegemonic domination is the recognition of the conditional character of working-class acquiescence to domination. Bourgeois hegemony is never finally and unequivocally "in place": it always has to be worked for. This involves the ruling class continuing, in Hall and his colleagues' terms, to "broaden and generalize the basis of class power" by encouraging the involvement of broad groups and social interests within particular parts of the state's activity. A classic instance of this generalization of power in the ultimate interest of capital would be the various instances of what is now widely called "corporatism" (the strategy of incorporating the trade union movement in state-level economic planning and decision making in "tripartite" commissions working "in the national interest")(see in particular Panitch, 1977). The point about such exercises, however, is that their success or failure is contingent on the mix of circumstances within a particular capitalist state (including the balance of ideological power); they are also affected by the condition of a particular economy or the narrow struggle continuing within it between employers and labour. In the now classic phrase, the determination of the economic operates "in the final instance": in any particular circumstance, however, the relations of capital and labour may be mediated through several levels of state representation and across a broad range of issues. It is by no means clear, therefore, that a crisis in the economy will produce a crisis of ideological hegemony, since that hegemony may be secured by virtue of appeals to a broad range of factors, of which the successful performance of the economy is only one.

For obvious reasons, the Gramscian theory of hegemony has been most popular and influential in European countries which have experienced serious economic and social problems over the last decade and a half but where there has still not been a successful challenge to bourgeois domination over the economy and civil society. But the theory has also been used to identify the conjuncture in those countries as involving both an economic and an ideological crisis. Speaking of the British situation in the 1970's, Hall and his colleagues put the point this way:

> the continuing attempt to bring off the project of social and cultural reproduction, as well as . . . economic production itself has had to be mounted in extremely unfavourable economic conditions, and in the face of a strong, though often corporate, working class with rising material expectations, tough traditions of bargaining, resistance and struggle . . . so each crisis of the system has, progressively, taken the

overt form of a crisis in the management of the state, a *crisis of hegemony*. Increasingly, the state has appeared to absorb all the pressures and tensions of the economic and political class struggle into itself, and then has been torn apart, by its conspicuous lack of success. (Hall et al., 1978, p. 214)

It is the existence of this crisis of ideological hegemony that forms the basis for explaining the development, and then the popular appeal, of Thatcherism in Great Britain. In place of the directive, top-down and "authoritarian-statist" interventions of the social democratic state, so obviously ineffective in reversing the widely experienced decline of the British economy, we are now offered the "authoritarian-populist" attacks of the Thatcherites on the welfare state and on centralized state planning of the industrial economy (Hall, 1979, 1980). An ideology that speaks now of "freedom" for individuals, and which indicts the authoritarianism of the welfare Keynesian state, creates a popular acquiescence for the rule of a government desperately committed to a return to the free-market as a "solution" to the current crisis of capital. The particular "conjuncture" which allowed the development of "Thatcherism" was not, however, specifically or exclusively economic. Margaret Thatcher was elected to the Tory leadership because of Edward Heath's failure in 1974 to convince the electorate of a Tory conception of the "national interest" that accepted much of the postwar social democratic settlement. Thatcher was elected to power in 1979 in the wake of a massive ideological campaign directed at the very philosophical and moral basis of postwar social democracy, not just at the ambiguous economic performance of the Labour Government of 1974-79. This ideological campaign focused heavily on the return of responsibility to the individual, on the need for moral and legal discipline, on the unity of interests of the British people (as against the sectional interests of trade unions), and on a variety of other largely social and political themes. Successive analyses of Thatcher's election victory of 1979 interpret the result as a product of a successful campaign to modify the ideological basis of class domination in Britain—away from a Keynesian compromise towards a new form of authoritarian populism.

The theory of ideological hegemony is not without its critics, either in Britain or in Europe. Abercrombie, Hill, and Turner, for example, have argued against the theory of "dominant ideology" being the primary source of working-class acquiescence to domination; in its place, these authors would prefer to restore a modified version of the realism of the later Marx, stressing the overwhelming influence of what Marx himself called the "dull compulsion of economic relations." They also cast doubt on the ability of writers in the Gramscian tradition to identify the existence and parameters of such dominant ideologies with any precision (see Abercrombie, Hill, and Turner, 1980). These seem an unhelpful attempt to resurrect economism. As Abercrombie and his colleagues note, they cannot "make . . . explicit claims about the relevance of our argument to other societies. We would not . . . be surprised if our argument had no relevance to capitalist societies in Europe and North America" (Abercrombie et al., 1980, p. 5). This is, in effect, an admission that an economistic account of domination is incapable of dealing with the differences between particular capitalist societies and, in particular, with providing any account of the different mix of struggle, conflict, and consensus that obtains in the political culture of individual capitalist societies. In particular, it appears unable to explain the now complete dominance of Thatcherism over the organized party of the ruling class in Britain (as well as the continuing influence of Thatcherism in a country still in massive economic decline) and the simultaneous *weakness* of the radical Right in a country like Canada, where there are now obviously quite severe difficulties with respect to the present and future structure and health of the economy. Economism yields no understanding of the specific ideological relations in particular national cultures.

HABERMAS'S THEORY OF LEGITIMATION CRISIS

At what is perhaps the opposite extreme to economistic approaches to the analysis of advanced capitalism stands the theory of the state and capital advanced by Jurgen Habermas. Habermas develops his analysis in broadly system-functional terms (rather than in terms of a class problematic); he sees the reproduction of capitalist economic relations as depending not on the ability of each ruling class to universalize its particular interest ideologically (a project of reproduction which, according to Gramsci, repetitiously confronts each new ruling-class formation). Rather, the emphasis in Habermas is on the performances and motivations of individuals within a "natural" system (that includes civil society, family, and work) which happens at present to be organized in the capitalist mode. For Habermas, the traditions which naturalized an individual's sense of citizenship, family responsibilities, and labour have become harder to sustain as natural adaptations, for reasons which require explanation.

At least two systematic reasons can be advanced for this "crisis in legitimation." One of these "crisis tendencies," as Habermas calls these system characteristics, is the growth of the public activity of the state itself and, in particular, the growth of the welfare state. Like some of the contemporary right-wing liberal critics of welfarism, Habermas is clear that the advance of welfarism *can* threaten capitalist economy by creating a sense of "state dependency" and, perhaps, individual "laziness". The particular term which Habermas himself evokes to deal with this disjuncture, however, speaks to a larger crisis in individuals' sense of purpose and meaning: he calls it a crisis of motivation. This crisis can have massive system effects, working back into the educational system and even into patterns of parenting or early childhood socialization.[9]

The other crisis tendency within advanced capitalism arises because of developments in the market, particularly the labour market. Advances in technology threaten not only to reduce the overall contribution of labour to the process of producing surplus value, but they also significantly devalue the value of labour itself in the individual act of production. Workers who once wielded individual tools with skill and craftsmanship are increasingly called upon to service machines that produce such tools by the million. This deskilling of labour is not actually an economic problem for capital (because it is a reduction in the cost of labour), but it is potentially a social control problem for capitalist states. There are not only massive increases in worklessness; there are also intensified problems of commitment and motivation in the workplace itself and, along with that, problems of the ability of the social and cultural system to work as a motivator of individual citizens and their children. Habermas's argument is that the reproduction of capitalist economic relations in the nineteenth century depended not upon some overt acceptance of the rationality of waged labour for capital, but upon the articulation in the public realm of much more extensive bourgeois (and even aristocratic-feudal) conceptions of authority in general. Values and beliefs were articulated to stress the importance of the patriarchal family, the moral value of status and wealth, the general validity of a fatalistic religious system and, an implicit celebration of the world and of nature as a place of art and beauty (within which labour achieved a dignity and purpose). All of these coalesce into two motivational patterns through which capitalist societies are reproduced: the patterns of "civil privatism" and "familial-vocational privatism."

In the twentieth century, according to Habermas, the ability of economic relations to reproduce themselves has been increasingly threatened by a decreasing sense of solidarity, group pride, and community self-respect within working-class neighbourhoods. In time, the cultural system's appeal to traditions of deference to authority and to the importance of family and community life—as a private preparation for a meaningful participation in public life—has lost force: in its place is left only the tradition of privatism itself. In turn, that privatization is left with only the market in which to explore itself, because there is no longer a viable link between private life and a meaningful public realm.

CHORNEY AND HANSEN: THE DECLINING RATE OF LEGITIMATION

In a recent, perceptive article, Chorney and Hansen have tried to apply Habermas's argument to the analysis of political culture in Canada. They begin by observing how Habermas's analysis is *prima facie* even more apposite in Canada than in Europe, since in Canada there is an overwhelming tendency towards consensus and integration. The instances of class conflict that do occur never even threaten to disrupt the routine function of the system. Moreover, "Canada itself combines all the integrative tendencies of modern capitalism with all the repressive fury of the nineteenth-century bourgeois personality" (Chorney and Hansen, 1980, p. 86).

For Chorney and Hansen the source of this enormous stress on consensus and on liberal individualism in Canadian political culture is a product of the particular history of the development of capital in the later nineteenth-century.[10] Though this development (for example, of capital expanding to the West, in the search for overall economic hegemony) has had broadly beneficial consequences for the mass of the population, it was a development which involved only small numbers of elite members in concrete political practice and representation. In an expanding capitalist society with no large organized working-class base, the consequence of the various economic struggles going on among "commodity producers" at the political level was the construction of an overwhelmingly bourgeois concept of politics. Not only was no party with an alternative, anti-bourgeois politics to emerge (until the CCF in the 1930's), but also the form of politics dominant at that time did not involve any fundamental political dispute between parties or interest. The public realm, therefore, was essentially depoliticized, in that visible "politics" had no structural connection to conceptions of collective interests or of alternative forms of moral order. The result is a peculiarly Canadian form of what Alan Wolfe has called "alienated politics." Chorney and Hansen's interpretation of Wolfe may be too instrumentalist, but the point is made:

> Alienated politics . . . is a politics designed to reinforce the competitive separation of people in objectively identical circumstances who might otherwise be capable of generating modes of collective action. This is possible because the state, and political institutions and practices generally in capitalist society, expropriate the common social power that individuals possess as potential members of a moral and political community and re-impose that power as an alien force directed against those from whom it was appropriated. (Chorney and Hansen, 1980, p. 86)

In alienated politics, political decision-making is reduced to a consumer decision: the choice between fundamentally similar products is decided according to the criteria of immediate individual self-gratification. This has brought about what Chorney and Hansen identify as a real decline in the quality of public life in Canada.

> Recent election campaigns confirm that politics at the electoral level has been reduced to widespread manipulation of public opinion with a heavy reliance upon professional pollsters, media specialists and advertising techniques. . . . The emphasis in recent campaigns on "leadership," the superficiality of popular journalism and the influence of dress and style on public perception confirm this decline. (Ibid., p. 69)

According to Chorney and Hansen, the decline of public life has some very strong negative effects. In particular, there is a real decline in people's interest in public issues and, indeed, in their interest in the public realm as such. There is a further accentuation of civic privatism. This has negative consequences not only for the progressive "statist" social policies advocated by Canadian Liberals but also for the vision of moral order based on integrated small communities and neighbourhoods supported by traditional Canadian Conservatism.

The decline of public politics, however, is evidence for Chorney and Hansen of a legitimation problem that has some potential progressive effect. They argue that "a significant portion . . . of the electorate . . . longs for a more substantive and meaningful politics" (ibid.). The evidence they cite for this assertion is the large number of undecided voters in the 1979 and 1980 federal elections. To this they could have added the tremendous decline in voting in federal elections since the early 1950's. In the federal elections of 1957, 1958, 1962, and 1963 (according to subsequent census enquiries), some 84 per cent, 80 per cent, 85 per cent, and 82 per cent of voters claimed to have cast their ballots. In 1974, the figure was down to 61 per cent. After a slight increase to 72 per cent in 1979, the figure in 1980 was back to 67 per cent. For Chorney and Hansen, therefore, there is some evidence of a popular withdrawal of legitimacy from the existing narrow form of bourgeois, consensual, and individualist politics in Canada. There is a chance that this disavowal of bourgeois politics could have constructive political consequences, especially in a situation where the economic rationale for working-class support for bourgeois parties is becoming less obvious.

EXCURSUS: POLITICAL CULTURE IN CANADA

As discussed in all the classic accounts, the development of capitalism in Europe in the nineteenth century involved the creation of a massive working class employed largely in manufacturing and in transport, ship-building and other industries connected to the requirements of profit-seeking, expanding imperialisms (see Hobsbawm, 1968). It was from that class that there emerged, in the late nineteenth century, state support for pensions, education, and health. In the twentieth century came the impetus for the creation of the labour parties that eventually realized the social-democratic reconstruction of many European societies after the Second World War. The economic and political advances of the working class in European capitalist societies have been considerable, though they have not, of course, extended to the abolition of capitalism. One of the important implications of the theory of hegemony, indeed, is that the acceptance of working-class influence within the state in Europe is "real," not an ideological deceit, and that the resilience of reformist, "class collaborationist," and other otherwise undesirable sentiments in the working class is explained in terms of the advantages which bourgeois social democracy *has* conferred on the working class in Europe (relative to conditions that would obtain in an unreformed free market capitalism). Another implication of the theory of hegemony, therefore, is that the form of ideological hegemony dominant in European social democracies until recently was not a pure bourgeois form but a social-democratic form.

The development of the Canadian capitalist economy and its associated social formation has moved along very different lines from those described by Hobsbawm for Europe. Industrialization has not at any time resulted in the employment of more than 25 per cent of the population in manufacturing and related industries, and, though it is obviously far too straightforward an association, the level of support for the organized party of labour has never exceeded that kind of figure either. Undoubtedly, workers employed in agriculture, mining, forestry, fishing, and other staple industries have created their own occupational and community cultures. Canadian labour historians like Stuart Jamieson, Gregory Kealey, Paul Phillips, and Bryan Palmer are also quite right to uncover examples of the vigorous popular culture and labour movement that exists in particular localities. But all this does not amount to evidence of a *national* working-class set of institutions and a body of culture actively at odds with the institutions and culture of the bourgeoisie.

Historical and sociological scholars of Canadian political economy have been at pains to identify and emphasize its distinctive features, from its "continental dependency" to its continuing reliance upon petty commodity production (Clement, 1977). Other accounts of the character of political and economic power in Canada have focused on the marked domination achieved by small numbers of elites over positions in politics and the economy at the national level (Porter, 1965; Clement, 1975).

But there have been few attempts to identify the connection between, on the one hand, these distinctive features of the history of Canadian political economy and its expression in the form of a narrow and undemocratic form of elite domination, and on the other, the specifically bourgeois form of hegemony that exists at the political level in Canada. Canada is, after all, extremely unusual within the advanced capitalist societies in that its two major political parties are *both* bourgeois parties. Neither of these parties even lays claim to represent or express the demands of labour or of specifically non-bourgeois forces (for example, in the way that the Democratic Party does in the United States).

Some scholarly work has emerged on the history of the bourgeois social formation of Canada, particularly with respect to the character of the educational and welfare systems. But much of this work has adopted a rather vulgar "instrumentalist" approach, wherein the history of educational and welfare practices is interrogated for evidence of farsighted bourgeois ideologies inculcating appropriate ruling-class values into the training and correction of troublesome working-class, native, habitant, and immigrant populations (see Curtis, 1983, Schecter, 1977).

A Gramscian would certainly take a very different approach to the explanation of the history of ideological relations in Canada. In particular, real attention would be given to identifying the specific, distinctive set of beliefs present in the development of social formation in Canada, which in turn find their expression in the political realm. Central to these beliefs appears to be a notion of "Canada" that carries particular and powerful connotations: a conception of Canada as an ordered and peaceable kingdom. From this perspective—unlike the dominant ideological theme in the United States of "America" as "a land of opportunity"—the advance of a free market economy is clearly a contingent rather than a primary concern, and the maintenance of a concept of social order and community is emphasized. It is a concept that finds its most succinct expression in the writings of the conservative nationalist George Grant, who distinguishes the concerns of the true conservative (the construction and defence of a moral community) from defenders of economic individualism (see Grant, 1965).

Canadian conservatism as expressed by writers like George Grant clearly derives its content and appeal from the days of pioneer settlement of Upper Canada and the founding provinces of Confederation. It is an expression of the real strength of the kind of bourgeois family and community that successfully survived the tempestuous early period of settlement in order to establish homesteads, villages, and towns in the rural waste. It is an image of the strong, resilient Canadian family settling the land.

Marxist readings of ideology can, of course, decode these beliefs as deceptions, that is as evidence of the false appeal of patriarchal or aristocratic-colonial Anglo-Canadian sentiment to women, Indians, or French Canadians. But such decoding cannot deny that the appeal of Canadian conservatism had some sort of rational basis in the real and lived relations of settler Canada. In particular, we should note the "moral promise" for all these groups during the nineteenth century of a hierarchical and patriarchal social formation as a guarantor of peace, social order, and economic survival in harsh and natural economic conditions and potentially conflictual interpersonal relations.

The advance of political Liberalism as a form of dominant ideology in Canada has never entirely extinguished the popularity of George Grant's version of Conservatism, especially in places like rural Ontario or the Atlantic provinces. What does seem to have happened, however, is that the advance of Liberalism has succeeded, until very recently, in persuading the mass of Canadians of an alternative agenda more conducive to the dynamic advances of capitalist economy.[11] In the absence of a developed working class contesting for power and influence nationally within the state, what emerges in Canada is not a social democracy, where the state is directly involved at the behest of labour in the intimate organization of both the economy and civil society, but a liberal democracy within a bourgeois social order with a longstanding conservative political culture. This "liberal democracy" certainly demands that the state engage in some general management of the social conditions on which the activity of capitalist economy depends, but it does not require that the state intervene directly or routinely in the everyday management of that economy. And Conservatives in Canada certainly demand that the key institutions of the liberal democratic state in this country, like the law, do not shrink from their proper role in the guardianship and reproduction of moral order. Provided, however, that a proper balance of general state management and particular economic freedoms is maintained, and provided also that there is no fundamental retreat by government from its responsibility in the moral realm, there appear on most occasions to be few grounds for fundamental ideological dispute between the two major parties.[12]

These remarks about political ideology in Canada obviously require considerable qualification. The impact of Conservatism and Liberalism has varied enormously across the country: the impact of bourgeois political ideology is different in provinces like British Columbia, where there is an oppositional labour tradition, to the impact felt in a province like Newfoundland or New Brunswick, where there is a much more secure ideological hegemony of the bourgeois parties. The importance of regional variations in Canada cannot be overlooked.[13] Any analysis of "dominant" ideology or class relations that looks accurate in central Canada becomes much more tentative the further one moves across the country. This is not an organic society; it is *not* on a par with geographically less dispersed European societies, dominated by powerful class fractions with both national and local representation.

But there can be too much emphasis on pluralism. While there may be enormous variations in the purchase of bourgeois ideology across Canada, this is still undoubtedly a country in which certain key images, such as that of "national unity" or of Canada as a traditional but moral society or an ordered cultural mosaic, continue to have considerable popular support. It is also a country with developed national institutions which represent the interests of different regional and national groups. And it is a country in which there is clearly a specific public rhetoric about Canada, "the economy," and national "politics" that is familiar to Canadians across the country. The significance of this public rhetoric may vary in fundamental ways across the different regions, but the rhetoric has an identifiable basis for all Canadians.

That basis is not merely institutional. The various institutions that identify Canada as a political and economic entity are also associated with certain cultural and ideological assumptions of what it is to be Canadian and what are considered the pressing issues and problems in Canada today. Some of these cultural assumptions undoubtedly derive from ongoing popular experience of the sheer size and varied geography of this country (see O'Neill, 1975; Blum and McHugh, 1978). Others derive from Canada's existence as an officially bilingual society, with a variety of immigrant cultures. Still other assumptions about "Canada" derive from the sense of being caught between the larger national influences of the United States and Britain and, in particular, from the sense that this is a national culture that has not yet developed and may not develop its own national literature, heroes, or autonomous rhetoric which could be capable of holding Confederation together in changing economic and political circumstances (see Armour, 1981). Many astute observers have interpreted the caution and conservatism of Canadians as a fear of the ever-present possibility of defeat of the culturally pluralistic, politically consensual, and essentially bourgeois concept of "Canada." There is widespread anxiety that the building is built on sand.

WHAT KIND OF CRISIS?

Over the last decade, Canadians have become much more accustomed to a new sense of "crisis" in the affairs of the country. In the late 1970's, an essentially political crisis dominated public debate, as the independentist movement in Quebec emerged. Simultaneously, serious disputes between the federal government and the province of Alberta seemed about to destroy the possibility of a national energy policy and wreak havoc on energy prices throughout an oil- and gas-dependent economy. In the fractious debates over the repatriation of the Constitution during 1981-82, serious doubts arose over the feasibility of a national agreement on a constitutional settlement (Carty and Ward, 1980), a controversy which continues to swirl around the Meech Lake Accord.

In the early 1980's, journalists and social commentators also began to find evidence of new strains in the fabric of social relations in Canada. Throughout 1981-82, a series of incidents of racism—ranging from Ku Klux Klan cross-burnings in Vancouver to systematic firings of Haitian taxi-drivers in Montreal—were reported in the national press; opinion polls revealed significant increases in antagonism toward non-white immigration.[14]

Most fundamental of all, the sense of political and social crisis was underpinned by the rapid escalation of popular anxiety over the condition of the Canadian economy. The sudden increase in the official unemployment rate from 8.1 per cent in February 1981 to 13.5 per cent two years later was not only a severe and often unexpected blow to those made redundant; it also had a fundamental effect on the sense of security experienced by Canadians. In November 1982, one-third of all Canadian adults reported to Gallup that they themselves (13 per cent) or some other family member (20 per cent) were "directly affected by unemployment" (*The Gallup Report*, 20 November 1982).[15] A heavy pessimism pervaded most discussion about the economy; Gallup reported in August 1982 that 55 per cent of Canadians described "business conditions" in their own community as "not too good" or "bad" (as compared with 29 per cent giving such a response in 1980). In the same period, a largescale study undertaken by Goldfarb Consultants in Toronto for a variety of business institutions reported that Canadians were, indeed, living "in the grip of fear": "[Canadians] watch their savings eroded by inflation . . . almost half surveyed feel someone in their household might lose his or her job in the next year [and] a significant proportion of them fear losing their homes to high interest rates." As a consequence, the report continued: "[People's] confidence in basic social insitutions is being lost at an alarmingly rapid rate. . . . The very underpinning of our whole economic system is being brought into question."[16]

The conclusion to the Goldfarb report seems positively Gramscian in alluding to the threats posed to "the underpinnings" of continued capitalist economic activity by the rise of unemployment and by rising interest rates. There was certainly very considerable anxiety in 1981-83 over the viability of familiar social and political institutions. In August 1982, Gallup reported a marked increase over the previous nine months in dissatisfaction among Canadians "with the direction in which our country is going" (81 per cent of respondents expressing dissatisfaction in 1982 in comparison with 64 per cent in November 1981).

This generalized anxiety also found a more specific expression in surveys revealing a marked increase in popular "fear of crime" in Canada. A Justice Ministry report released in May 1982 revealed that the "average Canadian" believed that between 40 and 55 per cent of crimes recorded by the police involved violence against the police; that prison inmates released on parole were almost certain to commit crimes of violence, and that the numbers of murders in Canada had increased since the abolition of capital punishment.[17] In November 1982, Gallup reported that 70 per cent of Canadians now favoured restoration of capital punishment in Canada (the figure on a similar poll in 1965 had been 54.8 per cent).

Popular anxieties were attacked at this time by the federal deputy Minister of Justice as misconceptions without any basis in existing statistical knowledge about crime.[18] But, as argued elsewhere (Taylor, 1983), the concern to deny the reality of popular fear of crime through references to statistical data may have missed the point. It seems clear that popular anxieties were (and are) activated not by knowledge of statistical rates but by popular interpretations of the changing character of crime or the continuing health of the social order. In part, these conceptions are abstractions, derived from print or television media reports (and in this respect are prey to all the "amplification" and exaggeration by journalists and their audiences so carefully dissected by liberally minded sociological labelling theorists). But the conceptions are also formualted in terms of expectations that people develop over time about social behaviour and social order in their own society, city, town, or neighbourhood. In Canada in 1982, many of these preconceptions were seriously disturbed by a series of homicides and incidents of violence reported in the national and local press.

The conviction of Clifford Olsen, early in 1982, for the murder of eleven young children in the Vancouver area[19] was followed in May by the revelation from the Attorney-General of Ontario that the deaths of forty-three young patients were under investigation at the Toronto Hospital for Sick Children and that a nurse was to be charged for four of these deaths (*Globe and Mail*, 24 May 1982). Later in the summer, the bodies of six members of the Johnson and Bentley families were found in a burnt-out car in isolated country near Clearwater, B.C., and a local "drifter" later admitted to their murders. Also in July, during a hostage taking in Archambault Penitentiary near Montreal, three prison guards were brutally killed and two prisoners committed suicide with cyanide. As I observed elsewhere, "whatever else we may say about all these various, quite different, killings, we did *not* have here a display of the image of the "peacable kingdom" of Canada to which many Canadians have traditionally been attached. We had, instead, a sense of the crime and the violence that is more characteristic of social relations south of the border" (Taylor, 1983, p. 4).

There is no question that this sense of a "social crisis" was fundamentally underpinned in 1982 by the anxieties which had been activated by the sudden rise in unemployment and interest rates. But, as we have indicated, the uncertainties of the economy also allowed Canadians to give expression to broader anxieties about the overall direction of the social order. The relative stabilization of economic conditions since 1982 does not seem to have extinguished these uncertainties in the Canadian population: economists and politicians alike, looking in vain for a national economic recovery led by a marked increase in consumer demand, have frequently had to admit to the absence of fundamental consumer confidence. The continuing high rate of unemployment has clearly played a major role in restricting a return of economic optimism throughout the population, but there are other specific features of the "conjuncture" in Canada in the middle 1980's which any useful theory of crisis must try to capture.

SPECULATIONS

Neither the Gramscian theory of hegemonic crisis nor the Habermassian theory of legitimation crisis seem to catch the specifics of the Canadian "crisis." There have been signs in Canada in recent years of the political polarization and unrest that were anticipated by Gramsci; for him, a crisis of ruling class hegemony

> occurs either because the ruling class has failed in some major political undertaking for which it has requested, or forcibly extracted, the consent of the broad masses . . . or because huge masses . . . have passed suddenly from a state of political passivity to a certain activity, and put forward demands which, taken together, albeit not organically forumulated, add up to a revolution. A "crisis of authority" is spoken of: this is precisely the crisis of hegemony, or general crisis of the State. (Gramsci, 1971, p. 210)

There was, of course, a marked collapse during the early 1980's of the electoral popularity of the Liberal government and its replacement by another government with a massive majority in 1983. But there is little evidence of a serious decline in the ideological hegemony of either bourgeois power or capitalist economy. Indeed, as Chorney and Hansen themselves anticipated, there is some evidence of an intensification of popular support for capitalist solutions to "the crisis" (specifically in the popular sentiment that "economic recovery" would be hastened if there were a reduction in government intervention). This antipathy to governmental "over-expansion" seems to be a contemporary variant of a much more fundamental theme in popular attitudes in Canada: the widespread feeling that it is "work" for purposes of sustaining oneself and one's family that is the real source of wealth. The adoption by government of a coherent national economic strategy, far from providing essential controlling parameters to the free market of capital, is broadly irrelevant to the process of wealth-creation. In Canada, in contrast to Britain, for example, very little is expected of the government itself in the sphere of economic activity; there is no "broad political undertaking" in the economy for which the Canadian state has obtained "the consent of the broad masses." There is also no real crisis in the overall form of dominant ideological relations in Canada. To speak of a fundamental crisis is to imply that the existing ideological relations are indeed "social-democratic" in the European sense—a corporatist settlement arrived at between warring social classes—and that, as a necessary response to the undoubted decline of the economic possibilities in Canada, there is to be a massive retreat by the state from such welfarist commitments. There *is* no such full-scale social democratic settlement in Canada. Retreats by governments from expenditure commitments on health and welfare could therefore occur without involving a fundamental and visible reconstruction of the state's declared relationship to civil society (of the kind being attempted via Thatcherism in the U.K.).

Habermas's account of the systemic working of bourgeois ideology is undoubtedly more persuasive as a description of the production of conformity within the Canadian social formation. It is particularly persuasive in its description of the way in which politics in Canada has become almost indistinguishable from consumer marketing, such that political issues in the nuclear age are almost invisible and the only important question is the appearance and technical competence of leaders and candidates.

But there are at least two major problems with the Habermassian account in the form that is applied to Canada by Chorney and Hansen, as well as in its original form. We are given no analysis of the real dynamics of this "alienated politics." There is the implication (or the hope) in Chorney and Hansen that the narrow form of consumer politics achieving dominance in Canada could elicit some sort of repugnant, critical reaction. But the conditions in which this might occur are not described. Would this be a reaction occurring in the middle class or in the working class? Would such a crisis (at the level of political discourse) only be provoked by a fundamental economic crisis in the country?

We are by no means alone in criticizing the Habermas account of legitimation and legitimation-crisis on the grounds that these concepts are not articulated specifically in terms of class content or in terms of its relationship to "the economic." But the criticism is sociologically and politically vital to an understanding of the Canadian conjuncture. To make the point as clearly as we can, we need to understand the limits of, or the contradictions in, the cultural and familial privatism that seems to underline Canadians' relationship to each other and the state. Gaucher's chapter in this collection makes a start by unpacking the historical roots of Canada as a culture that is "quintessentially bourgeois," even compared with its European progenitors. In place of the sense of neighbourhood and class "community" in older European capitalist societies in the nineteenth century, there was in Canada, in the same period, a much more individualistic pioneer culture. Insofar as there was a role for the Canadian state in its early years, it was not in the economy: the business of the state—for example in its use of the early militia and penal institutions—was to contain or expel the various non-bourgeois populations who posed "alternatives" to the pioneer lifestyle (Gaucher, this volume).

The contemporary form of this family-based culture of self-interest has found expression in the consumer marketplace. As the content of the various pullout sections of any Canadian newspaper proclaims, amassing material goods is a major preoccupation of the Canadian lifestyle. The generally North American preoccupation with the construction of status and esteem through conspicuous consumption was keenly observed by Robert Merton and by Vance Packard. But critical theorists working in the tradition of Habermas have been at pains to see this subordination of individuals to the market as the source of a general shift from the nineteenth-century bourgeois concern with the health of the "public realm" to the present elevation of exclusively private concerns at the centre of the conforming life (see Sennett, 1974). Christopher Lasch's analysis of various modern examples of this privatism (like jogging or health programmes) as a form of "narcissism" (Lasch, 1979) may not excite much support on the left in its more Freudian formulations (see Engel, 1980), but there is nonetheless a clear need to examine the source of the appeal and the character of these privatisms. Critical theorists have alerted us to the existence of these issues, but they have not helped us enormously with the analysis of the broad culture of conformity as it connects—and reproduces—the facts of class and capital.

The second problem with respect to the abstract Habermassian concept of culture is its essentially functionalist and undialectical character. There is not much sense of the contradictions that exist within culture; there is also no sense of what Gramsci refers to as "uneven development." And this is a vital silence in a culture of such fundamental regional variation as Canada. The volatility that has been evident recently in voting patterns in provincial elections in Saskatchewan and Manitoba, for example, could be taken as evidence of something like a provincial crisis of hegemony in the prairies (albeit a crisis of social democratic hegemony in Saskatchewan and a crisis of conservatism in Manitoba). Habermas's theory of the state and of ideology is only a very generalized statement on the question of political and social formation. It contains no guidelines for the analysis of localism or regionalism or indeed of national struggles going on within an established nation-state. In contemporary Europe, and certainly in different parts of Canada (Quebec and Western Canada), these are fundamental features of the present conjunctures.

In sum, there is a desperate need for a theory of national and regional culture within Canada and for a better understanding of the relationship between contemporary political developments (like the much-feared and, for Canada, exaggerated "rise of the Right") and changes in cultural and social relations. This chapter is an attempt to encourage conjunctural analysis in Canadian left scholarship along these general lines. Once such a theory is in place, analyses of the role of the Canadian state in setting the parameters of social control and diffusing challenges to bourgeois hegemony will develop more readily and will offer accounts that are much more adequate historically and also with respect to future possibilities.

NOTES

1. According to the Canadian Institute of Public Opinion, "unemployment" took over from "inflation" as "the most important problem facing this country today" at the end of 1982 and the beginning of 1983. It is some measure of the change in economic circumstances in Canada that while 61 per cent of Canadians questioned in November 1981 identified inflation as the most important problem and only 12 per cent named unemployment, by December

1984, 56 per cent were speaking of unemployment, and only 25 per cent of inflation, in such terms (*The Gallup Report*, 23 January 1982, 28 January 1985). In 1983, indeed, unemployment was being described as "the crisis of our times" by the Canadian Conference of Catholic Bishops (Archdiocese of Toronto 1983).

2. In 1980, the NDP had 19.65 per cent of the votes cast nationally and elected 32 members; in 1984, the share of votes cast was about 19 per cent, and only 30 members were elected.

   Note: this paper was originally written in 1983 and updated in 1985. The considerable gain in popular support for the NDP recorded in opinion polls in the spring of 1987 might be seen as a corrective to the argument developed in this paper; there is, however, little evidence that this advance in the fortunes of the NDP results from the public espousal by that party of any clear or essentially *political* position.

3. The attempt to move the provincial NDP in Ontario to the left, and the separate initiative for the creation of a new socialist party in that province—both of which were occurring quite vigorously during 1983—seem to have died. In Quebec, the Mouvement Socialiste has opened up an important space to the left of the Parti Quebecois, but severe strategic problems clearly exist in shifting from nationalist to socialist popular politics. Other important centres of socialist activity exist in Nova Scotia and British Columbia, in particular. But in no province could the left be said to be highly visible in popular politics or within realistic distance of challenging the overall domination of the familiar bourgeois parties.

4. Perhaps the most notorious example occurred in British Columbia in 1982, after the rapid emergence of Operation Solidarity. The provincial New Democrats were clearly very unsettled by the prospect of giving leadership to a mass movement that was apparently more committed to direct action politics than it was to parliamentarianism, and generally kept a "circumspect" distance from the radicalized trade union.

5. We have in mind the incidents on the Quebec/New Brunswick border during March to May, 1983, when New Brunswick workers attempted to block entry to workers living in and around Pointe-'a-La-Garde but travelling into Campbellton, New Brunswick, for work, as well as the events in Shippigan, New Brunswick, in April 1985 when over five hundred unemployed workers went on a rampage against the fishing vessels and port-based property of local employers.

6. See *inter alia* Alan Fotheringham "Socialist Hordes Reeling at Latest B.C. Setback," *Ottawa Citizen* (and other Southam Press syndicated newspapers) 7 May 1983.

7. A good example of the deceits to which the left is sometimes prey (in assuming the real popularity of socialist or progressive ideas and thereby completely underestimating the hold of bourgeois ideas amongst working people) is the Draft Manifesto produced by the Ontario Left Caucus of the NDP in 1983. A pivotal paragraph reads:

   A New Democratic Party government will seek to give political power to unorganized and organized working people, to farmers, women, students and all groups subjected to national oppression. A New Democratic Party government will develop a plan to legislate the key elements of its democratically determined program as the first step towards transforming Canada into a socialist society. Such a government will seek to educate and mobilize in defence of its legislative program against entrenched power blocs that may seek to thwart *the will of the majority* [my emphasis].

8. In the work of groups like the Institute for the Study of Labor and Economic Crisis in California, for example, it is clear that a conspiracy is thought to exist on the part of a united and organized capital strategically to mislead labour on the "facts" of the current crisis. This work of misleading and confusing labour involves a variety of tactics on the part of capital: the task of socialist analysis is to identify what particular ideology or false account is being proffered in particular moments, in order that these ideologies can be overturned in practical struggle.

9. The relationship between legitimation crises and problems occurring in child socialization was originally discussed by Habermas in his essay on "Moral Development and Ego Identity," written given first in German in 1974 (Habermas, 1979).

10. Chorney and Hansen place rather more emphasis than we would, however, on the growth of the State (and, in particular, on "social democracy") in Canada as a source of individualism and consensus. We have already indicated that we see no evidence of a full-blown social democratic settlement in Canada. The source of the individualism in Canada must surely be explained in terms of the continuing primacy of market relations over individuals and the basis of the always rather urgent search for "consensus"—seen as the rather precarious self-concept of a national bourgeoisie with no strong sense of its historical mission.

11. It cannot be a burden of this paper to argue the point at length. But with observers on the left like Patricia Marchak as well as with conservative writers like George Grant, we could see Liberalism as a politics that encouraged the orderly advance of a free market economy in twentieth-century Canada, by legitimating "possessive individualism" as a desirable form of social relation (over and above the conservative stress on moral order and community). It did this within broad parameters governed by the state and with the state acting also as a guarantor of minimum living standards via the development of a public health and welfare system (Marchak, 1981; Grant, 1969).

12. Possibly the last occasion when there were grounds for fundamental ideological dispute over the government's role in the management of moral relations was during Prime Minister Trudeau's involvement in permissive legislation (for example, on questions of sexual behaviour) during the late 1960's. Accusations made against him in this period were suddenly abated in 1970 subsequent to his unequivocal invocation of the War Measures Act to deal with the threat of social democracy in Quebec.

13. An interesting, but programmatic rather than substantive, attempt to locate the question of "region" in a Marxist theory of the Canadian state can be found in Legaré (1983).

14. A Gallup Poll undertaken for the then Minister of Multiculturalism, Dr. James Fleming, and released in March 1982, revealed that 12 per cent of respondents now opposed non-white immigration altogether, while 31 per cent said they would support organizations that work "toward preserving Canada for whites only" (*Globe and Mail*, 6 March 1982). A further Gallup Report, released in December 1982, reported that 50 per cent of the Canadian population expected an increase in racial problems "over the next five years" (*The Gallup Report*, 4 December 1982).

15. The proportion of young Canadians under 30 years of age "directly affected by unemployment" was significantly higher than for adults, with 23 per cent reporting themselves and 21 per cent some other family member (*The Gallup Report*, 20 November 1982).

16. Untitled report of Goldfarb Consultants, Toronto, quoted in *Globe and Mail* ("Measures in Budget in Accord with Poll," 15 July 1982).

17. All of these popular fears *are* ungrounded in the statistical evidence about crimes committed by parolees (the vast majority of paroled inmates do not recommit), about the proportion of all offences known to the police which involve violence (between 6 and 8 per cent), and the impact of the abolition of capital punishment on homicide rates.

18. The release in 1984 of the findings of the Canadian Urban Victimization Survey, conducted by the Ministry of the Solicitor General, showed the limitations of the earlier reliance on official criminal statistics. This self-report study (based on interviews with 61,000 Canadians in seven urban centres) suggested that in 1981:
    > there were more than 700,000 personal victimizations of people over 16 (sexual assault, robbery, assault, and theft of personal property) and almost 900,000 houseold victimizations (break and enter, motor vehicle theft, theft of household property and vandalism) in the seven cities surveyed. Fewer than 42 per cent of these incidents had been reported to the police. Quite simply, a large number of Canadians were victimized, many more than the Uniform Crime Report statistics would suggest.

    This 1984 report did affirm that the majority of these incidents "did not involve those offences which evoke our greatest fears" (particularly sexual assaults and robberies with violence). But it did concede that the thefts of property which comprise the bulk of the "victimizations" are often far from "painless" and that they are much more frequent than official statistics reveal.

19. The Olsen trial came fairly soon after the conviction in 1981 of Peter Sutcliffe, "the Yorkshire Ripper," in England for the murder of thirteen women and the conviction of Wayne Williams in Atlanta, Georgia, accused of killing a total of twenty-eight young blacks. Perhaps unsurprisingly, the coincidence of these highly publicized trials fuelled an anxiety, which was given expression on a *W5* programme on CTV on 7 February 1985 that "there's a strange and frightening phenomenon in our society. . . . mass murder [and] it's on the increase."

REFERENCES

Abercrombie, N., S. Hill, and B. S. Turner. 1980. *The Dominant Ideology Thesis.* London: George Allen and Unwin.

Archdiocese of Toronto. 1983. *Canada's Unemployed: The Crisis of Our Times.* Report of the Hearing Panel on "Ethical Reflections on the Economic Crisis". Toronto: Archdiocese of Toronto (Mission Press).

Armour, Leslie. 1981. *The Idea of Canada and the Crisis of Community.* Ottawa: Steel Rail Publishers.

Blum, Alan, and Peter McHugh. 1978. "The Risk of Theorizing and the Problem of Place: A Reformulation of Canadian Nationalism." *Canadian Journal of Sociology* 3, no. 3: 321-48.

Carty, R. K. and W. P. Ward, eds. 1980. *Entering the Eighties: Canada in Crisis.* Toronto: Oxford University Press.

Chandler, D. B. 1976. *Capital Punishment in Canada: A Sociological Study of the Repressive Law.* Toronto: McClelland and Stewart.

Chorney, H., and P. Hansen. 1980. "The Falling Rate of Legitimation: The Problem of the Capitalist State in Canada." *Studies in Political Economy* 4 (Autumn): 65-98.

Clement, W. 1975. *The Canadian Corporate Elite: An Analysis of Economic Power.* Toronto: McClelland and Stewart.

_____. 1977. *Continental Corporate Power.* Toronto: McClelland and Stewart.

Curtis, B. 1983. "Preconditions of the Canadian State," *Studies in Political Economy* 10 (Winter): 99-01.

Engel, Stephanie. 1980. "Femininity as Tragedy: Re-examining 'the new Narcissism.' " *Socialist Review* 53: 77-104.

Gaucher, R. 1983. "Canada: The Quintessentially Bourgeois State," pp. 167-97 this volume.

Gramsci, Antonio. 1971. *Selections from the Prison Notebooks.* London: Lawrence and Wishart.

Grant, George. 1965. *Lament for a Nation: The Defeat of Canadian Nationalism.* Toronto: McClelland and Stewart.

Habermas, Jurgen. 1979. "Moral Development and Ego Identity." *Telos* 19 (Spring 1974), reprinted in J. Habermas, *Communication and the Evolution of Society.* Boston: Beacon of Society. Boston: Beacon Press.

Hall, Stuart. 1979. "The Great Moving Right Show" *Marxism Today* 23, no. 1 (January).

_____. 1980. "Popular-Domocratic versus Authoritarian Populism: Two Ways of 'Taking Democracy Seriously.' " In Alan Hunt, ed., *Marxism and Democracy.* London: Lawrence and Wishart.

_____., John Clarke, Chas. Crichter, Tony Jefferson, and Brian Roberts. 1978. *Policing the Crisis: Mugging, the State and Law and Order.* London: Macmillan.

Hobsbawm, E. J. 1968. *Industry and Empire.* London: Weidenfeld and Nicholson.

Lasch, Christopher. 1979. *The Culture of Narcissism.* New York: Warner Books.

Legaré, Anne. 1983. "Canadian Federalism: A Marxist Theory." *Studies in Political Economy* 8: 37-58.

Marchak, M. Patricia. 1981.*Ideological Perspectives on Canada.* Toronto: McGraw-Hill Ryerson.

Massey, Doreen, and Richard Meegan. 1981. *The Anatomy of Job Loss: The How, When and Where of Employment Decline.* London: Methuen.

Mouffe, Chantalle, ed. 1982. *Gramsci and Marxist Theory.* London: Routledge and Kegan Paul.

O'Neill, John. 1975. "Facts, Myths, and the Nationalist Platitude." *Canadian Journal of Sociology* 1, no. 1: 91-106.

Panitch, Leo. 1977. "The Development of Corporatism in Liberal Democracies." *Comparative Political Studies* 10, no. 1 (April).

Porter, John. 1967. *The Vertical Mosaic.* Toronto: University of Toronto Press.

Schecter, S. 1977. "Capitalism, Class and Educational Reform in Canada." In L. Panitch, ed., *The Canadian State: Political Economy and Political Power.* Toronto: University of Toronto Press.

Sennett, Richard. 1974. *The Fall of Public Man: On the Social Psychology of Capitalism.* New York: Vintage.

Taylor, Ian. 1981a. *Law and Order: Arguments for Socialism.* London: Macmillan.

_____. 1981b. "Policing the Police." *New Socialist* 2 (November-December): 42-46.

_____. 1983. *Crime, Capitalism and Community.* Toronto: Butterworths.

10

Theorizing on the Canadian State and Social Formation

ELIZABETH COMACK

In recent years, the efforts of Marxist academics have been directed toward a gaining a better understanding of the nature and role of the capitalist state in Canada. In carrying out this task, attention has been focused on such issues as corporatism, foreign ownership, and regionalism.[1] The papers by Gaucher and Taylor can be viewed as part of this more general effort to increase our understanding of the Canadian state and society. In particular, both authors sensitize us to the need for both an historical and theoretical specificity in understanding Canadian society. The differing historical preconditions and historical path of Canadian capitalism, in contrast to other capitalist countries, has resulted in a different configuration of the state-civil society relationship, different strategies of control, and a different situation vis à vis the current crisis. Given this historical specificity, one issue that emerges is the extent to which theoretical constructs formulated to analyze European countries are relevant when applied to the Canadian experience. As Gaucher argues, there is a need for "grounded theory"; our theorizing must be based on an analysis of the material life of Canadian society.

In their analyses of Canadian society, both Gaucher and Taylor have characterized Canada as a "thoroughly bourgeois social formation."[2] Gaucher bases this depiction on an analysis of the petit-bourgeois settler society of the pre-Confederation era (which, he notes, is to serve as the basis for further analysis), while Taylor focuses on what he perceives to be "the relatively unproblematic character of the domination exercised by the bourgeois state over civil society in Canada." The purpose of this chapter is to examine in detail this depiction of Canadian society as "thoroughly bourgeois." More specifically, such a depiction raises issues which have a direct bearing on both theorizing on the state and mechanisms of social control and developing appropriate strategies for social change in Canada.

A THOROUGHLY BOURGEOIS SOCIAL FORMATION?

One obvious question which needs to be addressed is: What does it mean to say that Canadian society is "thoroughly bourgeois"? In the extreme form, such a depiction is compatible with the liberal vision of a fundamental harmony between capital and labour. There is no inherent or inevitable class conflict. To use the analogy of William Lyon Mackenzie King, capital and labour are "the two blades of the shears which, to work well, must be joined together by the bolt of mutual confidence, but, if wrenched apart, are both helpless and useless."[3] While such imagery may be fitting for liberals, it is certainly problematic from a Marxist approach, since it precludes any discussion of a socialist alternative, given that the main motor of social change—class conflict—is absent.

Interpreted another way, "thoroughly bourgeois" suggests a lack of class awareness on the part of the working class. This second interpretation appears to come closer to that intended by both authors. Gaucher, for example, asserts that there has been an absence of significant class consciousness and class struggle in the history of Canadian society. Acceptance of this assertion (and hence the depiction of Canada as "thoroughly bourgeois") requires some understanding of what is meant by "significant" levels of consciousness and struggle. Short of a full-fledged class revolt, has there been no working class resistance? Has bourgeois domination been all that easy? Taylor clarifies the issue somewhat when he suggests that while examples of a vigorous popular culture and labour movement have occurred in particular localities, there has been an absence of a national working-class set of institutions and a body of culture actively at odds with the institutions and culture of the bourgeoisie at the national level.

Gaucher and Taylor advance this position in opposition to that of the "new" labour historians (such as Kealey and Palmer) who are accused of trying to invent a Canadian working-class history. Granted, in comparative terms the Canadian working class has been one of the less successful of the western working classes in forging political, economic, and cultural unity (see Panitch, 1984). But does this admission necessarily lead to the conclusion that Canadian society is "thoroughly bourgeois"? In short, is it possible to reject the position advanced by Gaucher and Taylor without becoming too doctrinaire (Marx said there *should* be class conflict so there *must* be) or being accused of romanticizing the past (by imputing class awareness to workers' actions)? Clearly, the answer to such questions will hinge on how "class conflict" and "class awareness" *are conceptualized*. Panitch, for one, offers some guidance:

> When it is said that a class is formed through conflict or struggle, this is *not* to be construed to mean that the history of a class is predominantly one of revolutionary consciousness and purpose. . . . It means rather that it is through workers' attempts to establish their autonomy *vis à vis* capital and the state that the working class becomes more than a collective object (with workers having only a structurally given exploitation and domination in common) and becomes a collective subject, an active, living force in society and history. The struggles workers engage in may be about wages or dignity, organization or control, elections or revolutions, but however mundane or lofty these struggles they become the stuff of class formation as they yield collective experiences, ideas and associations which are more or less autonomous and distinctive from those of other classes. In this respect . . . working class defeats no less than victories can contribute to the making of a class: it is in the process of coming together for the struggle that collective identities are formed. (Panitch, 1984, pp. 221-22)

In response to Gaucher and Taylor, therefore, I would like to argue for a specifically class analysis of Canadian society; one which can account for the nature of class formation and class structure in Canada over time. While a detailed analysis cannot be accomplished here, what can be offered is an indication of the general direction in which a class analysis of the Canadian social formation would proceed—an analysis which yields quite different kinds of conclusions and theoretical and practical possibilities than those arrived at by Gaucher and Taylor.

The starting point for a class analysis of capitalist society is the contradictory relationship between producer and nonproducer—between capital and wage labour. Here we can reiterate a point made by Gaucher: that relationship as it emerged in the Canadian context was "historically specific." European societies were confronted with the problem of transforming the "undisciplined" labour of the feudal era into the "disciplined" labour required for capitalist production. In contrast, the Canadian experience was characterized by the absence of a feudal stage of development. With no feudal restraints, the obstacles to capitalist development were more easily overcome in Canada than in most European countries.

This is essentially what Gaucher demonstrates in his analysis of the events leading up to Confederation and the formation of the bourgeois nation-state. Economically, Canada was a society of independent commodity producers and economic concerns centred largely around the sale and control of land. Politically, the social formation was characterized by the absence of an articulate alternative in opposition to bourgeois development. The labour organizations which did exist were essentially conservative in nature. They constituted a "labour aristocracy" with a "producer ideology" (Palmer, 1979). As such, there were relatively few problems of control, and those which did exist were managed (following Gaucher) by the strategies of containment, selective immigration, education, expulsion, and migration.

Nevertheless, the pre-Confederation era was a formative period in capitalist development. Gaucher himself recognizes that the creation and maintenance of an industrial working class was a secondary consideration at this time. Indeed, the Canadian economy during this period can be described as "pre-industrial." To quote Rinehart:

> the continued hegemony of the mercantile class derived from activities connected with the staples trade, land speculation, and control over the credit market rather from the appropriation of a surplus (and capital) through ownership of the means of production and regulation of the labour process. (Rinehart, 1975, p. 28)

Moreover, the underdeveloped state of the market signified a rudimentary division of labour. Artisans, for example, were relatively free of constraints in that they established their own production goals and patterns of labour. As late as Confederation, "blacksmith, coopers, wheelwrights, tinsmiths, and many other artisans practiced their trades much as they had been practiced for centuries" (Harris and Warkentin, cited in Rinehart, 1975, p. 27). In other words, labour had considerable autonomy and control over the work process during this formative period.

In order to comprehend the nature of class formation and the degree to which class awareness was present, we need to examine what transpired once industrialization began to take root, that is, once the Canadian social order was transformed from a petit-bourgeois settler society based on independent commodity production (of which Gaucher speaks) to one based on industrial capitalist commodity production. It was only once this transition began that the creation and reproduction of an industrial working class became a primary consideration and workers' control over the production process began to erode. Both of these developments generated particular problems of control to which capital and the state had to respond.

While there are some minor discrepancies among Canadian historians, most agree that by the 1870's the stage was set for the creation of an industrial capitalist political economy in Canada. The period from 1870 to 1890 is usually characterized as one of the rise of industrial capitalism and the ascendancy of the capitalist class; the period between 1890 and 1920 is characterized by the concentration and centralization of capital and marks the consolidation and entrenchment of industrial capitalism in Canada.[4]

During the initial phases of capitalist development in Canada, control over the production process by capitalists was neither assured nor complete. The formation of privately owned, profit-seeking corporations did not itself signal a fully developed capitalist mode of production. Even though corporate owners had an upper hand through their control of access to markets, workers in many industries still maintained considerable domination over production (for example, through control of wages, hours worked, and admissions to their craft), thus acting as barriers to expanded profit making and capital accumulation. Capitalist ascendancy, therefore, required breaking the last vestiges of workers' control.

Indeed, there were three general developments which characterized the changes in the production process during the period of capitalist ascension in Canada, developments which had also taken place at an earlier period in European countries. These included: the monopolization of Canadian industry, which in part allowed for greater capitalist control over production inputs such as labour; the increasing rationalization of the production process through mechanization and the use of scientific management techniques; and the subsequent "de-skilling" of the labour force.[5] Each of these developments contributed to the erosion of workers' control, thus furthering the entrenchment of capitalist class dominance. Therefore, in terms of the dynamics of class and class formation (not to mention problems of control stemming from the material base), the struggle for control over the workplace was at the heart of the rise of industrial capitalism in Canada.

At the same time that capitalist rise to dominance was characterized by developments which had transpired in other countries, capitalist development in Canada was also "specific," given the reality of Canada as a staples-producing economy. This meant that economic development progressed unevenly and with a fragmented labour market. One major consequence was that working-class formation was itself uneven and fragmented. For example, increasing mechanization in the late nineteenth century produced an "industrial proletariat" in the factories of central Canada, while the development of the mining, fishing, and timber industries which accompanied the opening of the west led to the creation of a "resource proletariat." The net result was what Drache (1984) has referred to as the "distinctive configuration" of production relations of resource capitalism.

The fragmented nature of the working class also meant that the response of workers to various developments (particularly as they altered the structure of the labour process and workers' control over production) varied considerably across the country in both form and intensity. Indeed, the working class itself was often divided over the appropriate forms of organization and political strategies with which to respond to capital. Conflict between the craft and industrial workers, the American and Canadian unions, the national and regional labour centres, and the labourists and socialists have all been well documented by historical research.[6] Taken together, these conflicts could be said to have mitigated against the formation of a unified, national working class. But is that to say that class awareness was absent? Does the lack of a unified working class mean that bourgeois domination, as Taylor argues, has been "relatively unproblematic"?

Granted, the interests of capital and labour did often coincide. The best example of this is the National Policy. Although a source of contention for labour because of its immigration component (it encouraged the influx of cheap, unskilled labour which was perceived as a threat to job security), the National Policy was not entirely at odds with the interests of Canadian workers. As Craven and Traves note, the tariff component of the National Policy posed a confusing dilemma for labour: "to the extent that it was the *sine qua non* of the industrial system, workers had a vested interest in its maintenance: to the extent that the tariff was a mechanism for redistributing real income from workers to capitalists, it was anathema" (1979, p. 15).

As well, Marxist socialism—although prominent in the mining communities of Nova Scotia, Alberta, and British Columbia—never did become a widespread phenomena in the Canadian working-class experience. Other segments of the working class, such as the labourists, were more willing than were socialists to co-operate with capital. Nevertheless, while the labourists were less radical than the socialists, they were certainly no less militant in their beliefs. To quote Heron:

> If these working class politicians [labourists] were not always fundamentally at odds with capitalism, they were certainly opposed to the version of it which was reshaping Canadian society. This was not a revolutionary challenge, but it was a *resistance movement*. (Heron, 1984, p. 84; emphasis added)

The issues of class awareness and bourgeois domination can be approached even more directly by considering Gaucher's example of the Winnipeg General Strike of 1919. Gaucher defines the Winnipeg confrontation as a "rare" moment of conflict in an area in which bourgeois hegemony was not yet fully established. Other writers, however, have presented a very different interpretation of the strike. Rather than a "rare" moment, it is argued that the Winnipeg strike cannot be viewed in isolation from the events of the previous decades or from other occurrences in the same year.

The labour movement had been growing in strength since the turn of the century. An increasing number of workers were becoming unionized,[7] and there was a growing demand for industrial unionism.[8] What is even more significant was the extent of strike activity. Jamieson (1971), for one, argues that Canada is a country which has had the most difficulty industrializing, given the level and intensity of strike activity around the turn of the century. Work stoppages were not simply "bread and butter skirmishes" but reflected a more fundamental conflict. Heron and Palmer (1980, p. 57), in their examination of strikes in Southern Ontario between 1900 and 1914, found that 50 per cent of the strikes which took place concerned "some aspect of control of the work place."

The year 1919 marked a peak period of labour unrest in Canada. The number of strikes, workers involved, and man-days lost far exceeded any previous period in Canada's history (Jamieson, 1971, p. 185). In this regard, Reilly asserts that the Winnipeg General Strike was not an isolated confrontation between capital and labour but was "only the tip of the iceberg of class conflicts that stretched from Nova Scotia to British Columbia" (1984, p. 8). Furthermore, Kealey presents documentation to show that the revolt was national in character and that "its seeds were not rooted in any unique regional fermentation" (1984, p. 15).

Clearly, such intense militancy makes it difficult to suppose that Canadian workers simply accepted capitalist dominance. However, an even more telling indicator of the extent to which working-class resistance to bourgeois domination prevailed was the use of coercive measures by the state. Police harassment and imprisonment of "dangerous agitators" was not an uncommon occurrence. Sam Scarlett, for example, was arrested "about 160 times" by Canadian and American police for his organizational work with the Industrial Workers of the World and the Communist Party (Avery, 1978). On a wider scale, the state regularly used the militia to break strikes and force labour back to work. Macgillivray, for example, notes that from 1867 to 1933 the military came to the aid of civil power in Canada on at least 133 occasions (1983, pp. 116-17). The threat or apprehended threat of domestic disorder was the primary justification for both the retention and expansion of military forces throughout the period. One half of the incidents in which military forces were used involved labour disputes.

The Winnipeg General Strike was one of those incidents. In addition to military force, the state relied on arrest, imprisonment, deportation, the suspension of democratic rights and freedoms (including the right to strike and freedoms of association and publication), and an extensive propaganda campaign to defeat the workers' organizations and discredit their leaders. The collapse of the strike (and similar strikes in other cities), followed by the fall of the One Big Union, took the steam out of the labour movement in the ensuing decade. But it did not permanently end labour unrest, nor did it signal the end of state coercion. Indeed, part of the state's legacy from the Winnipeg General Strike included the creation of the RCMP, which with its high degree of centralization and breadth of powers went on to prove its "utility" for breaking strikes, smashing radical trade unions, controlling the unemployed, and hounding political dissenters during the 1930's (see Brown and Brown, 1973).

In sum, a class analysis yields a different depiction of the Canadian social formation than the one advanced by Gaucher and Taylor. To say that Canada is "thoroughly bourgeois" implies that capitalist development proceeded unhindered. However, a class analysis suggests that the advance of capitalist industrialization and the subsequent erosion of labour's control over the production process was met by the resistance of workers. While the form and intensity of that resistance varied across the country, Canadian workers *did* respond. Moreover, in contrast to the pre-Confederation period (on which Gaucher bases his argument) Canadian capital and the state were confronted with very different problems of control in the post-Confederation period, especially given that the reproduction of a capitalist labour force had become a primary consideration with the rise of industrial capitalism. Consequently, strategies like expulsion and migration were no longer feasible solutions. Quite the opposite, the state was often placed in the position of having to accede to the demands of labour to ensure that wide-scale migration did not occur.[9] In addition, the "threat" which workers' resistance posed to the stability of the capitalist order meant that the state had to respond with both co-optive and coercive measures.

A class analysis of the Canadian social formation is sensitive to the fact that capitalist development and working-class formation, when they did occur in Canada, were "specific." But the analysis stops short of suggesting that the pattern of development and class formation in Canada was somehow "exceptional"; that is, that without a sustained national working-class presence, Canada has been deviant, deficient, and bereft of class consciousness.[10] Such exceptionalist arguments are problematic to the extent that they assume either a preconceived, fixed image of a monolithic, homogeneous working class or at least some ideal notion of what class formation and class consciousness should look like. Clearly, if we are to maintain a sensitivity to the specific nature of the Canadian social formation, it would be wise to avoid exceptionalist arguments.

Exceptionalism is further cast into doubt by the recognition that the social process of industrialization in European countries was in many ways mirrored in Canada once industrialization proceeded. This would also suggest that perhaps there is something of value in European Marxist theories for understanding the Canadian conjuncture. Ultimately, our theorizing must be "grounded" in concrete material reality. But there is also a need—at a more general theoretical level—to make sense of the Canadian state in both its form and the content of its activities (including state disciplinary institutions). Such theoretical generalizations could both inform, and be informed by, historical analysis. In addition, an explicit theoretical framework can serve to clarify points of divergence and convergence in the continuing debate over the nature of the Canadian social formation (not to mention discussions on the appropriate strategies to be used for its transformation).

SOME THEORETICAL AND PRACTICAL CONSIDERATIONS

One of the more troublesome aspects of depicting Canada as "thoroughly bourgeois" is its ramifications for social change. In effect, what it suggests is that bourgeois rule is secure in Canada; there is a "resolute attachment" to existing economic, social, and political arrangements. As Taylor asserts, economic, social, and political crises have occurred and, while they have led to an increased anxiety among the general population (over crime, violence, racial unrest, and the like), they have not resulted in a serious decline of capitalist hegemony. Given this picture the prospects for the emergence of a socialist alternative appear slim, if not altogether non-existent. Nevertheless, one could argue a different scenario.

What is especially attractive about Gramsci's (1971) concept of hegemony is that it captures the tenuous nature of bourgeois rule. Hegemony— the universalization of capitalist class interests—was for Gramsci not an automatic condition but a continuous and pervasive effort conducted within civil society and by the state. The scope and forms of hegemonic control— and hence its impact—varied greatly from society to society. As Boggs (1976) notes, Gramsci was one theorist who brought his own theoretical generalizations down to earth. Although his primary focus was Italy, Gramsci also devoted attention to several other countries. His comments on the United States are noteworthy, since they could just as easily have been made of Canada. Gramsci saw the United States as the best example of a society in which the ruling class had established an almost complete ideological hegemony. This, he suggested, was largely owing to the absence of a feudal stage of development in that country (Boggs, 1976, pp. 50-51). Nonetheless, hegemony was never total nor static. Because it was not automatic, and because of the contradictory nature of the system in which it operates, hegemonic control was subject to periodic crises.

Hegemonic crises, according to Gramsci, can result from a number of different causes. They are not necessarily the outcome of an economic crisis, although an economic crisis could create the conditions for one by putting capital and the state in a position of making mistakes in responding to economic problems. A "crisis of hegemony" could result from unpopular actions of capital and the state or from increased political activism by previously passive masses (see Carnoy, 1984, pp. 78-80). Whatever the specific causes, a hegemonic crisis amounts to a "crisis of authority" of bourgeois rule. There is a loss of consensus. The domination of capital and the state is based on the exercise of coercive force alone.

If a "crisis of hegemony" is seen not simply as an event or even a series of events, but as a process, then there emerges a somewhat different interpretation from Taylor's of the current crisis of Canadian capitalism. Taylor himself provides us with the basis for this interpretation (1983, Chapter 3).

In discussing the restructuring of public expenditure that has taken place in Canada during the late 1970's and early 1980's, Taylor suggests that what has been emerging during this period is a new "law and order state." While welfare state expenditures (on health, welfare, and education) have continued to fall over the last decade, expenditures in the areas of social control and criminal justice have increased considerably. For instance, expenditure on police, courts, and corrections rose from about $100 million in the early 1960's to $1 billion in the late 1970's (Demers, Chan, and Ericson cited in Taylor 1983, p. 141). The expenditure on the administration of justice in 1973-74 of $1.2 billion has been projected to an expenditure in 1985-86 of $7.5 billion (cited in Taylor, 1983, p. 141). This massive inflation of expenditure on "law and order" has been accompanied by an expansion of state disciplinary activity which, when taken together, have given credence to the opinion that "Canada is being transformed into one of the most heavily policed of western societies, with one of the highest rates of imprisonment in the West" (Taylor, 1983, p. 141).[11]

This reconstruction can be viewed as part of the overall effort by capital and the state to manage the effects of the current crisis. What is significant is that it marks a definite shift away from "consent" (providing welfare state services) and toward "coercion" (maintenance of law and order).[12] The viability of this strategy, however, may be in doubt. Withdrawal of welfare monies only aggravates the plight of those hit hardest by the economic crisis, such as the poor and the unemployed. Legitimizing increased state disciplinary activity will only be possible so long as the public's fear of crime and social disorder can be tapped. In short, what we may be witnessing is a hegemonic control that is *in the process of breaking down*. And if this is the case, then there is a real need to explore appropriate strategies for the left in Canada to pursue.

According to Gramsci, the erosion of the ideological hegemony of capital and the state could only create the possibility of advancing towards socialism. Social transformation also depended upon the capacity of the left to take advantage of the situation and create a "counter hegemony." In other words, the struggle for change would not simply be structural in nature (dependent upon the level of organization and unity of the socialist movement); it would be *ideological* as well. The position of the dominant class would have to be demystified at the level of popular beliefs and then replaced by a more liberating set of values. In this respect, socialist academics in Canada could contribute to the formation of a counter hegemony by penetrating the "false world of appearances" rooted in the dominant belief system (Boggs, 1976, pp. 40-42).

As Taylor has noted, political culture in Canada has traditionally centred on certain key images: "peace and security," "national unity," and so on. Such conceptions are not false in that they do have a real appeal and support among the general population. Nevertheless, these images are also very much a part of the ideological defence—the "official world view"—that is perpetuated by state and cultural control systems within society (such as the media) to ensure the stability of the class order of capital. In this respect, one of the central features of ideology is that it distorts. Conceptions of Canada as an "ordered and peaceable kingdom" or the popular image of the RCMP as the "guardians of democracy" serve important ideological functions; they cannot be accepted unconditionally.[13] What needs to be distinguished, therefore, is the difference between "fake accounts" and "appearances." As Hall and his colleagues state:

> The notion of "appearance" as used in Marx is not the same as the commonsense meaning of the term "false appearances," if by that we understand something which is simply an optical illusion, a fantasy in men's imagination. The term "appearance" in Marx implies a theory of *darstellung* or representation—a theory that a social formation is a complex unity, composed of different levels and practices, where there is no necessary identity or correspondence between the effects a relation produces at its different levels. Thus "appearances" in this sense are false, not because they do not exist, but because they invite us to mistake surface effects for real "relations." (Hall et al., 1978, p. 198)

Critical analysis, therefore, must uncover how the "culture of conformity" is maintained and reproduced, not only historically through the generation of a particular political culture, but also currently in terms of defining the very nature of the crisis. For example, rather than viewing media-generated reports of crime and racism as evidence of people's cultural understanding of the kind of crisis they are experiencing, we need to question the role which such phenomena—as "appearances"—may themselves play in the production of capitalist hegemony.

One might argue, for instance, that to successfully mediate class conflicts and re-establish working-class consent, problems have to be dealt with in other than class terms. From this perspective, the emphasis in the media on racial conflicts and the increasingly violent nature of crime could be interpreted as part of a more general effort to promote a particular definition of the situation. Indeed, in the hands of the media, talk of crime has generated all manner of misplaced fears and perceptions among the public. Similarly, racism has been utilized by the media and politicians to influence people's cultural understanding.[14]

This is not to suggest that such phenomena are illusory. Crime is a very real fact in our society, and racist sentiments have been prevalent among Canadian workers.[15] What is being suggested, however, is that such phenomena need to be situated in the social relations out of which they arise. Otherwise, the picture that emerges is that the crisis we are experiencing is neither an economic nor a class one. Rather, problems are rooted in the changing nature of crime or the existence of racism; hence, the appropriate solutions would be in fighting crime (by reinstituting capital punishment, for example) or alleviating racial tension (such as through more "selective" immigration policies). In short, the *class-based nature* of the crisis is never questioned.

The creation of a counter hegemony, therefore, must include a continual defining and redefining of crime and race issues in political-economic (class) terms. At the same time, there is a need to address the real anxieties which such issues have generated among the public. The left, for example, has typically shied away from "law and order" issues. As a result, the right has not only been able to capitalize on the public's fears and anxieties but has also had a relatively free rein in defining the terms and parameters of how law and order issues are to be resolved.

The demystification or unmasking of "appearances" is one step toward the formation of a counter hegemony. However, the creation of a working class hegemony will also require organization and unity at the political and economic levels. As Taylor has noted, the left in Canada has failed to offer a political programme that can stand as a real alternative to existing bourgeois political parties. Economically, working class hegemony will have to confront the obstacle of the historically fragmented nature of the Canadian working class. Overcoming this obstacle will require the continual expansion of consent of not only workers, but other diverse groups (such as women and Natives). Clearly, the Canadian left does have much work to do, and one should not be overly optimistic about the prospects of a socialist alternative emerging in Canada. Nevertheless, the class analysis of the Canadian social formation which has been suggested here does offer a set of theoretical and practical possibilities for realizing a socialist alternative. On that basis, it merits further consideration.

NOTES

1. For a comprehensive review of these developments see Stevenson (1983).
2. See also Taylor (1983, Chapter 1).
3. Canada, *Sessional Papers* (1903) No. 36, "Report of the Royal Commission on Industrial Disputes in the Province of British Columbia," p. 66.
4. See for example Rinehart (1975); Cross and Kealey (1983: General Introduction).
5. All of which, it should be noted, occurred unevenly in terms of the different industries and regions of Canada. See for example Kealey (1976); Marglin (1974); Meyers (1972); and Heron and Palmer (1980).
6. See, for example, Phillips (1967); Robin (1972); and Heron (1984).
7. Logan (1948) documents the growth of unions based on *Labor Gazette* surveys.
8. The United Mine Workers of America, for example, grew from a membership of 10,000 in 1897 to 400,000 in 1913 (Avery, 1979, p. 56).
9. Ostry (1960) has suggested that the National Policy, which was first proposed by the Tories during the election of 1872, was inextricably connected with the passage of the Trade Union Act (which protected workers from the charge of criminal conspiracy for membership in unions) that same year. Ostry notes that one of the main ingredients of the National Policy's strategy was the provision and maintenance of an adequate skilled labour force. But skilled Canadian workers had been emigrating to the U.S. in search of higher wages. So long as unionization was prohibited, and no effective check was available to prevent employers from reducing wages, emigration would continue. Added to this, British workers, who had already won the right to unionize, would refrain from moving to Canada. To gain the co-operation of labour, therefore, John A. Macdonald had to present himself as a "working man's friend," a "simple cabinet maker" with the workers' interests at heart. Consequently, the Trade Union Act can be interpreted as a necessary (although not sufficient) condition for the success of the National Policy.
10. See Wilentz's (1984) argument against exceptionalism as it is applied to the American labour movement.
11. This expansion of state disciplinary activity is evidenced by the increased numbers of police officers (1.8 per 1,000 people in 1969 to 2.3 per 1,000 in 1977) and admissions to Canadian penitentiaries and jails (237,103 in 1980-81,

a 14 per cent increase as compared to 1978-79) (cited in Taylor, 1983, pp. 141-42).

12. The movement away from consent and toward coercion is also evidenced in the state's involvement in labour relations. Panitch and Swartz (1984) note that this shift toward coercive measures is most graphically reflected in the rising incidence of *ad hoc* back to work legislation at both federal and provincial levels.

13. See also Osborne's (1979) discussion of the portrayal of workers in Canadian history texts.

14. At the turn of the century, amid increasing class conflict, Asians in British Columbia (many of whom were brought to Canada under labour contracts) became easy targets for such a scapegoating technique. See for example, Roy (1974).

15. Although usually in combination with a strong anti-immigration stance, see Watt, 1959; Ostry, 1960; Craven and Traves, 1979; and Kealey, 1980.

REFERENCES

Avery, Donald. 1978. "British Born 'Radicals' in North America, 1900-1941: The Case of Sam Scarlett." *Canadian Ethnic Studies* 10, no. 2: 65-85.

————. 1979. *Dangerous Foreigners: European Immigrant Workers and Labour Radicalism in Canada, 1896-1932.* Toronto: McClelland and Stewart.

Boggs, Carl. 1976. *Gramsci's Marxism.* London: Pluto Press.

Brown, Lorne and Caroline Brown. 1973. *An Unauthorized History of the RCMP.* Toronto: James Lorimer.

Carnoy, Martin. 1984. *The State and Political Theory.* New Jersey: Princeton University Press.

Craven, Paul, and Tom Traves. 1979. "The Class Politics of the National Policy." *Journal of Canadian Studies* 14, no. 3: 14-38.

Cross, Michael, and Gregory Kealey. 1983. *The Consolidation of Capitalism 1896-1929: Readings in Canadian Social History.* Volume 4. Toronto: McClelland and Stewart.

Drache, Daniel. 1984. "The Formation and Fragmentation of the Canadian Working-Class: 1820-1920." *Studies in Political Economy* 15 (Fall): 43-89.

Gramsci, A. 1971. *Selections from the Prison Notebooks.* New York: International Publishers.

Hall, Stuart, C. Critcher, T. Jefferson, J. Clarke, and B. Roberts. 1978. *Policing the Crisis: Mugging the State, and Law and Order.* London: Macmillan Press.

Heron, Craig. 1984. "Labourism and the Canadian Working Class," *Labour/Le travail* 13 (Spring): 45-75.

————., and Bryan Palmer. 1980. "Through the Prism of the Strike: Industrial Conflict in Southern Ontario, 1901-1914." In P. Grayson, ed., *Class, State,*

Ideology and Change. Toronto: Holt, Rinehart and Winston, pp. 47-71.

Jamieson, Stuart. 1971. *Times of Trouble: Labour Unrest and Industrial Conflict in Canada, 1900-1966*. Ottawa: Information Canada.

Kealey, Gregory. 1976. " 'The Honest Workingman and Workers' Control': The Experience of Toronto Skilled Workers, 1860-1892." *Labour/Le Travail* 1: 32-68.

_____. 1980. *Toronto Workers Respond to Industrial Capitalism, 1867-1892*. Toronto: University of Toronto Press.

_____. 1984. "1919: The Canadian Labour Revolt." *Labour/Le Travail* 13 (Spring): 11-44.

Logan, H. A. 1948. *Trade Unions in Canada: Their Development and Their Functioning*. Toronto: Macmillan.

Macgillivray, Don. 1983. "Military Aid to Civil Power: The Cape Breton Experience the 1920's." In M. Cross and G. Kealey, eds. *The Consolidation of Capitalism 1896-1929: Readings in Canadian Social History*. Volume 4. Toronto: McClelland and Stewart, pp. 116-40.

Marglin, S. 1974. "What Do Bosses Do? The Origin and Functions of Hierarchy in Capitalist Production." *Review of Radical Political Economy* 6, no. 2: 33-60.

Myers, G. 1972. *A History of Canadian Wealth*. Toronto: James Lorimer.

Osborne, Ken. 1979. "Hard-Working, Temperate and Peaceable: The Portrayal of Workers in Canadian History Texts." *This Magazine* 13, nos. 5-6: 21-26.

Ostry, B. 1960. "Conservatives, Liberals and Labour in the 1870's." *Canadian Historical Review* 41: 93-127.

Palmer, Bryan. 1979. *A Culture in Conflict: Skilled Workers and Industrial Capitalism in Hamilton Ontario, 1860-1914*. Montreal: McGill-Queen's University Press.

Panitch, Leo. 1984. "Review of 'Working Class Experience: The Rise and Reconstitution of Canadian Labour, 1800-1980' by Bryan Palmer." *Labour/Le Travail* 14 (Fall): 221-25.

_____., and Donald Swartz. 1984. "Towards Permanent Exceptionalism: Coercion and Consent in Canadian Industrial Relations." *Labour/Le Travail* 13 (Spring): 133-57.

Phillips, Paul. 1967. *No Power Greater, A Century of Labour in British Columbia*. Vancouver: BC Federation of Labour.

Reilly, Nolan. 1984. "Introduction to Papers from the Winnipeg General Stike Symposium, March 1983." *Labour/Le Travail* 13 (Spring): 7-10.

Rinehart, James. 1975. *The Tyranny of Work*. Toronto: Longman Publishers.

Robin, Martin. 1972. *The Rush for Spoils: The Company Province, 1871-1933*. Toronto: McClelland and Stewart.

Roy, Patricia. 1974. "The Oriental 'Menace' in British Columbia." In M. Horn and R. Sabourin, eds., *Studies in Canadian Social History*. Toronto: McClelland and Stewart, pp. 287-97.

Saywell, J. R. 1951. "Labour and Socialism in British Columbia: A Survey of Historical Development Before 1903." *B.C. Historical Quarterly* 15: 09-50.

Stevenson, Paul. 1983. "The State in English Canada: The Political Economy of Production and Reproduction." *Socialist Studies/Etudes Socialistes: A Canadian Annual*, pp. 88-128.

Taylor, Ian. 1983. *Crime, Capitalism and Community: Three Essays in Socialist Criminology*. Toronto: Butterworth.

Watt, F. W. 1959. "The National Policy, the Workingman, and Proletarian Ideas in Victorian Canada." *Canadian Historical Review* 40: 1-26.

Wilentz, Sean. 1984. "Against Exceptionalism: Class Consciousness and the American Labour Movement." *International Labor and Working Class History* 26 (Fall): 1-24.

CONCLUSION

11

Epilogue: Law, Justice, and the State

JOHN L. McMULLAN

The articles in this book debate the ideology of criminal justice reform, the utility of the concept of relative autonomy in understanding law and the state, and the nature of the state, its evolution, disciplinary institutions, and class character. In different ways, they explore practical, historical, and theoretical problems. The conclusions are sometimes pessimistic about criminal justice reform and about overcoming current economic, political, and legal crises in Canada; sometimes they are optimistic about legal change in the criminal justice arena. All of the essays probe the major issues central to developing a coherent sociology of the state and of social control. The starting points are usually the postulates of a broadly defined conflict criminology, whether informed by elite theory about interest groups and power relations or by more explicitly Marxist conceptualizations. Eclecticism is compounded further by divisions within a radical perspective. Instrumentalists, structuralists, and class conflict theorists, for example, are critical of each others' formulations, especially on topics such as the role of the law, the importance of ideology, and the imperatives of the economy. In a manner similar to research in the United States and Britain, the critical study of law and the state in Canada "has not developed as a monolithic enterprise consisting of a single theoretical perspective" (Beirne and Quinney, 1982, p. 16). There are powerful concerns about being one-sided, reductionist, or deterministic in research and analysis.

Ericson and McMahon sensitize us to the fact that the state in Canada is bent on increasing and widening the nets of social control. Policing reform is much more likely to re-form the policing function and to restructure the justice system in favour of property relations and class domination than it is to allow for a democratic reordering of policing practices, procedures, and institutions. Criminal justice reforms, they say, must be seen for what they really are: a set of partisan social, economic, political, and cultural instruments, the underlying purpose of which is the reproduction of domination "over the lower orders" under the guise of progress or benevolence. However, this instrumentalist line of argument is not without difficulties. Aside from Fattah's observations about the problems of judging reform and about overcoming analytical despair, their analysis does not easily consider how the strategies and actions of various powerful interest groups are actually limited by impersonal structural forces and constraints. They have difficulty accounting for the existence of laws and reforms that are not in the interests of a power elite or dominant class fraction; where such laws do exist, they imply that capitalists are immune from criminal sanction when they violate them. There is certainly much truth in this. The state and its legal and criminal justice systems do serve as important mechanisms for securing the social relations of domination, but not all the consequences of the "rule of law" are negative ones for the dominated classes. As Thompson notes:

> The rhetoric and rules of society are a great deal more than sham. In the same moment they may modify in profound ways, the behaviour of the powerful, and mystify the powerless. They may disguise the true relations of power, but at the same time, they may curb "that" power and check its intrusions. (1975; p. 265)

Indeed, the struggles for reform, as Fattah and Comack convincingly argue, do result in outcomes that bring about substantive change in justice politics and the social order, changes not sponsored or approved by a dominant class. Not all reforms are "bourgeois" or in the interests of a "thoroughly bourgeois" social order.

In contrast to this instrumentalist discourse, a structuralist position rejects the notions of the state and the law as mere weapons in the hands of ruling groups. As Ratner, McMullan, and Burtch argue, the state organizes and mediates class relations on *behalf* of, rather than at the *behest* of, capital. Whether in the areas of accumulation, legitimation, or coercion, the state's role requires a degree of autonomy, not from the structural needs of the economy but from the direct control and manipulations of state programmes and activities by dominant class-based groups. This does not necessarily mean, as Mandel assumes, a confusion of appearance with reality or an ignorance of the despotism of the capitalist marketplace. The state is neither the unfolding of the will of capital nor the functional requirements of presupposed economic needs. Mandel's assertion that "bases need superstructures and they get the superstructures they need because they need them" is problematic. Aside from its tautological features, this form of thinking reduces the state to a political effect of the demands of capital, a potentially misleading formulation in that it can block recognition of the degree to which the state has become an important arena of class conflict. Mandel's interpretation, while unequivocal, is rather one-sided and not sensitive enough to the contradictory process of capitalist production and reproduction, where, in both the marketplace and the state, the very foundations of the production and reproduction of surplus value are constantly suspended and regenerated. As a result; "the state is not a functional agency that can *resolve* these contradictions. It is rather a complementary form through which capital attempts to pursue the class struggle in a vain attempt to suspend its contradictory character" (Clarke, 1983, p. 121).

In their study of the Law Reform Commission of Canada (LRCC), Hastings and Saunders adopt a modified structuralist approach emphasizing the process of the relative autonomy of law. They reveal much about criminal justice reform and they do not fall prey to what Cohen calls analytical despair or adversarial nihilism (1985, p. 240). They make sense of the politics of the LRCC by showing how, as an agency, it was shaped by a problematic and contradictory process where the relations of class forces were determinant. They show how the LRCC was fashioned as a mechanism of social control to manage a perceived crisis of morality, legitimacy, and authority in the 1960's and 1970's. In this regard, the LRCC's main virtue was in depoliticizing social issues "by dictating and legitimating the definition of a problem, the proper terms of public debate, and the allowable repertoire of strategies of intervention." In the process of doing this, the LRCC compromised their autonomy as a state agency and, in the name of political realism and expediency, aligned themselves more and more as a technical branch of the justice department. The have unequivocally adopted the view of law-reformers and are, in the apt words of their president, "smoother-outers, adjusters . . . not revolutionaries." They now exercise reform in the areas of least political significance—procedural and administrative law—a far cry from their earlier mandate. This is not because LRCC reforms were prescribed failures, or because their employees were servants of the state, suppliers of alibis, or primarily legitimators of dominant forms of power. The LRCC reform agenda failed because it was politically defeated. Hastings and Saunders's basic point is that the struggle for reform waged in the LRCC was undercut by decisive ideological, political, and radical shifts occurring within the wider context of Canadian society. The creation of the LRCC was not an instrumental response; it was much more complex than a conspiratorial reflex, although in the end, the Law Reform Commission confirms the wisdom "Beware the State Bearing Gifts."

In assessing the LRCC, Hastings and Saunders warn about the limits of criminal justice reform politics. At bottom, like Ericson, and Ericson and McMahon, they reveal the co-optive power of the state, whereby its selective mechanisms ignore potential progressive reform or translate it into a self-serving agenda via state-hired professionals. But they differ in explaining how this is accomplished. Hastings and Saunders are more dialectical in their thinking and theoretically opposed to "we blew it" or "we told you so" explanations (Cohen, 1985). Their work represents an important effort to outline abstract ideas about law and the state in Canada.

It should be clear from these comments that the development of the capitalist state is not a smooth evolution of the desire of capital, nor is law a mere instrument of class domination. The state is something formed through trial and error in the unfolding of class conflict, conditioned to a considerable degree by the direct agency of sections of the capitalist class. However, behind the direct representation of capitalist class interests lies the more fundamental, if less obvious, relations between capital and the state to obtain the control of the capitalist class over the state, thus securing the political-legal subordination of labour. This is accomplished only provisionally and through struggle, and this means the active involvement and intrusion of the working class into the state arena. In Canada, capitalist development did not proceed unhindered. Panitch has shown that the relative strength of independent commodity producers retarded a smooth transition to industrial capitalist development (1981, pp. 7-34). The Canadian business class had a hard struggle to advance industrialization, as Comack has noted, addressing certain omissions in Gaucher's and Taylor's work. Workers' resistance meant that the state had to accede to the demands of labour and respond not just to co-optive measures but to coercive ones as well.

An adequate theorization of the state, law, and criminal justice politics requires, therefore, a more radical attention to class conflict and a less sanguine interpretation of bourgeois hegemony. Raymond Williams's observation "that no mode of production and, therefore, no dominant social order and, therefore, no dominant culture ever in reality includes or exhausts all human practice" (1977, p. 125) deserves serious consideration in light of explanations that promote the "quintessentially bourgeois" thesis or that see in Canada the simple, uncomplicated production of a conforming people "hooked" on bourgeois values. The growing despotism of the world economic system and the spread of "alienated politics" in Canada, as Mandel and Taylor observe, do speak to the power of capitalist relations of production and to the relative strength of class ideology and government. Yet it must not be forgotten that while subaltern classes are frequently the objects of state power, the working class does not simply abandon its collective aspirations in accepting admission to the political franchise and in organizing trade unions. It continues to wage class-based struggles. The labour legislation of the 1940's, which ushered in the era of reform in industrial relations in Canada:

> did not evolve suddenly from the progressive minds of legislators, judges and industrial relations experts, nor had capitalists miraculously been transformed into far-sighted social philosophers . . . rather [it] was a product of an unparalleled shift in the balance of class forces. (Panitch and Schwartz, 1985; p. 18)

Of course, the 1970's and 1980's have witnessed the dismantling of many of these workers' "rights" and "freedoms." The rebirth of exceptionalism, ideologically and in specific acts of coercion—such as back-to-work laws, removal of the right to strike within the public sector, and anti-inflation programmes—are part of a class process, the purpose of which is a new subordination of labour within capitalism. Yet the boundaries of the "economic" and the "political," the definitions of the "rights" of capital and of the working class, and the forms of conflict, are all a constant object of class politics, with the working class regularly pressing beyond the limits accorded to it by capital and the state. Thus, workers occupy factories, wildcat strike, encroach on the rights of management, sabotage the workplace, and mobilize against state policies. Moreover, the state has had to concede a growing political role to the collective organizations of the working class.

One must not overestimate the dominance of capital and the state. It is necessary to be sensitive to the double meaning of "rights" and "freedoms" and to the contradictions of the current crisis in Canada. Hard-won struggles and victories are more than bourgeois cunning. If not, then there is a true confusion if appearance with reality and a pronounced conflation of the superstructural nature of law and state, with near complete political impotence on the part of the working class.

But let us be clear on this point. We do not deny that the form and content of legal discourse remains dominated by the dynamics of class formation, conflict, alliance, and crisis which reflect the character of the dominant mode of production. Yet what must be avoided are the orthodoxies of economism and class reductionism. As Sumner notes, the concept of law insofar as it is negative ideology is not to be equated necessarily with the false, the bourgeois, the political, the systematic or the economic reflex, but rather that on the positive side, it can be enlightening, revolutionary, practical and sustained in sites of oppositional culture" (1983, p. 197).

What about criminal justice politics? In their article on "Relative Autonomy and Criminal Justice in the Canadian State," Ratner, McMullan, and Burtch point out that the state is a complex of contradictions determined by the social relations of production but intruded upon by working class politics. It possesses a degree of freedom to act autonomously because it has acquired a powerful surveillance function, because it has assumed increasing amounts of institutionalized control over the use of violence, and because it has become the constitutional guarantor of general legal relations. There is an implication that reform is politically feasible and that the state is an arena of class struggle, because it is an important agency facilitating the material power of capital and because it opens up a space for potential social justice reform. We argue the importance of paying attention to the strategic loopholes, exceptions, ambiguities, and positive benefits that exist within the state as a prime agency for social change: reducing economic inequalities, providing some legal safety, and struggling for rights in the public and private spheres. In our view, the state is not a uniform expression of "capital."

Alongside a class-based analytical view of current social control practices must be placed a pragmatic politics of preferred values and radical legal/social change. For Canada, this entails a radical decentering of power in the criminal justice area and an agenda of state reform via legal challenge, local reform, and democratic accountability. Such an agenda has been successful in some of Britain's urban centres where Labour Party activities have delimited police powers and created new imaginative local policies on crime prevention (Taylor, 1982). In the United States, there have been similar movements for authentic forms of popular policing, justice, and punishment. They have been communally generated and have achieved crime prevention beyond the surveillance and control offered by the state (Einstadter, 1984, pp. 199-212; Michalowski, 1983, pp. 13-23).

In Canada, there are three immediate tasks:

1) Fighting Forward on the Ideological Front. This includes:
   a) countering the misinformation of liberal and conservative governments and policies, showing how their "get tough" policies do not work, do not make communities safer, nor provide real assistance to victims, and demonstrating that their programmes are not cost effective;
   b) making efforts to delimit coercive control by continuing the fight for offenders' rights and by opposing prison construction, determinate sentencing, and repressive correctional practices

now filling the vacuum created by the abandonment of the rehabilitative ideal; and

c) reaffirming rehabilitation as an appeal against repressive justice policy and exploring the avenues toward a principle of punishment based on a vision of a "pain-reduced" society (Christie, 1981).

2) Democratizing the state system from within, including a deliberate democratization of police work, the courts, prisons, and community custodial institutions. This entails reconstructing a popular form of justice based on a politics of localism (Taylor, 1983). Most importantly, this means specifying the content of popular justice and the principles upon which it rests, as well as clarifying the agency of reform, their class-based politics, and related organization strategies for carrying forward a progressive substance to punishment that avoids the appeals to formal changes in representation on police, prison, and local boards and committees.

3) Defining and developing a politics of localism. This entails reconsidering the "quintessentially bourgeois state" and "collapse of community" theses for Canada and constructing a realistic, multi-pronged strategy that both recognizes the divided nature of the contemporary community and tries to amalgamate the different sections into a productive whole to deal more effectively with crime and social justice. What must be clarified are the material conditions, strategies, and tactics of municipal socialism. The attractive and radical power of localism needs to be infused with clear-sighted understandings of the substance of local interests, the nature of progressive alliances, the strengths and weaknesses of the local state and its ability to carry forward a progressive content for decentralized governance, and an assessment of the likelihood of short-term and circumscribed reform programmes becoming the basis for a truly national strategy. Pragmatic substance must be breathed into appeals for popular, democratic crime policies (McMullan, 1986).

There are, of course, other important fronts for criminal justice politics. At scattered points in the social system are programmes and agencies which were set up as radical alternatives and continue to satisfy such an agenda: rape-crisis centres, informal justice projects, prisoners' organizations, self-help and counselling networks, neighbourhood policing, and community youth projects. These are not only, or even primarily, net-widening or disguised coercion. Gains have been registered, despite an overall system bent on trying to eliminate or contain these changes. Alternative services, resources, contacts, and therapies tied to the strategic use of social control have opened up wider opportunities for social improvement and social solidarity. Community crime-prevention programmes, as Cohen observes, while not eliminating crime in city areas, have succeeded in achieving "intermediate links," "incidental effects," or "means" which have displaced the fear of crime, overcome apathy and isolation, and contributed to neighbourhood redevelopment (1985, p. 265).

Our point is that a case can be made for channelling welfare resources into genuine reform projects, especially if they are alternatives to escalating repressive programmes. In Ericson's, MacMahon's and Ericson's, and Mandel's work, there is a tendency to conclude that "nothing works the way it is supposed to." Perhaps nothing can be done! Reforms have a way of confirming the order of things. Or worse still, "it's all a trick"! False hopes get turned around and impede a true radical course of action. The analytical merit of their work is hindered by a kind of cynicism. To them, the ironies of reform are the negative, unintended consequences—more social reform begets more social domination. But what about the ironies of social and state intervention? The notion of muddled or unintended consequences must logically allow for positive results. Reforms may turn out to be better than expected because unknown bad features of a previous condition have been removed or because reforms turn out to contain unrecognized beneficial features (Henshel, 1976, Chapter 3). We need a cautious reaffirmation of a pragmatic alternative agenda which states preferred politico-moral values and which is able to confront squarely the problems of utilitarianism in crime control policy and local justice in the community. The key features of this programme are:

1) struggling to abolish the criminogenic features of the system which liberals and conservatives are committed to preserving or enhancing;
2) halting the process by which the state and society keeps classifying, excluding, and controlling more and more groups according to age, sex, race, class, behaviour, moral status, ability, or psychic state;
3) breaking up the concentrated and centralized system of expertise and professional knowledge and restructuring them so that they are in the service of local neighbourhoods, worker's groups, community networks, women's organizations, and so on;
4) demarginalizing offenders by integrating rather than separating or excluding them. This means promoting community justice programs, victim restitution schemes, and decarceration as viable alternatives to prisons;
5) working for pre-emptive deterrence in order to prevent crime before

it is committed, rather than punishing after the fact. This entails working out strategic relations between citizen groups, patrols, and the police as a way of offering safety in housing blocks and slum zones;

6) formulating a policy of punishment and responsibility within clear limtis based on:
   a) the nature of the offender, the violation, and the victim,
   b) the minimal use of pain to achieve social control, and
   c) allowing for mitigating circumstances on a systematic level;

7) developing a doctrine of human diversity that recognizes that cities and smaller communities should be places where differences, tensions, and disorders can be tolerated, rather than being divided up into antiseptic zones; and

8) encouraging a parallel debate about the realities of social control and the need for protection from state repression in existing socialist societies (Christie, 1981; Greenberg, 1983, pp. 313-27; Taylor, 1983; Cohen, 1985, Chapter 7).

Philosophically, this is a reaffirmation of an agenda for living with paradox, contradiction, and ambiguity in criminal justice politics. In our view, a tough-minded politics in the present conjuncture demands a reconsideration of the theoretical search for essences and ultimate causes. We have been blunted by the pursuit of absolutes and certainties. One important step forward is the establishment of achievable progressive reform priorities in the current period. Noble wishes are no substitute for making and implementing radical moral choices in the crime policy area which, as Cohen notes, itself generates absolute values—justice, rights, freedoms, mercy, betterment—which are often incompatible with each other.

However, caution must guide our politics. There is ample evidence from this book and others that good ideas can make awful practices. Various pre-emptive and inclusionary visions sometimes fail to confront adequately the moral issues of wrong-doing, harm, danger, and fear which are raised by the crime question. A minimal statist message with a non-interventionist stand may easily become a benevolent licence for neglect. A conservative government in Canada now uses laissez-faire ideas to abdicate responsibility for welfare and caring for its weaker citizens while increasing its overall powers of moral surveillance and regulation (Ratner and McMullan, 1983, pp. 31-43). Community inclusionary policies may also inadvertently lead to the creation of new agencies, institutions, and professional bodies whose purpose and modes of operation may undercut authentic reform and lead to new forms of classificiation, exclusion, and the dispersal of social control (Cohen, 1985).

Nevertheless, we must be realistic without being fatalistic. The struggle for social justice demands a struggle over law. Legal rights, as Sumner notes, express the "relative social power and political coherence of different classes, class fractions, and social groups" and are "key movements and weapons in the development of the working class" (1981, p. 68). This includes the fight for basic liberal-democratic legal rights as well as the building of a movement based on the pursuit of social rights. Such a movement would oppose the current ideological focus on competitive individual rights with a campaign for collective rights based on social need. In the present period this includes: social wage needs such as adequate housing, education and medical services; workplace rights such as health and safety provisions, and the rights to work and to strike; labour law reform, especially the rejection of legal and ideological stigma which outlaws certain types of workers' actions and which allows for the use of the full repressive force of the state; rights to a safe living environment; cohabitation rights for women such as rights to a shared home, rights to and for children, and rights to security (Bottomley et al., 1985; White, 1986, pp. 97-103).

A campaign for social rights holds out a strategic advantage: unity of interests and forces on a broad front. The political logic is the commonality of people's needs, not the individualism of personal rights or goods. This requires the advancement of "coalition politics" linking relatively powerless groups like the unemployed, the poor, native peoples, ethnic and sexual minorities, and women, with strong organizations such as the union movement or progressive religious institutions. People from radically different cultures, classes, and regions can be mobilized in common action over rights issues. As White notes, "the idea of social rights implicitly challenges the right-wing grip on the ideological terrain where social issues are fought" (1986, p. 100). In our view this is central to advancing a new political agenda around justice.

REFERENCES

Beirne, P., and R. Quinney, eds. 1982. *Marxism and Law*. New York: John Wiley.
Bottomley, Ann, Katherine Grieve, Gay Moon, and Angela Weir. 1985. *The Cohabitation Handbook*. London: Pluto Press.
Christie, Nils. 1981. *Limits to Pain*. Oxford: Martin Robertson.
Clarke, Simon. 1983. "State, Class Struggle, and the Reproduction of Capital." *Kapitalistate*: 10/11:113-30.
Cohen, Stanley. 1985. *Visions of Social Control*. London: Polity Press.
Einstadter, W. J. 1984. "Citizen Patrols: Prevention or Control." *Crime and Social Justice* no. 21-22: 199-212.
Greenberg, David. 1983. "Reflections on the Justice Model Debate." *Contemporary Crises* 7 (November): 313-27.
Henshel, Richard. 1976. *Reacting to Social Problems*. Ontario: Longmans.
McMullan, John L. 1986. "The Law and Order Problem in Socialist Criminology." *Studies in Political Economy* no. 21.
Michalowski, Raymond. 1983. "Crime Control in the 1980's: A Progressive Agenda." *Crime and Social Justice* no. 19: 13-23.
Panitch, L. 1981. "Dependency and Class in Canadian Political Economy." *Studies in Political Economy* 6 (Autumn): 7-34.
Panitch, L., and D. Schwartz. 1985. *From Consent to Coercion: The Assault on Trade Union Freedoms*. Toronto: Garamond Press.
Ratner, R. S., and John L. McMullan. 1983. "Social Control and the Rise of the Exceptional State in Britain, the United States and Canada." *Crime and Social Justice* no. 19: 31-43.
Sumner, Colin. 1983. "Rethinking Deviance: Toward a Sociology of Censure." *Research in Law Deviance and Social Control* 5: 187-204.
_____. 1981. "The Rule of Law and Civil Rights in Contemporary Marxist Theory." *Kapitalistate* 9: 63-91.
Taylor, Ian. 1982. *Law and Order: Arguments for Socialism*. London: Macmillan.
_____. 1983. *Crime, Capitalism and Community*. Toronto: Butterworths.
Thompson, E. P. 1975. *Whigs and Hunters: The Origin of the Black Act*. Middlesex: Penguin Books.
White, R. D. 1986. *Law, Capitalism and the Right to Work*. Toronto: Garamond Press.
Williams, Raymond. 1977. *Marxism and Literature*. Oxford: Oxford University Press.